Lexis Complexes

Nelson Hilton

Lexis Complexes

Literary
Interventions

**The University
of Georgia Press**

Athens & London

© 1995 by the University of Georgia Press
Athens, Georgia 30602
All rights reserved
Designed by Walton Harris
Set in 10/14 Electra by Tseng Information Systems, Inc.
Printed and bound by Braun-Brumfield, Inc.
The paper in this book meets the guidelines for permanence
and durability of the Committee on Production Guidelines for
Book Longevity of the Council on Library Resources.

Printed in the United States of America
99 98 97 96 95 C 5 4 3 2 1

Library of Congress Cataloging in Publication Data

Hilton, Nelson.
Lexis complexes : literary interventions / Nelson Hilton.
p. cm.
Includes bibliographical references and index.
ISBN 0-8203-1687-3 (alk. paper)
1. Discourse analysis, Literary.   2. Criticism.
3. Psychoanalysis.   4. Semiotics.   I. Title.
P302.5.H55   1995
808'.0014—dc20   94-15271

British Library Cataloging in Publication Data available

For Holly

Contents

Acknowledgments   ix

1   Lexis Complexes and Intentions in Tension   1

2   Before the Milk of the Word: Nipple-Eyes   23

3   Restless Wrestling: Johnson's *Rasselas*   38

4   Mary Godwin's Remonstrance   56

5   Keats, Teats, and the Fane of Poesy   72

6   Tears, Ay, Dull Tears: Tennyson's Idle Idol-Idyl   99

7   Under Brontëan Thunder   119

8   Hypograms, Hypocrits, and Hippos: Conrad's *Heart of Darkness*   142

9   Sylvia on Aurelia Plath   159

Notes   187

Works Cited   201

Index   219

Acknowledgments

This short book has been long enough in process to amass debts beyond its means. I am grateful to the Georgia Research Foundation for support over the summer of 1984, and to the Center for the Humanities, University of Georgia, for additional research hours in the spring of 1989. Various individual chapters have benefited from readings by Margaret Dickie, Bill Kretzschmar, Anne Williams (all at the University of Georgia), Irene Tayler, and Renato Almansi. An early version of chapter 6 appeared in *Essays in Criticism* (1985), and chapter 5 began as a paper for a conference on the theme "Romanticism and the Imagination" (Melbourne, 1989), which was published in *Imagining Romanticism: Essays on English and Australian Romanticisms*, edited by Deirdre Coleman and Peter Otto (West Cornwall, Conn., 1992).

As the work is so molded with the red clay of my years at the University of Georgia—the continual rereading of texts for the sophomore survey, ENG 232, not least—I am pleased that it issues from the University of Georgia Press, to one of whose anonymous readers I am obliged for the most cogent and comprehensive critique I have yet encountered.

My first book celebrated my parents' fortieth anniversary; this can note another dozen years of "more knowing together." That interim, too, has brought an essential reeducation in childhood from superb and untiring instructors, Theo and Alice. Holly Compton Hilton has lived for years with this text (and subtext, and context); its inscription marks her trust, hope, and love, which made it possible.

Lexis Complexes

1
Lexis Complexes and Intentions in Tension

> *A bon entendeur ne faut qu'une parole.*
> —RABELAIS

Lexis transliterates the Greek word λέξις, or "speech," "diction, style," and "a single word or phrase." The word first appears outside its mother tongue in late Latin, though it could hardly thrive there in the shadow of the crucial Latin word *lex*, "law." English also deferred *lexis* before the ongoing powerful associations of the Latin word, as embodied, for instance, in the 1644 title *Lex Rex*, but the growing concern for "lexicons" and "lexicographers" (first *OED* citations are 1603 and 1658) kept the Greek root in circulation. By the middle of the twentieth century, however, *lexis* found itself fully lexicalized in English, in part, perhaps, to mark a contrast to the more evidently vocal root of *vocabulary* and *diction*. Today, the *lex* of law Latin grows more antique, and the associations of *law* and *word* meet upon more equal terms, as in the legal data-base and retrieval system LEXIS®.[1]

Complex derives from the Latin verb *complecti* (past participle *complexus*), "to embrace," "to grasp," "to encircle": Ovid describes the merging Hermaphroditus and Salmacis as knit *conplexu tenaci*, "in a tight embrace" (*Metamorphoses* 4.377). Just as with the Old English *fathom*, the Latin verb also means "to embrace something intellectually," and, a result of such comprehension, "to express or explain a multitude of objects," "to sum up." The echo of *complicare*, "to fold together," complicates the meaning of the word: a complex comprehends something already plaited or intertwined. Early in the twentieth century, *complex* gained another particular reference, owing to C. G. Jung's use of the term to denominate the "special psychic contents" or "secondary mind" ("Complexes" 599, 601), which he identified as the cause of certain disturbances in subjects' responses to the word-association experiments he began in 1902. The complex linked together various private ideas with a common emotional tone, and, being "relatively independent," could drive "at certain intentions . . . contrary to the conscious intentions of the individual" ("Complexes" 601). An approving Freud related in a 1906 article specifically conscious of *lexis* and *lex* ("Psycho-analysis and the Establishment of the Facts in Legal Proceedings") that

> the connection between the stimulus-word and the reaction-word could not be one of chance, but must be determined by a pre-existing group of ideas in the mind of the person reacting.
>
> It has become customary to call a group of ideas of this kind, having an influence on the reaction to the stimulus-word, a "complex." The influence works either by the stimulus-word actually touching a complex directly or by the complex succeeding in getting into touch with the word by intermediate links. (14)

Eight years later, directly after the split between the two analysts, Freud regarded *complex* more critically as "a convenient and often indispensable term for summing up a psychological state descriptively. None of the other terms coined by psycho-analysis for its own needs has achieved such widespread popularity or been so misapplied" ("History" 313); Jung, however, continued to maintain that "the *via regia* to the unconscious . . . is not the dream, as [Freud] thought, but the complex" ("Complex Theory" 101).

Freud had been thoroughly primed to follow a connection between lexis and complex. In *Studies on Hysteria* (1895) he had come upon "the genesis of hysterical symptoms through symbolization by means of a verbal expression" (179) in cases like that of Elisabeth von R., whose facial neuralgia was related to a much earlier traumatic conversation with her husband and an insult that "was like a slap in the face" (178). Another case turned on "the emergence of isolated key-words" that Freud and his patient had "to work into sentences" (276), and which proved to articulate a childhood sexual trauma. Two years later Freud states in a letter that he has found confirmation that the locality at which the repressed breaks through is the *word presentation* and not the concept attached to it. (More precisely, the word memory.) Hence the most disparate things are readily united as an obsessional idea under a single word with multiple meanings. The tendency toward breaking through makes use of these ambiguities as though it were killing several flies at one blow. (*Letters* 287)

The obsessional ideas, he adds, "frequently are clothed in a characteristic *verbal vagueness* in order to permit such multiple deployment" (288). He imagines the thought content behind such words as corresponding "to a ramifying system of lines and more particularly to a converging one": the meeting of two or "often" more threads determines (or "overdetermines") a nodal point as, for instance, a "symptom"—which might itself be "an isolated word" or apparently "meaningless series of words" (*Studies* 290, 276).

Reporting the case of an obsessional patient whose breakdown was triggered by hearing the account of a torture with rats, Freud characterizes the story itself as a "complex stimulus-word" to which the patient reacted with "his obsessional idea" ("Notes" 353). Indeed, classification of the Rat Man's pathology required Freud's identifying a series of "verbal bridges" in "the rat delirium" that linked the stimulus to the patient's investment not only in the word *Ratten* ("rats"), but also *Raten* ("installments"—as in the payments for this therapy in words), *Spielratte* ("gambler"—evoking his shame over his father's gambling debt), and *heiraten* ("to marry"—reflecting an ongoing conflict). Such patients, writes Freud, "*do not know the wording of their own obsessional ideas*" (359) and in the "secondary defensive struggle" against their unwanted thoughts generate "deliria" or seemingly incoherent bits of narrative, wordplay, and injunctions in order both to struggle with and to maintain their pathology. The obsession, writes Freud, can be "protected" by "indefinite or ambiguous wording," and "after being misunderstood, the wording may find its way into the patient's 'deliria,'" which "constantly tend to form new connections with that part of the matter and wording of the obsession which is not present in consciousness" (382).

The "rat obsession" might also be seen as an instance of the unconscious dynamic of "condensation" in the way it constitutes an abridged translation of the patient's anal-erotic and oedipal conflict. "Condensation," or *Verdichtung* in German, can suggest the dynamic of poetic work through its homophonic connection to *Dichtung* ("poetry," "fiction") and the thought that, for Freud, "the work of condensation in dreams is seen at its clearest when it handles words and names" (*Interpretation* 330). It is under the heading of *Verdichtung* in *The Interpretation of Dreams* that Freud dwells on what he now calls the *Knotenpunkt*, the knot or nodal point or "switch word" at which, in which, different themes and interpretations intersect and overlap. The nodal point is a kind of revolving door—or complex gate—that multiple, perhaps conflicting motivations each utilize in reaching expression, even while maintaining, through such communal use, an appearance of collective unity or identity. Concluding the discussion of his "Dream of the Botanical Monograph," Freud reflects that "the elements 'botanical' and 'monograph' found their way into the content of the dream because they possessed copious contacts with the majority of the dream-thoughts, because, that is to say, they constituted 'nodal points' upon which a great number of the dream-thoughts converged, and because they had several meanings in connection with the interpretation of the dream" (317–18). These elements, he continues, turn out to have been "overdetermined," or "represented in the dream-thoughts many times over" (318). Regarding another dream and its highlighted neologism *tutelrein*, Freud finds that the word "could be analyzed in three directions, and led in that way to three of the subjects represented in the dream-thoughts" (332). These subjects included "a legal term for 'guardianship'" (*Tutel*), "a vulgar term for a woman's breast"—"'Tutel' (or possibly 'Tuttel')"— and the concluding portion *rein* ("clean"), which by analogy with another compound suggested *zimmerrein* or "house-trained," and, "in addition, sounded very much like the name of a member of the dreamer's family" (332). A more succinct example, based this time on elision, comes in Freud's comment regarding "the meaning which references to Italy seem to have had in the dreams of a woman patient who had never visited that lovely country: '*gen Italien* [to Italy]'—'*Genitalien* [genitals]'" (265).

In *Jokes and Their Relation to the Unconscious*, Freud identifies the process of condensation as the principle technique of verbal *Witz* and regards its production of "multiple use of the same material, play upon words, and similarity of sound" as intending to obtain pleasure in the "localized economy" of the words—something that "had been permitted at the stage of play but had been dammed up by rational criticism in the course of intellectual development" (169). Such condensations, he adds, "arise automatically . . . during thought-processes in the unconscious" (169), that is to say, during the never-sleeping "unconscious thought-processes . . . produced in early childhood," that period of life "in which we were accustomed to deal with our psychical work in general with a small expenditure of energy" (170, 236). Jokes, puns, and condensations are all marked by a concern for economy, "a tendency to compression, or rather to saving," and Freud punctuates the discussion of such frugal oration by quoting Hamlet's "Thrift, thrift, Horatio!" (42). This notion of economic motivation can be related directly to the poetic function of language characterized by Roman Jakobson as the projection of the "principle of equivalence from the axis of selection into the axis of combination. Equivalence is promoted to the constitutive device of the sequence" (358).

One of Jakobson's examples is the memorable political slogan of the 1950s in which the selected or intended sentiment "I admire Eisenhower" or "Vote for Dwight" is made "poetic" by the projection of the principle of equivalence (various possible forms of the content) into the choice of sounds/words actually combined to derive the exemplar of similarity, "I LIKE IKE." Jakobson suggests that the inclusion of *Ike* in *like* offers a "paronomastic image of a feeling which totally envelops its object," while the inclusion of *I* in *Ike* supplies a "paronomastic image of the loving subject enveloped by the beloved object" (357).[2] The point is that the jingle, with its paronomasias or puns, is more highly motivated than other slogans one might construct, as its popularity proved (a bon mot has mo'-*mot*-motivation). Its effectiveness is overdetermined by the declarative import, the communally sanctioned projective identification (Ike [daddy] and I are one), and also by the childlike pleasure in the chiming words which at once screens and prepares that identification—makes the speaker a tyke, so to speak. The economy of the formulation satisfies regressive impulses and, what amounts to the same thing, resistance in the face of logical, demanding discourse (*reasons* why one supports Ike). The lexis complex simplifies complex logos, and this reduction or economizing or reformating or "data compression" can be seen as the knowledgable making—poesis—behind "the poetic function."

For another example, consider the successful advertising campaign of the early 1980s that asked, "Where's the beef?" Because the customer's complaint or belief or "beef" supposedly concerned the lack of real meat or "beef" in the competition's burger patty, one could unpack the three words as "Here's my beef, which is, where's your beef?" There is also, one supposes, an element of suggestion that prompts the audience to salivate and wonder where to buy some beefburgers, and to decide at the same time certainly not to bother with those places that leave one asking, "Where's the beef?" From another angle, one might point to an abundance of repressed, infantile anger and hostility to account for popular identification with such aggressive questioning, and speculate that the potential hazards and guilt accompanying such self-assertion dictated the advertiser's creating a physically nonthreatening caricature old lady as the speaker. The history of these two slogans also suggests that the pleasure or interest they convey, as with jokes, lasts only as long as the material is tightly packed and unfamiliar. The delight they activate is bound up in experiencing the packed or overdetermined nature of their message, but not in a fully conscious manner—once the material appears more clearly to consciousness, through either analysis or saturation, its pleasure evaporates. Furthermore, in the case of these slogans, the message can easily become conscious because it is carefully plotted (test marketing, audience-response surveys, and so on)—as Jakobson says of "I like Ike," the poetic function is only secondary. Perhaps the transience, the short shelf life of such advertising ploys bespeaks the poverty in the intention to urge consumption rather than to satisfy it.

The question of intention has begun to emerge in these last paragraphs, and with that the question of what it means. Take, for an example, an anagram formed by the initial letters of the third stanza of Blake's "London," lines bracketed by the poem's two direct declarations, "I hear":

> The mind-forg'd manacles I hear
>
> How the Chimney-sweepers cry
> Every blackning Church appalls,
> And the hapless Soldiers sigh
> Runs in blood down Palace walls
>
> But most thro' midnight streets I hear.

Though unrecorded for almost two centuries, this seems an effect intended by the author, given the occasional occurrence of such anagrams in earlier poetry, the statistical improbability of the word's random formation, the priming context, the evidence of revision, and the apt interpretation it supports (in a poem about the necessity of altering perceptions—language first of all—the anagram offers an object lesson, a literal parable for the revelation possible in a revision of normal perceptual paradigms: who have eyes to see, let them [see] "hear" here).

A more problematic example comes from Ferdinand de Saussure's *Cours de linguistique générale* and its celebrated discussion of the arbitrary nature of the sign, "l'arbitraire de signe." By this Saussure means that the signifier, or sound-image, "is unmotivated, i.e. arbitrary in that it actually has no natural connection with the signified [i.e., 'concept']" (69). Curiously enough for someone obsessed with identifying anagrams in Latin poetry (see Starobinski), the signified Saussure chooses to illustrate *l'arbitraire* is the sign *l'arbre* ("tree"). This seems unintended, in comparison to Blake's anagram, but not arbitrary—motivated in other words, if only by the opportunity to conserve a quantum of mental energy through hewing to preexisting arboreous associations for language (cf. Saussure's later comparison, accompanied by an illustration, of linguistics to a plant stem cut transversely and perpendicularly; and also the standard branching "tree" of languages). Jacques Lacan, one might note, seizes on the "anagram of '*arbre*' and '*barre*'" to show how "our word 'tree'" crosses "the bar [*barre*] of the Saussurian algorithm" of signifier/[bar]signified, having attached to it "a whole articulation of relevant contexts" (*Ecrits*, 154).

Intention, and its etymological doublet, *intension*, derive from the notion of stretching or straining (Lt. *intendere*): the stretched or strained or forced point is, by this light, the one most intended. *Intension* has been applied to the tightening of instrument strings, to the augmentation of force (tension) generally and, specifically, to contrast intensification-as-*ex*tension, and to the "comprehension" or connotation of a term (again, in contrast with its "extension"). *Intention* similarly has been applied to instrument strings and to the idea of intensification—even as the "eagerness of desire" and "vehemence or ardour of mind" that head Samuel Johnson's 1755 definition of the word—but it now trafficks more in the mental realm of purpose, goal, meaning, end: the "aboutness" or "directedness" of tendency. It bears remark, though, that the colloquialism denoting purpose-to-marry recognizes the complexities of that single act by privileging the plural form, intentions. The strong association of intention with consciousness derives from philosophical concepts relating principally to the use of the term in phenomenology "to denote, roughly, the relation between an act of perception and the real object perceived" (Patterson 137).

But perception, it appears, is a multistage process operating to a great extent unconsciously, one in which, for instance, an "enormous amount of visual processing is necessarily carried out automatically and without awareness" (Marcel 199)—as in the dynamics, measured in milliseconds, of the eye's saccade (leap forward), fixation, and regular regression in its sweep over a line of print, eight or so characters at a time (your eye here and right now, for instance). Cognitive psychology demonstrates in many ways the surprisingly limited channel capacity of conscious experience (cf. Dixon 3–4, 261) and the existence of a hierarchy of processing stages that serve to *limit* the representation of input. The utility of such limiting is all the more evident as we realize that much perceptual processing occurs in parallel rather than seriatim (see Gazzaniga). For our "linear intelligence," as Robert de Beaugrande terms it, "overloading is never very far away" (31); hence all of us, most of the time, rely on already existing mental representations. One might be reminded here of Freud's comment in *Beyond the Pleasure Principle* that "*protection against* stimuli is an almost more important function for the living organism than *reception of* stimuli" (21), and his haunting suggestion that consciousness itself serves as a kind of "protective shield" (hence "blindness and insight"—the more one focuses on z, the more one forgets a–y). In any event, with such complexities attending the notion of perception, one can hardly be surprised to find Stanley Cavell taking up the idea that intentions must be conscious, only to conclude, "It is not clear what that means, nor that it means anything at all, apart from a contrast with unconscious intentions; and it is not clear what that means" (233). Richard L. Gregory writes, still more directly, "Just what an intention is, in terms of brain processes or anything else, is exceedingly hard to say" (383).

Questions of linguistic intentionality and authorial intention do, however, loom large in *The Structure of Complex Words*, William Empson's impressive 1951 study of complex lexes. Empson's project might be seen as one working out of complications in Wittgenstein's sense that "intention is embedded in its situation, in human customs and institutions" (*Philosophical Investigations* 108)—taking those customs and institutions as language. Committed to "linguistics not psychology" (31), Empson is interested in "the covert assertions in single words" (47) of the cultural lexicon as used by an individual, and in how there might be "an inner grammar of complex words like the overt grammar of sentences" (253). The "complex words" seem at first rather ordinary ones, such as *fool, dog, honest, sense*; but Empson employs them to study the way in which the contemporary bearing of these words, "referring their users to a background of shared understanding, comes to suggest an implicit ideology" (Norris 26). An Empsonian instance apropos of our critical and theoretical concern would be "intention" itself as the once hotly contested word embodying a desire to establish some control on response, some gauge that would permit "validity in interpretation," or, finally, Truth. But in attempting to decide what might constitute an intention, one discovers the complicity of the concept with the idea of subjectivity, usually of the conscious, present-to-itself, sound-mind-and-body variety. A knowledge of intention, for instance, might serve the desire for the self-validation of being the recipient of a message or communication from an authoritative figure, with whatever empowerment such validation might bestow (the idea, as Northrop Frye puts it, of the literary work's being the author's pie stuffed with "a specific number of beauties or effects" that the critic, like Little Jack Horner, has only to pull out with the self-congratulation "O what a good boy am I" [17–18]). To receive a message one has already assumed a very great deal about the nature of messages (and texts, and teaching) and the intentions behind them, particularly that the intentions of the other reciprocate with one's own. The simplest assumption is that the text embodies some sort of direct communication or representation—Wordsworth's "man speaking to men," for example—and that the reading relation mimes a version of Saussure's speaking relation, with its single direct line going from speaker's mouth to receiver's ear. More experienced *entendeurs* will at least sympathize with the contention of the surrealist Michel Leiris that such a utilitarian notion of language as "born to facilitate men's mutual contacts" appears a "monstrous aberration" (in Ahl 18).

With regard to the "complex words" he brings forward, Empson feels that the term *head sense* ought to sum up and recall "a real field of activity for the critic" as one who "needs to know the general flavour and proportions of any crucial word in the minds of the audience primarily intended, and he needs to know whether other uses of the word by the author in hand show that he does something special with it" (75). "Head sense" makes the argument in a pun, combining "leading dictionary definition" with individual "mental ability"; but the conception of "the audience primarily intended" raises the question of history and psychocultural change. Empson finds "an historical locus for *Complex Words* in the Restoration and Augustan periods," that is, with authors writing in an age when "conventions were deep enough to achieve conviction without private backing" (Cavell 226), and for whom "complexity is a matter of social nuance, of tactful understatement and ironic self-regard" (Norris 101). The writers I will discuss in terms of some of their "lexis complexes" (a few from a wide range of possibilities) come from a later era, when the continuing evaporation of Christianity has weakened conventional reliance on words and the Word. The poet's "intention," for Empson, "is located precisely in the knowing play of attitude, ironic and self-critical, that keeps both poet and reader from an unreflecting state of immersion in the poem's metaphysical conceits" (Norris 134); later writers (and readers) have less faith in "knowing play" and may seem more preoccupied with constructing projections and displacements adequate to contain (temporarily) their needs and conflicts.

In his appreciative critique of Empson, Christopher Norris identifies "two basic dimensions in the understanding of a Complex Word: the informing background of historical context and the implications *of* and *for* the semantic grammar of its usage" (107). The consideration of lexis complexes, on the other hand, finds its stamping ground in biography—especially as concerns early object relations, inaccessible and textualized though they must be—and in the inflections and associations to be found in the individual's semantics. *Nature* and *reason* are complex words in Samuel Johnson's discourse, *restless* one example of its "complexemes." Empson takes *sense* as a complex word in *The Prelude*, where a sense of lexis complexes would include *since* and *presence/absence*, even *incense* (cf. "smoke / Sent up, *in silence*" ["Tintern Abbey"]) and "in[-]no[-]cence". Rather than gauging a complex word's intentions and "covert assertions" (Empson 47, 255), the study of lexis complexes pursues covert associations the word holds in tension.³ With its rationalist, phenomenological orientation, Empson's *Complex Words* has little place for the unconscious, whereas the psychoanalytical bias in the imagining of lexis complexes takes the unknown as given.

The bottom line for the usual question regarding intention appears in Norris's remark that "a line must of course be drawn between the critic's own virtuosity—meanings patently 'read into' the text—and the content he can claim to have uncovered" (33). Similarly, Umberto Eco, having specified an intention of the author, of the work, and of the reader, distinguishes between "interpretation" as research into the first two, and "use" as the "imposition" of the latter (62, 50). We move here toward the rhetorical world made familiar by reader-response criticism, where reality is a matter of what positions achieve communal recognition; in that bizarre marketplace of ideas or ever-evolving textual ecosystem, the stretching or far-fetching of some points to make space for others seems a necessary part of critical response-ability. In the ensuing conflict or dialectic of readings one discovers, as Norris quickly acknowledges, that "there is no absolute distinction, no possible demarcation between what is 'in' the text and what is produced by the critic's active involvement" (34).⁴

A "pragmatic" way of formulating the question, then, recognizes the reader's necessary cooperation in producing the text and finds intention in the implication of its words. In this view, initiated by H. P. Grice in over thirty years of occasional lectures and articles collected as *Studies in the Way of Words* in 1989, conversation—including the relation of writer and reader—proceeds and depends upon certain shared assumptions. These Grice organizes according to four general maxims regarding quantity ("Give the right amount of information"), quality ("Try to make your contribution one that is true"), relation ("Be relevant"), and manner ("Be perspicuous") (26–27)—maxims that even in being flouted are confirmed. Modified by a generation of scholars (including Geoffrey Leech, John Searle, and Dan Sperber), such principles are still taken to govern the complex inferencing strategies by which we understand invisible or "implied" meaning. For Grice, recognizing a speaker or author's intention equals identifying the act he or she performs in all its implications, but as pragmatic critics who actually confront poetic effects have come to see, there are in such cases a vast continuum of implicatures ranging from fully determinate to very indeterminate, and poetic metaphors in particular access a wide range of weak implicatures (see Pilkington 53–56). Here once again we confront the practical need of limiting input, and because the inferencing of implicatures offers endless possibilities, considerations of relevance operate to constrain inferencing. Relevance in turn depends on context, the scenario one builds around the text; and criticism, including the chapters that follow, inevitably emphasizes or "privileges" a more or less limited context. The creation of a plausible context returns us to the familiar rhetorical considerations of any attempt to persuade—ethos, pathos, and logos.

We might consider, for an example, a literary text that Grice uses to illustrate the flouting of the maxim of manner, "Be perspicuous" (with its subordinate maxims: "Avoid obscurity of expression," "Avoid ambiguity," "Be brief," "Be orderly"). For an instance in which "the speaker intends or expects [ambiguity] to be recognized" and "the problem the hearer has to solve" is why this should be so, he offers "Blake's lines: 'Never seek to tell thy love, love that never told can be'"—though "to avoid the complications introduced by the presence of the imperative mood," Grice casts the sentence in first-person declarative, past tense ("I sought") (35). He notes the double reference of "my love" to a state or an object of emotion, and how the second line means either that the love cannot be told, or if told, cannot continue to exist, and concludes "that the ambiguities are deliberate and that the poet is conveying both . . . though no doubt the poet is not explicitly saying any one of these things but only conveying or suggesting them" (35–36).

Further work with this example requires greater context, beginning with the literal text of the poem as it was available in the standard edition when Grice wrote:

> [Never (seek *del.*) pain to tell thy love
> Love that never told can be;
> For the gentle wind does move
> Silently, invisibly. *del.*]
>
> I told my love, I told my love,
> I told her all my heart,
> Trembling, cold, in ghastly fears—
> Ah, she doth depart.

> Soon as she was gone from me
> A traveller came by
> Silently, invisibly—
> [He took her with a sigh *del.*]
> O, was no deny.
>   (Keynes 161)

The revision of "seek" can indeed give readers "pain," because the rare intransitive usage with its obsolescent reflexive sense ("to take pains"; the latest OED example is 1529) greatly complicates the imperative mood, but unless we are proposing an example without much relevance to an actual text, the particulars and context must matter. Generalizing the largest implications ("Never," "never") from the seemingly slender basis of one experience (an act that carries implications of its own), the speaker presents a complex picture of message and audience. The awkward sequence of the tenses—especially the present indicative "doth depart" (which parallels "does move")—the ambiguity of "love," and the vague reference of "she" ("my heart," the already ambiguous "love"), all work to take us into an unstable ego we might most naturally overhear as directing imperatives to itself. At this point our interpretation could take a psychoanalytical turn into the world of object relations and find the manifestation of an unconscious depressive ambivalence highly relevant to the expression of ambiguity centering on a female-gendered love. But it should already be imaginable that "pain" in part implicates the speaker's subjective state, and its inner tensions are what the text—if not the hypothesized speaker—intends. Regarding the text as the representation of an illocutionary act rather than some direct communication in itself does not resolve the question of its motivation, though the additional displacement may suggest that such texts, like the productions for the dream work for Freud, *"are not made with the intention of being understood"* (*Interpretation* 377).

Words present particularly complex objects for individual and cultural processing in view of the contention, stated by R. Hudson, that "there is no known limit to the amount of detailed information . . . which may be associated with a lexical item" (in Aitchison 12). To "know" a word fully would entail the impossibility of complete knowledge of the various systems in which it was implicated, including idiosyncratic personal references and the ongoing operant processing system. Of more immediate concern for lexical processing is polysemy, the condition of a word's having several or more meanings. Experimental research suggests that all the available known meanings of a polysemous word, and even homonyms, may be activated preconsciously, although only one meaning will be selected (see Dixon 256; Aitchison 182–83). As with spontaneously reversing figure-ground designs where one cannot see simultaneously the profiles and the goblet, or the duck and the rabbit, there is for the polysemous word a fixed conscious capacity limitation (Dixon 233). The linear intelligence guiding the organism does not long or well tolerate dissonance, poets' pleas for "negative capability" or a "willing suspension of disbelief" notwithstanding. Like humans in other aspects of life (cf. Gazzaniga 175), readers seek parsimonious and unified explanations for the logic governing texts, and hence, as Stephen Booth observes, "most people who talk about poetry will not admit secondary senses or overtones or invasions of logically impertinent contexts unless the presence of such ideational static is capable of promotion to the distinction of full-fledged, syntactically admissible ambiguity and therefore capable of interpretation" (370).

Recognizable ambiguity has long offered a kind of special-case logical category for literary criticism. According to the influential argument of Cleanth Brooks's *The Well Wrought Urn* (1947), a poet may "choose ambiguity and paradox" because the task "is finally to unify experience" (212). As the poet "perforce" dramatizes "the oneness of the experience, even though paying tribute to its diversity," his or her "use of paradox and ambiguity is seen as necessary" in giving us "an insight which preserves the unity of experience and which, at its higher and more serious levels, triumphs over the apparently contradictory and conflicting elements of experience by unifying them into a new pattern" (213, 214). But to see paradox plainly, Brooks contends, "will require a closer reading than most of us give to poetry" (11), in fact, "the closest possible examination" (xi). The library's groaning shelves testify that we have risen to the occasion, and a half-century of ever closer reading finds us long past the parody of *The Overwrought Urn* (published in 1969) and through the looking glass of the text to face "the overdetermined yearn."[5] The deconstruction of the "unified," "total" structure or "oneness of experience"; awareness of parallel—plural—processing; new sensitivities to the discourse of language and ideology, and to the psychodynamics of language acquisition and use, can combine to make undecidable what was before merely ambiguous or paradoxical. As per Heisenberg's uncertainty principle, once we enter the detailed realm of "the closest possible examination," the force of our observing itself touches our sense of verse and universe. To recall overdetermination, one has only to consider a favorite text and its train of widely varying critical commentary, more than one portion of which probably receives assent. All the determinations, like a sum of vectors, are at work (or play) in and on "the total experience" (Brooks 75) of the text's passage to materiality, the word's present instantiation: "the word, directed toward its object, enters a dialogically agitated and tension-filled environment of alien words, value judgments and accents, weaves in and out of complex interrelationships, merges with some, recoils from others, intersects with yet a third group: and all this may crucially shape discourse, may leave a trace in all its semantic layers, may complicate its expression and influence its entire stylistic profile" (Bakhtin 276).

One set of determinations difficult to formulate involves the author's life, particularly with regard to that individual's accession to language in early childhood and the acquisition of characteristic "in-tensions." At least during the flowering of individual subjectivity that has produced so much literature, the artist's life constitutes an indispensable context for the work. If a primary function of literature is "to convert a sector of reality (whether psychic or external) into literary reality" (Green 342), then that extraliterary reality forms an important reference. And if "the artist cannot take us where he himself has never been" (Rickman 307–8), and if "home is where we start from" (D. W. Winnicott), then some sense of early emotional, psychic, and perceptual states traversed will be implicated in understanding her or his work. Charlotte Brontë's *Jane Eyre* offers a memorable instance in the heroine's three major encounters with different families, each *re*presenting the author's sibling configuration of two sisters and a brother. Of all the states through which an author has passed, however, that of learning language with Mama supplies the least data, and the little we have of that absent, silent, mum period are "always already" textualized. But like the cosmic event or big bang accessible only theoretically, the birth into the symbolic order perhaps leaves some trace of its occurrence in a background noise we can attune ourselves to hear.

Freud's passionate interests in the "talking cure," verbal symbolism, and "the antithetical sense of primal words," make all the more remarkable the extent to which he overlooked what we call, owing to the fixation he institutionalized, the "*pre*oedipal" stage of development. It is during this period, prompted by a genetically encoded timetable, that the baby (*in-fans*, "not speaking") passes from "being" to a being merged with the body of the mother/world to a child split off from that former being, gaining the problematic compensation of a body of or being in words and accompanying prohibitions, injunctions, names. Speculations concerning this speechless period are rich and strange—from Wordsworth's image of his "intercourse of touch" and "mute dialogues with [his] mother's heart" (*Prelude* [1805] 2.282, 283) to Julia Kristeva's sense of a "psychosomatic modality" embracing "the connections between the (glottal and anal) sphincters in (rhythmic and intonational) vocal modulations, or between the sphincters and family protagonists" (28–29). In this matrix of mutter-matter the earliest word symbols "are fused not only with the object that is the ostensible referent, but also with the mother herself who taught the word" (Rosen 163). Margaret Mahler and her associates characterize the preoedipal stage in terms of separation-individuation and see language as "instrumental in creating a special pocket of maternal reserve" that can be called upon—even in the parent's absence—for the "emotional refueling" necessary to untroubled development (Shapiro 150). Already in two-and-a-half-year-old children one sees the internalization of language as they play on their own with words before going to sleep—language forms a kind of teddy bear or security blanket, a "transitional object" that opens the realm of illusion that can unfold in art (Shapiro 42). At least in some cases, perhaps, the writer's or critic's obsessive probing of language reflects or enacts or sometimes "works through" his or her insecure possession of such a "maternal reserve." So Jean-Jacques Lecercle, thinking of the insecurity that language engenders, suggests that "one writes about and against one's mother, one's mother tongue, in order to get rid of the anxiety of influence" (238)—the anxiety of lack, of loss, of having to use words.

But some do seem to work through to a re-membering and creating anew Mother tongue in poetic words. Tracking her own profoundly ambivalent maternal relationship, the American poet H.D. (Hilda Doolittle) undertook some analytical sessions with Freud in 1933; from these she became convinced that "mine is absolutely FIRST layer. I got stuck at the earliest pre-OE stage, and 'back to the womb' seems to be my only solution" (in Friedman 313). So in her account she writes of her mother, "One can never get near enough, or if one gets near, it is because one has measles or scarlet fever. *If* one could stay near her always, there would be no break in consciousness" (*Tribute to Freud* 33). Some ten years after that recognition, in her *Tribute to the Angels* (ἄγγελος, "messenger"), she offers this remarkable consideration of the most profound maternal complexus in the Western cultural archive:

> Now polish the crucible
> and in the bowl distill
>
> a word most bitter, *marah*,
> a word bitterer still, *mar*,
>
> sea, brine, breaker, seducer,
> giver of life, giver of tears;
>
> Now polish the crucible
> and set the jet of flame
>
> under, till *marah-mar*
> are melted, fuse and join
>
> and change and alter,
> mer, mere, mère, mater, Maia, Mary,
>
> Star of the Sea,
> Mother.

In acquiring language, writes Victor Rosen, "each individual goes through idiosyncratic processes of associating tactile, auditory, and other sensory stimuli (signals), childhood theories, fantasies, and experiences (signs) to the conventional word symbol" (187). This quotidian history of such intimate life is laid out for all to read in Joyce's *A Portrait of the Artist as a Young Man* and its construction of Stephen Dedalus. The fiction builds up models of overdetermination as it commodiously recirculates through various nodal words such as *nice, murmur, order, sin,* and

Simon (the name of Stephen's father). It shows how words, the meanings of which are unknown to Stephen, guide him toward a cultural/symbolic order and reverberate "the echoes of certain expressions . . . in remote caves of [Stephen's] mind" (157) as his subjectivity gels. Joyce's novel offers a potted case for training a kind of (psycho-) "analytic attitude" in the way it demands and quickly begins to reward and reword the reader's evenly suspended, free-floating attention. So when, at the prospect of a religious retreat, "Stephen's heart . . . withered up like a flower of the desert that feels the simoom coming from afar" (108), the momentary flicker over the book's singly occurring "simoom" is soon reinforced by an invocation of "the name of the Father" to reverberate the reader into an oedipal Simon complex reaching back to Stephen's "*swoon* of sin" (101—itself following his loss of self in the carved letters "Foetus" and the initials that fuse his name and his father's, S.D.), and extending forward to one attraction for Stephen in joining the priesthood, the possibility of knowing (at last) "what was the sin of *Simon* Magus" (159). This example highlights the oedipal dynamic that engages Joyce before the "abnihilization of the etym" in *Finnegans Wake*, a dynamic so foregrounded, one might argue, because it distracted, even "soothed his eyes which still saw the image of his mother's face" and "soothed his ears in which his mother's sobs and reproaches murmured insistently" (*Portrait* 224; cf. "The mar of murmury mermers to the mind's ear" of the *Wake* [254]). With its deep cunning, *Portrait* gives the name of Stephen's mother only once (30), though as the Blessed Virgin it saturates the text; unlike the name given Stephen's father, Mary was in fact the name of Joyce's mother.

The complexly overdetermined lexis of the author is complicated still more in its reception by the reader's associations and intentions. At the same time that Cleanth Brooks was putting forward his examples of "closer reading," Leo Spitzer described how such readings came about for him. "The only way," he reports, describing one version of *attention flottante*, "is to read and reread, patiently and confidently, in an endeavor to become, as it were, soaked through and through with the atmosphere of the work." Then, "suddenly, one word, one line stands out," making "the characteristic 'click' . . . which is the indication that detail and whole have found a common denominator" (*Linguistics* 26–27).[6] Other readers can no doubt summon up analogous versions of this experience, certainly one of the most delicious that professional reading affords. Spitzer's "one word, one line," by virtue of its standing out, would be for the contemporary theorist Michael Riffaterre an example of the anomaly or "agrammaticality" that "marks a moment at which one shifts from a referential to a poetic code" and by which the analyst "can identify one of the transformational systems at work in the text" (de Man 34). For Riffaterre, Spitzer's "common denominator," at least in the case of a poem or poetic segment, will be in turn some preexistent word or word group that he labels the "hypogram" or "matrix" and sees as generating the text and authorizing a definitive reading. The poem is a complex built around a word repressed by the text, and reading is completed by pulling out that verbal plum, with the concomitant perception of the text as "the ultimate word game, that is, as literary" (Riffaterre, *Semiotics* 42). The "hidden hypogram," one commentator notes drily, can seem "very little compared to the intricacy of the work that was needed to disguise it" (de Man 38). According to this formalist endeavor, "the matrix is semantic, and not lexical or graphemic," and the resulting text "exteriorizes the inner semantic configuration of the nuclear word" (Riffaterre, *Text* 77) with little place for whatever complex affect may have marked the configuring of the word's semantic content.

The Spitzerian "click" when one word suddenly stands out can be taken in other ways, of course. It suggests an experience like laughter at a joke, when, as Freud saw it, the seemingly irrational "primary processes" become conscious and energy thus liberated must be discharged (*Interpretation* 644), or like the frisson before the uncanny, or like the "flutter of jubilant activity" when the infant assumes an *I* in Lacan's "mirror stage" (*Ecrits* 2). It reflects feelings of mastery and power, pleasurable relief at the lowering of tension now that "a common denominator" opens the way to intervene, a door to further discussion. This reposes an ongoing question behind our consideration of complexes: Does the affect accompanying the "click" stem from the sense of having in some degree demystified the text through identifying and denominating a possibly complex pattern? Or does it come from having found, at last, unawares, a way of "cathecting," investing, projecting a complex of one's own into the text and making it speak oneself?[7]

In his method of "psychocriticism," contemporary with Brooks and Spitzer, the French analyst Charles Mauron "superimposes" a writer's texts (ideally the entire oeuvre) to detect latent patterns. "Guided by the notion that the key to an expression or a work is to be found in other expressions or work," Mauron has "listened to resonances, followed associations, and sought out persistent groupings" in order to locate "underlying networks necessarily linked to the unconscious. . . . forming complexes and structuring the creative imagination" (52, 2). These networks correspond to affective themes that, expressed in recurring and evolving fantasies, embody the "personal myth" of the author. But given Mauron's repeated discovery of an obsession with the mother (e.g., in Racine, in Baudelaire, in Mallarmé), Wendy Deutelbaum can point tellingly to the presence of Mauron's own "personal myth" and its profound implication in a psychoanalytic myth and cultural ideology. In a conclusion that bears pondering, perhaps particularly by men who would pursue complexes, Deutelbaum writes that her criticisms "do not discredit Mauron's readings. Mauron does find common patterns; and these reflect real places of 'coincidence' between his own and other myths. His very partiality is a source of his work's strengths as of its limitations. By repressing part of his own subjectivity, Mauron weaves a delusion of 'objective explanations.' His explanations repeat a monotonous albeit real patriarchal theme of ambivalent maternal fixation" (96).

For the essays that follow, the Spitzerean "click" took, more often than not, the form of a homophonic "common denominator" linking aspects of the particular teaching text, corpus, and pertinent past and present corporeal realities. Arguing for an "applied grammatology," Gregory Ulmer imagines teaching a "new mimesis . . . based on homophonic resemblance" (187) in which the "puncept" would figure with the "concept." Such a pedagogy, derived from "the fully developed homonymic program at work in Derrida's style" (168) and amply evident in present critical writing, would seize on the puns or homophones as precisely the device that, at the level of language, is "capable of relating elements with the least motivation, hence with the greatest economy of speed" and "generating the greatest 'information' [i.e., negentropy]" (170, 172). Such synthetic terms may offer an instance of the "higher-order bootstraps" students will need to think a massive cultural inventory soon instantly accessible by the terabyte, in hypertext: as the neurologist Gerald Edelman observes, "Thinking occurs in terms of *synthesized* patterns, not logic, and for this reason, it may always exceed in its reach syntactical, or mechanical, relationships" (152). The puncept may suggest such a synthesized pattern that works to tie together, or suture, in highly economical fashion, a variety of logical considerations and procedures. Then there is the issue of a paradoxically revived presence of the author, or critic, if we agree with Lecercle that "in paronomasia, it is I who speak. I make language do my bidding. I take an untrodden path, only faintly indicated by language—I force my way through words" (80). Such exuberance may be intriguing and playful, or threatening and off-putting as a violation of the "cooperative principle"—the customary groan at a pun suggests the latter—but it will ensure at least against "a delusion of 'objective explanation.'" The "puncept" or lexis complex becomes at its best a word of art, a bit of critical poetry, that act defined by Wimsatt and Beardsley as "a feat of style by which a complex of meaning is handled all at once" (4).

The pun or homophone thus offers a kind of *Knotenpunkt* linking various signifieds in its common denominator. At issue is whether—as it were—you travel outward from a word, letting the sounds generate conceptual material in "free" or even mechanical association, or whether, working from a mass of text, you try to home in on homophonic connections that might tie it together. The wager of *Lexis Complexes* is that these two movements constitute a double cone or vortex (each enmeshing with the other like those Yeats describes in *A Vision*), and that the second type of approach (by the reader) finally might suggest some sort of time-reversed and compressed experience of the first (by the writer). This doubled vvord-text might also image the originally interacting realms of lexis and individual childhood psychological environment that combine in the author's particular psychosemantic inflections (including stylistic invariants as instances of repetition compulsion). So it is that many of the words soon to surface here are proper names and simple nouns, adjectives, and phrases typically encountered early in childhood (for example, "Don't be restless"; "Don't be idle"; "moon"; "Aurelia"). Such "archeonymes," writes Derrida, describe "beneath the articulation of a sentence and a scene, a multiple economy of places, instances, and safes" (xlvii) and can be imagined, in part, to motivate our present penchant for puns and possibly lead us, like Thomas Pynchon's "dreamer whose puns probe ancient fetid shafts and tunnels of truth," to enact some "special relevance to the word, or whatever it is the word is there, buffering, to protect us from" (95).

Before we turn to some words, the following chapter tries first to suggest one aspect of "whatever it is" whose special relevance might work to overdetermine those words.

2
Before the Milk of the Word: Nipple-Eyes

~

—ANON.

"At their mother's moist'ned eyes babes shall suck," says Shakespeare's Duke of Bedford fifty lines into *Henry the Sixth, Part 1*. Foreseeing the posterity of wretched years now to follow on the death of the king, Bedford adds, developing the image, that England shall "be made a nourish of salt tears." Implicit here is the metaphor of eye for nipple, face for breast first studied by Renato Almansi in an essay entitled "The Face-Breast Equation," published in 1960. Almansi's article builds in turn on earlier research that calls first for review.

In 1938 the Viennese analyst Otto Isakower published his classic paper entitled "A Contribution to the Patho-psychology of Phenomena Associated with Falling Asleep," describing what has come to be termed "the Isakower phenomenon." As described by a later researcher, this hypnogogic event

> is characteristically remembered or re-experienced by the individual as the visual sensation of a large, doughy, shadowy mass, usually round, growing larger as it comes nearer and nearer to his face, swelling to a gigantic size and threatening to crush him, and then gradually growing

smaller and moving further away. Often there is an indistinct perception of a purplish shape like the nipple area of the breast. The approaching mass slowly seems to become a part of him, obscuring the boundaries between his body and the outside world, and blurring his sense of self more and more. All of this is typically accompanied by sensations of tactile roughness on the skin and inside the mouth, and a milky or salty taste in the back of the throat. Often there are feelings of floating or loss of equilibrium. In some individuals there is, interestingly, a memory of voluntarily producing the experience or prolonging it. (Bromberg 600–601)

Isakower argues along Freudian lines that "when we fall asleep, the ego withdraws its interest and its cathexes [investments] from the external world" (336). This gradual withdrawal permits the "revival of very early ego-attitudes," and Isakower contends that the phenomena he reports represent imprints from "mental images of sucking at the mother's breast and of falling asleep there when satisfied" (341). H.D., whose preoedipal concern was noted in the previous chapter, offers a possible analog to the phenomenon in the seemingly hallucinatory experience she described to Freud as "the transcendental feeling of the two globes or the two transparent half-globes enclosing me"—Isakower's paper not having yet appeared, Freud evidently acquiesced to the poet's supposition that she had gotten back to the womb in "some form of pre-natal fantasy" (168).

Bertram Lewin, in a series of papers dating from 1946 to 1953, discussed the Isakower phemenonon in relation to what he called "the dream screen" and also "the class of blank dreams." For Lewin, "the dream screen" constitutes one visual element in the Isakower conglomeration of relatively formless visual and nonvisual hallucinations. As the name suggests, Lewin's "dream screen" constitutes the background on which the dream projects its imaging: "it is flat, or virtually so, like the surface of the earth, for it is genetically a segment of the baby's vast picture of the mammary hemisphere" (197–98). Lewin's third category, the class of blank dreams, "consists of various subgroups, having in common an absence or near absence of formed, manifest, visual detail and plot. They may be simple, visually manifest blanks, or they may be composites of various features of the Isakower phenomena, or they may be blended with later impressions. They are often not describable in concrete terms but only by means of metaphor, and they may resemble feelings and affects rather than pictures" (198). Lewin concludes that "genetically, Isakower phenomena, dream screen, and blank dreams are in essence the same thing; they reproduce some of the impression that the smallest baby has at the breast" (198).

The gifted clinician and theorist René Spitz responded to the "extraordinary fertile" work of Lewin and Isakower in his 1955 study of "the genesis of perception and its role for psychoanalytic theory," "The Primal Cavity." Spitz's detailed direct observations on infants had led him to conclude "that the [infant's] first visual percept is the human face," or, more exactly, "a Gestalt configuration *within* the human face" (216). He makes the crucial point that "the nursing baby does not look at the *breast*. He does not look at the breast when the mother is approaching him, nor when she is offering him the breast, nor when he is nursing. He stares unwaveringly, from the beginning of the feeding to the end of it, at the mother's face" (218). Spitz thus proposes that "the Isakower phenomenon does not represent the approaching breast" but "the visually perceived human face" (218). For the infant, nursing and staring at the same time, "breast and face are experienced as one and indivisible" (219), and the concomitant tactile sensations in the oral cavity are united with visual perceptions into one undifferentiated unity, "in which any one part of the experience comes to stand for the total experience" (222). Given his sense of the infant's developmental program, Spitz characterizes the Isakower phenomenon and the dream screen as two stages of regression. The dream screen he imagines to go to the level of the memory traces "laid down somewhere between" the ages of six months and one year, while the Isakower phenomenon "harks back to a [still] earlier period, that which precedes the reliable laying down of visual mnemic traces" (232). These regressions are thus presented as the counterpart to the ontogenetic development of perception via the mouth as the primal cavity where—anticipating Julia Kristeva's more recent conception of the "chora"—"the earliest sensory experiences . . . are dealt with on the level of the primary process, yet they lead to the development of the secondary process" (238). So for Spitz the dream screen is not the visual image of the breast but much more probably "the result of a composite experience, which in the visual field represents the approaching face of the mother, but in the field of the other percepts involves the sensations within the oral cavity" (232). "This," he adds, "is perhaps also an explanation of the fact that in so many of the dream screen reports the dream screen appears dark, at other times colorless, amorphous." What Lewin sees as "a blending of different images of the breast," Spitz labels "a synesthesia of many different senses, the visual constituent of which is derived from the percept of the face" (233). In the condensation of the face with the breast image, it is, fascinatingly enough in this hypothesis, the image of the face that is most repressed.

Spitz's observations are amply confirmed by contemporary researchers who have repeatedly established, as Michael Carroll summarizes, that an infant of two to four months will fixate more upon the eyes than upon any other facial feature. Of the several explanations offered for this effect, "the most common is that this preference for 'eyes' derives from a set of more general visual preferences that characterize the infant at this age"— including preferences for curvilinearity, concentricity, and contrast density (Carroll 183). Hence early infants prefer bull's-eye patterns over other graphic designs, a finding with noticeable impact on the latest generation of mobiles for babies. The physical similarity of eye and nipple appears in the word *areola*, by which English refers both to the concentric and pigmented iris of the eye and to the pigmented area surrounding the nipple. If we grant that young infants fixate upon the eyes because of a generalized preference for certain physical characteristics, concludes Carroll, then it follows that they "would fixate upon the tip of their mother's breast for the same reasons, since the tip of the breast manifests these same traits" (184).

Renato Almansi's attention to "the face-breast equation" was prepared by earlier work on the hypnagogic phenomenon of a scopophilic and orally oriented patient in whom "intense frustration and anger toward the mother figure had come to the fore":

> The visual components of this phenomenon appeared to result from the fusion of two percepts: the image of a face, which was identified as loving and inviting at times and as angry and forbidding at other times; and the image of the breast, which had probably been perceived at a later stage of development. In this patient, the latter image, i.e., the breast, screened the former almost completely; only through the patient's numerous associations and his statement that a voice emerged

from inside of a breastlike cloud was it possible to ascertain that, in effect, the breast concealed the percept of a face. (43–44)

This clinical example, and the theoretical concepts behind it, encourage Almansi to speculate that the fusion of the two percepts of breast and face, the screening of one by the other, and their equation may occur more frequently than is commonly realized.

In "The Face-Breast Equation" he offers several additional clinical examples. The first concerns an ophthalmologist, the eldest of eight children, whose mother weaned his siblings by painting her nipples with a mixture of vinegar and charcoal in order to bring about revulsion in the child. His presenting symptoms included the fact that "when he operated on a patient's eye with the assistance of a female attendant, he was under tremendous tension, which he attributed to the fear that his hand might slip and that he might thrust the knife forcefully into the patient's orbit." Speculating "why this symptom was present only in the presence of his nurse, . . . he realized that while he had only been consciously aware of his wish to fondle her breasts, actually he felt strong aggressive impulses against her" (45).

Another of Almansi's examples is a lawyer in his middle thirties who also revealed "strong, latent aggressive impulses, which were directed against the women in his family, and frequently against his female clients as well." When a termination was set, this patient began obsessively doodling naked female figures, as in the examples Almansi reproduces (fig. 1) with the comment,

> At times, he elaborated on these figures by adding a semicircle to the semicircle representing the breasts, which transformed them into complete circles; he would then draw a line, joining the two circles to make a pair of glasses, and would shade the area between the breasts to make it look like a nose. Occasionally, in his drawings, [the patient] would enlarge the navel, to give it the appearance of a mouth. Thus, finally, he completed his representation of a face. (46–47)

The resolution of some of the patient's most obstinate residual problems came one day when, after several weeks of this activity, during an analytic session he drifted into a hypnagogic state in which he visualized with great clarity the dark, benevolent eyes of his mother, isolated and suspended in

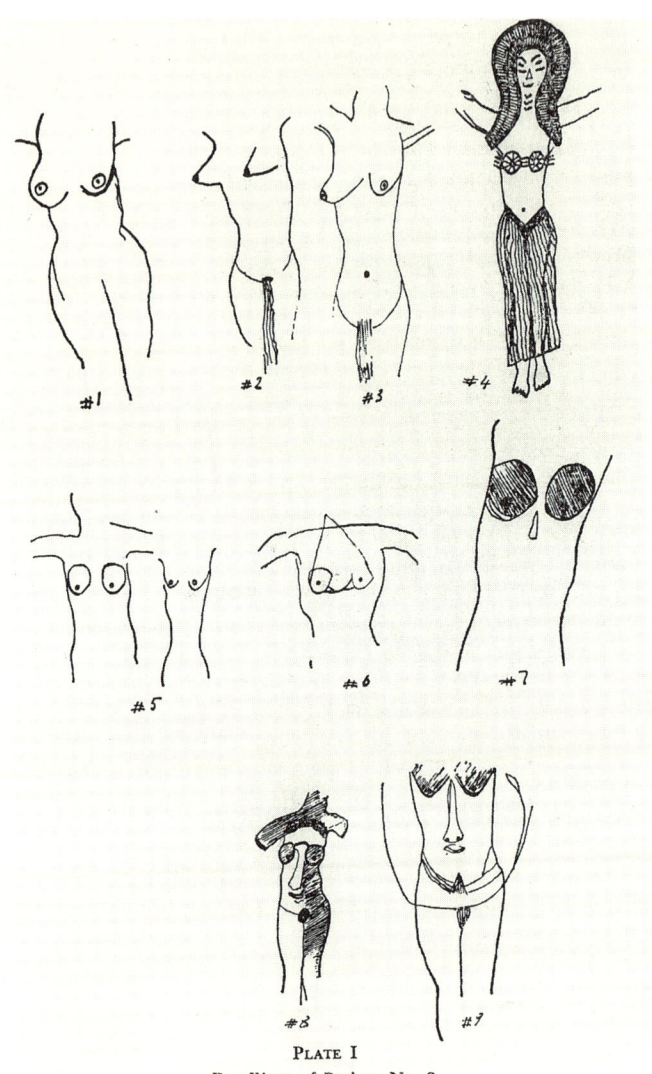

PLATE I
Doodlings of Patient No. 2.

Fig. 1. Doodlings of Dr. Almansi's patient. Renato J. Almansi, "The Face-Breast Equation," *Journal of the American Psycho-analytic Assocation* 8, no. 1 (1960).

space, looking down upon him (47)—a description suggestive of Odilon Redon's 1882 lithograph "On the horizon, the angel of certitudes, and in the somber sky, a questioning gaze" (fig. 2). The patient's visualization and Redon's image can anticipate our later discussion of moon-moms in Keats, Plath, and Charlotte Brontë, whose Jane Eyre receives her only vision of her dead mother when the moon becomes that human form "inclining a glorious brow earthward" which "gazed and gazed and gazed" on her (281). This vision also prepares us for the role of the moon in linking (like a satellite relay) the mom's face and the mom's breast: for some, the moon is the breast *and* the eye of night.

In addition to the case material, Almansi develops the "face-breast equation" with graphic material, including cartoons. In one of these a small male figure looks at female breasts, which in turn regard him; the female figure has neither a nose nor eyes—these being displaced downward—but her mouth is indicated. Almansi also includes some findings from a Sumerian temple studied by the archaeologist M. E. L. Mallowan; dated at approximately the third millennium B.C.E., it was "adorned with a frieze depicting a very large eye; and many thousands of votive objects were found inside" (61). These idols represent the outline of a woman in which the eyes are situated where the breast ought to be, and Mallowan believes that "the Eye-Idols are the abstract symbols of some divinity . . . who, if not the Mother Goddess herself, had the same powers of reproduction and generative force" (153) and which, at this site, for some unknown reason, were expressed in the form of the "magic eye." Some specimens (fig. 3) present a cross between "the naturalist form of eye-idol" and the "spectacle-topped" variety (34–35), to produce an idol that seems to equate eyes and nipples.

From all these data Almansi concludes that "on a primitive perceptual level the face may be equated with the breasts, and that there is a particularly strong correlation between the nipples and the eyes." He notes that in all the cases he reports the phenomena involved "were indissolubly bound to the liberation of large amounts of aggression," specifically reactive to oral deprivation. This aggression he relates to repeated frustration experienced at the breast at about three months, when, at the same time, the infant as a result of its deprivation fuses the percepts of face and breast. The infant reacts to its frustration with the "hallucinatory projection of the

A l'horizon, l'Ange des CERTITUDES, et dans le ciel sombre un regard interrogateur.

Fig. 2. Odilon Redon, "A l'horizon, l'ange des certitudes," from A *Edgar Poe* (1882). Courtesy of the Fogg Art Museum, Harvard University Art Museums, Gift of Philip Hofer.

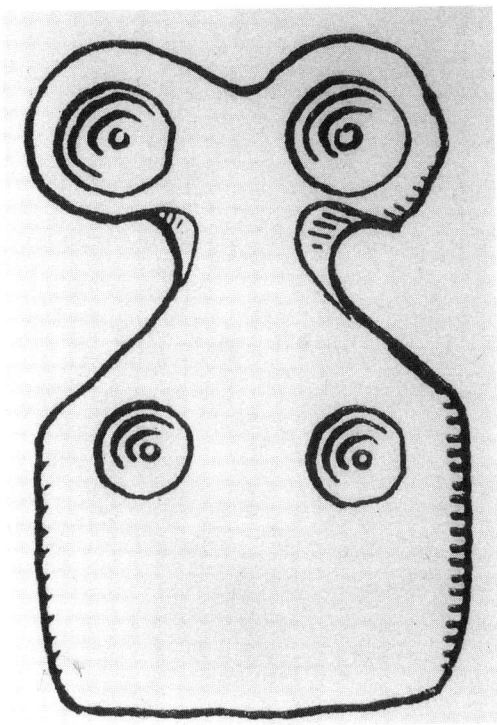

Fig. 3. "Eye-Idol." M. E. L. Mallowan, "Excavations at Brak and Chaga Bazar," *Iraq* 9 (1947), fig. 6.

satisfaction-giving object, in an attempt to recreate, in part at least, the primitive perceptual cluster consisting of the sensation of the nipple in the mouth and the concurrent vision of the mother's face. The interruption of this cluster by the withdrawal of the nipple is a powerful determinant in the differentiation between the 'I' and the 'non-I,' in the division between what is experienced internally and what is seen as external" (68). Almansi suggests that phenomena he describes "relate precisely to a period when the dividing line between the 'I' and 'non-I' was still not sharply drawn." The " 'looking and being looked at' motif" expressed in the cartoons and in many of his clinical cases pertains to such a lack of differentiation and embodies dynamics of both identification and projection. Almansi's formulations correlate significantly with Melanie Klein's conceptualization of the infant's early object relations and her sense that it is precisely during this same period between the second and fourth month that the infant moves from what she terms the "paranoid-schizoid" position to a depressive position fraught with ambivalent feelings toward the breast. Indeed, through a consideration of the crucial role Klein gives to envy, Michael Carroll's study of the psychological origins of the familiar folk belief in the evil eye argues that "the association between 'eyes' and the 'good breast,' and the association between 'envy' and the 'good breast' are probably among the earliest of all the associations formed in the mind of the human infant. That the adult's projection of the infantile memory of the good breast would be represented as an 'eye,' or that envy directed at the good breast should become—through projection [of repressed hostility]—envy coming from the 'eyes' of another individual, is therefore not at all surprising" (184).

Such dynamics are known to students of English Romanticism through a curious incident related by John William Polidori, who was serving as Byron's physician during the famous summer of 1816, which saw Byron, Shelley, and Mary Godwin meet at the Villa Diodati and undertake the ghost-story contest that resulted in Mary Godwin Shelley's *Frankenstein* (discussed in chapter 4). According to Polidori's eyewitness account, after midnight on 18 June 1816, "Byron repeated some verses of Coleridge's *Christabel*, of the witch's breast"—no doubt the climactic lines concerning "a sight to dream of, not to tell!"—"when . . ." But first, *Christabel*. Though never explicitly presenting the nipple-eye, the poem offers a telling embodiment of its thematic, combining as it does in the figure of Geraldine a crucial breast image ("the most important in the poem," as one critic says [Twitchell 47]) and a character whose "daemonic aggression resides in her eye" (Paglia 223). In the poem's unforgettable scene Christabel watches as Geraldine

> unbound
> The cincture from beneath her breast:
> Her silken robe, and inner vest,
> Dropt to her feet, and full in view,
> Behold! her bosom, and half her side—
> A sight to dream of, not to tell!
> O shield her! shield sweet Christabel!
> (248–54)

Earlier, while she was leading to her room the "lady strange" who had appeared suddenly from behind a "huge, broad-breasted, old oak-tree,"

> Christabel *saw* the lady's eye,
> And nothing else *saw* she thereby,
> Save the *boss* of the shield of Sir Leoline tall,
> Which hung in a murky *old* niche in the wall.
> (160–63; italics added)

The association of *boss* with bosom, or breast, appears in the *OED*'s definitions for the word: "1. A protuberance or swelling on the body of an animal or plant; . . . 3. A round prominence in hammered or carved work." One might think as well of the conventional armor of Wagnerian Valkyries. Coleridge seems to play with the association through a verbal echo in the second part of the poem as Christabel, viewing "the joyous look" her father, Sir Leoline, receives from Geraldine, recalls the key scene of the preceding night, and

> Again she *saw* that *bos*om *old*,
> Again she felt that bosom cold.
> (457–58; italics added)

"The touch of this bosom" has, however, left Christabel—like the author—unable to specify what Geraldine refers to as "this mark of my shame, this seal of my sorrow" (270). This ancient mar in her[1] appears in part the projection of Christabel, who regresses, in simile, first to a child sleeping with her mother (301) and then an infant (318), all the while "dreaming that alone, which is— / O sorrow and shame!" (295–96), that is, Geraldine's "mark of her sorrow" and "seal of her shame." For Coleridge, as for Freud, the unconscious knows not time, and

> neither heat, nor frost, nor thunder,
> Shall wholly do away, I ween,
> The marks of that which once hath been.
> (424–26)

To return to the early hours of 18 June 1816 and Polidori's account: Byron repeated some verses of the poem, "of the witch's breast; when silence ensued, and Shelley, suddenly shrieking and putting his hands to his head, ran out of the room with a candle. . . . He was looking at Mrs. Shelley [Mary Godwin], and suddenly thought of a woman he had heard of who had eyes instead of nipples, which taking hold of his mind, horrified him" (Holmes

329). Mary Godwin, who even as a child had heard *Christabel*'s author recite his poetry at her home, reportedly knew firsthand that "the horror that Coleridge meant to attach to the Ladie in Christabel was two eyes in her bosom" (Sunstein 112 and n.) and no doubt shared this image with her lover, so preparing the way for the hallucination of which she herself was to be the victim. Already in *Alastor* Shelley had fused "that snowy breast, those dark and drooping eyes" (line 601), and in *The Witch of Atlas*, the appearance of "bosom-eyed" figures (line 136) suggests a familiarity with residual effects and affects of unsuccessful early nurturing in a projected fearful sense of parental reproach, the consequence of the infant's anger and frustration over oral deprivation.[2]

One of the more striking images to be generated out of surrealism, René Magritte's *Le viol*, "The Rape," was produced in several versions and media between 1934 and 1948. The image was initially regarded as so scandalous that in the 1934 surrealist Minotaur exhibition in Brussels, it was hung in a private room and shown only to initiates (Koslow 78), though in that same year André Breton used Magritte's design for the cover of his pamphlet *Qu'est-ce que le surréalisme?* (fig. 4). It is perhaps an instance of the cunning or unconscious of history, that in illustrating this question with this image, these dedicated surrealists are transposing a representation out of their cultural archive—even an emblem of "Reason," as imagined in the early years of the French Revolution (fig. 5). Elizabeth Wright considers Magritte's image "a metaphor for [Lacan's sense of] any gaze, signifying desire and an invasion of the other's desire ('The Rape')" (118). Lacan identifies the gaze as the "lodging of desire in looking," that is, an expression of the subject's "search for a fantasy that represents for him/her the lost phallus" (in Wright 117) or primal object that can be, paradoxically enough given the terminology, the mother. This dynamic appears already in Wordsworth's *Prelude*, where the orphaned poet, himself fixated on "drinking in" external nature, blesses "the infant Babe,"

> Nurs'd in his Mother's arms, the Babe who sleeps
> Upon his Mother's breast, who, when his soul
> Claims manifest kindred with an earthly soul,
> Doth gather passion from his Mother's eye!
>
> ([1805] 2.240–43)

Fig. 4. André Breton and René Magritte, *Qu'est-ce que le surréalism?* (cover, 1934). Photograph courtesy of the Art Institute of Chicago.

Fig. 5. "Reason." © Bibliothèque Nationale Paris.

The gaze, one might say, is an attempt to recover or reestablish the lost object, the "object perdita" that Lacan calls the "*object petit a*" that in its basic form would return us to the infant staring "unwaveringly, from the beginning of the feeding to the end of it, at the mother's face" (Spitz 218). As Lacan puts it, "the breast . . . represents that part of himself that the individual loses at birth, and which may serve to symbolize the most profound lost object" (in Silverman 156). Of course, no reality of the present can ever correspond to that infantile wish, and, moreover, the equally unwavering desires of the other must be reckoned with; so, for Lacan, pessimistically, "*what I look at is never what I wish to see*" (*Concepts* 103). By this account, for example, our enduring cultural fixation on the female breast (see, e.g., Plath's *Journals* 22; below, chap. 9) might be seen as a function of reluctance to enter the symbolic order and acknowledge the I/eye of the other. This rape or "seizure" of the subjectivity of the other also represents the defensive move of a desire not to be objectified by the gaze of the mother— the drive not to be an other for those eyes peering deep into one's self. Magritte, as an artist reordering the intersection of the imaginary (or private) and symbolic (or cultural) order, disturbs the narcissistic, regressive-tending gaze of the viewer with an image that makes the viewer see "the ubiquity of the libidinous" (Wright 118)—that is, the always scandalous picture of our ongoing infantile sexuality.

These considerations may resonate with the preceding chapter's conflicting approaches to the "other" of the text. And it might be argued that even as the dynamic guiding the chapters to come sets out to "nipplize" the text in search of what the gospel calls "the sincere milk of the word" (1 Peter 2:2), at the same time the endeavor displaces the face of the text with its own object/reflection/regard. However that may be, the homonym, paronomasia, pun can epitomize the full word, full precisely with its flowing links to or glances at or segues into other contexts, some of which look back to where we start from ("home-nymic" associations, perhaps), while others trace our destiny.

3
Restless Wrestling: Johnson's *Rasselas*

We are now again invading the habitations of the dead.
—*Rasselas*

Samuel Johnson's *Rasselas* can be seen in part as the personal (a word rooted in Latin *persona*, "a mask") meditation one might expect given its presenting occasion, the death of the author's mother and his ostensible need for money to cover funeral expenses, and its composition in a weeklong, scarcely revised outpouring. On or near the book's publication date Johnson writes that such powers as we now find in *Rasselas* are necessitated only by "great exigencies"—these "happen but seldom, and therefore those qualities which have a claim to the veneration of mankind, lie hid, for the most part, like subterranean treasures, over which the foot passes as on common ground, till necessity breaks open the golden cavern" (*Idler* 51, 7 April 1759). *Rasselas* (R) suggests, in part, personal meditation, because, as with most any literary text, the book and its author disclose many things. Like the palace described at the end of the first chapter, "built as if suspicion herself had dictated the plan," the text is riddled with "open and secret passage[s]," [1] though the "upper stories" are no doubt better known and more accessible than the "subterranean passages." Like the palace, the text seems joined with a cement—a semantics—that, as with the force of habit, "grows harder by time" (R 41).[2] In this written palace "many of the columns," we read, have "unsuspected cavities" concealing treasure whose accumulation, only to be revealed in "utmost exigency," is recorded "in a book" (in *its* columns, one supposes) "itself concealed" (41). For Johnson, as for Wordsworth after him,

>   books are yours,
> Within whose silent chambers treasure lies
> Preserved from age to age; more precious far
> Than that accumulated store of gold
> And orient gems, which, for a day of need,
> The Sultan hides deep in ancestral tombs.
>   (*The Excursion* 4.564–69)

One can find Johnson everywhere just around the corner in *Rasselas*—in the old man at the end who has "neither mother to be delighted with the reputation of her son, nor wife to partake the honor of her husband" and who regrets time "lost in idleness and vacancy" (136), in the astronomer who "has drawn out his soul in endless calculations" (127),³ in the anonymous auditor of chapter 22, "more affected with the narrative than the rest" (87), in the roving Arab beset with "an intestine conflict" (126), and in the "wise and happy man" overcome by the death of his closest female relation. This latter encounter, in chapter 18, W. K. Wimsatt finds "the only part of the whole book that verges on the uncomfortable" ("In Praise" 128), and in that reflects our general lack of ease with raw affect. Yet it seems perfectly in keeping with some logic of the unconscious that this wise and happy man who speaks with the greatest energy on "the government of the passions" is the very one who must endure the passion of realizing that "what I suffer cannot be remedied, what I have lost cannot be supplied." With the death of his only daughter, he continues, "my views, my purposes, my hopes are now at an end: I am now a lonely being disunited from society" (R 81). Johnson's *Idler* 41, published 27 January 1759, five days after his mother's death, echoes his language: "The life which made my own life pleasant is at an end." A month later he writes his stepdaughter, still in the tone of the bereaved philosopher, "I am now very desolate" (1 March, *Letters* [L] 121).

A decade earlier, when his mother was eighty and it was then a mere nine years since he had last made an excursion to Lichfield to visit her, Johnson was already anticipating her death as "one of the few calamities on which I think with terrour" (L 31). Little wonder that some critics have been curious about young Sam Johnson's relationship with his mother, Sarah, already forty when he was born her first child. Such concerns are of course colored by presuppositions: so one critic feels that "there can be no doubt of his love for her" since "in later life he wrote of his 'dear mother' with obvious feeling" (Clifford 20), but for another, "if he felt love, it was clearly a love overlaid and warped by other emotions; not once in his private diaries and prayers did he call his mother 'dearest,' though commonly using the term for his female friends" (Porter 73). Johnson's own comment is curiously ambivalent and might raise doubts, as well, about his reading of the word *love*: "I did not respect my own mother, though I loved her: and one day, when in anger she called me a puppy, I asked her if she knew what they called a puppy's mother" (Piozzi 69). Whatever the exact age we are to give Sam in this scene, the son's slur testifies to his internalization of what he later reported as the parents' mutual "contempt" (Clifford 17).

"My mother," Johnson said, "was always telling me that I did not *behave* myself properly" (Piozzi 68); to Boswell he related that "Sunday was a heavy day to me when I was a boy. My mother confined me on that day, and made me read 'The Whole Duty of Man'" (Boswell, *Life* 50). Such early, repeated confinement seems a precondition for Johnson's now much discussed "padlock" and the associated diary entry, in 1771, "De pedicis et manicis insana cogitatio" (*Diaries* 140); in 1773, under the same roof with his by then securely established reparative object, Hester Thrale [later Piozzi], Johnson wrote her, in French, that "if it seems best to you that I should remain in a certain place" it "will not cost you more than the trouble to turn the key in the door twice a day" (Newton 104; cf. L 323–24). These obsessions with imprisonment may lead us to recontextualize one familiar anecdote: "Dr. Johnson said, that one day at Oxford [when he was nineteen], as he was *turning the key of his chamber*, he heard his mother distinctly call *Sam*. She was then at Lichfield" (Boswell, *Life* 1138; first italics added). Perhaps the key to this account is not the "supernatural" (Boswell) or nostalgia (Clifford), but the dynamics of unconscious association: Johnson's mother was certainly an ongoing internalized object, and Johnson told of another incident in which "a long time after my mother's death, I heard her voice call *Sam!*" (Piozzi 125), though here also we do not learn whether the sounds of a key in the door triggered the memory.

Even the most abbreviated view of the "world of bad internal objects" (Newton 113) that young Johnson incorporated in Lichfield, that "place of confinement" (*Rambler* 165), requires mention of Johnson's father and brother. From his father Johnson felt he had inherited "a vile melancholy"

(Boswell, *Life* 27), and he looked back on the bookseller Michael Johnson, fifty-two years his senior, as "a foolish old man" (Boswell, *Life* 31). The deeper complexities to the relationship, not to mention the timelessness of the unconscious, are marked in Boswell's picture (p. 1357) of Johnson, in his seventies, standing in the rain at the spot where his father's market stall had been, to expiate the "prideful" refusal to tend it of a half-century before (perhaps when his father was dying in 1731). As for Johnson's brother, Bernard Meyer ("Application") draws attention to the possible psychological connection between Nathaniel's birth, when Sam was three, and the celebrated incident of the three-year-old's chancing "to tread upon a duckling, the eleventh [11 = 1 + 1] of a brood" and composing a quatrain for its epitaph (according to Johnson, his father wrote the verses and wished to pass them as his son's). Johnson's near-total silence regarding his brother speaks for his jealousy of this "rival for the mother's fondness" (Piozzi 63). "Natty" died mysteriously, perhaps a suicide, when Johnson was twenty-seven and leaving Lichfield for London, but twenty-two years later, recording a prayer for his mother, just dead, Johnson adds, "The dream of my Brother I shall remember" (*Diaries* 67). So much for the sentiment he penned contemporaneously that "he that is once buried will be seen no more" (R 107).

On 23 March 1759, two months after his mother's death, Johnson mentions his "little story book" as soon to be published (L 122). Unlike his author, the character of the story whose name soon came to denominate it has neither a dead mother, a dead father, a dead brother, nor a dead wife, but rather a "dear" (R 97) sister, Nekayah. The incantation of her name, however, might recall the Greek Νέκυια (Nekuya), which, as a note in Pope's translation details, traditionally names the eleventh book of the *Odyssey* owing to the calling up of the dead (*nekus*) therein, including, memorably, the shade of Ulysses' mother. Johnson, after all, was an old hand at deriving significant names from his classical heritage, as evidenced by the ferociously arrogant Ferocula, furious Furia, unhappy Misella, the suitor Hymenaeus, calm Tranquilla, the traveling Viator, or the maxim-wise minimal critic, Dick Minum of Johnson's periodical essays (themselves offered through his self-personifications as Mr. Rambler or Mr. Idler). The added terminal letter of Nekayah (like that of the other named woman, Pekuah) perhaps also points towards Sara*h* Johnson.

While the narrative of *The Prince of Abissinia* (the title under which was first published what we have come to call *Rasselas*) opens and remains for some chapters in "the *happy valley*" of Abissinia, the concluding sentence reports only that the company "resolved, when the inundation should cease, to return to Abissinia." One still encounters the blithe assumption that the party returns to the happy valley (e.g., Meyer, "Notes" 334), but after George Sherburn's 1951 query, "Rasselas Returns—To What?" and the increasing recognition of Johnson's "uncustomary obscurity" (Wasserman 20) regarding this point, readers have become more comfortable with the fearful symmetry of the story's inconclusive conclusion. Steven Lynn sounds a contemporary tone when he writes, "We do not know if the travellers carry out their resolve 'to return to Abyssinia.' Nor do we know for sure what it would mean if they do" (125). Edward Tomarken, reviewing in 1989 interpretations of the conclusion, reports confidently that "now we are able to understand why it took two centuries for the meaning of the term 'Abyssinia' to be fully understood," even as he himself remains sure that "they return to Abyssinia" (102). It is striking, first of all, that the narrator abandons us in a rising flood: the nothing that is concluded (to invoke the final chapter heading) concludes with and includes "the inundation of the Nile." The pilgrimage began in Abissinia and, we now learn, intends to return there—what concerns us here, especially given the closing flood, are some possible connotations of the word/space whence the protagonists came and into which they are to return. This trajectory—as old, at least, as Bede's bird passing from the darkness into the brightly lit feast hall and out again—suggests that, despite the red herring *i* for *y*, Abissinia is another name for the abyss, or, in the definition of Johnson's *Dictionary*, "a depth without bottom," "a great depth," and "in a figurative sense, that in which anything is lost." The attempt to find the lost object thus carries one into the abyss; in the *Idler* essay directly following his mother's death, Johnson reports that "the loss of a friend . . . is a state of dreary desolation in which the mind looks abroad impatient of itself, and finds nothing but emptiness and horror" (no. 41, 27 January 1759). Abyssinia is, of course, a geographical entity, but the vagaries of Johnson's effort in translating Father Lobo's *A Voyage to Abyssinia* (note the *y* there) suggest that the homeland of Rasselas translates "the abyss of meaninglessness that [Johnson's] big writing projects always encounter" (Kernan 168). "Since college days at least," writes Joseph Krutch, Johnson "had known that the abyss was just beside whatever path he trod" (108). But Rasselas's Abissinia is more a name and mental space than a geographical locale—the "real scene of *Rasselas*," remarks Irvin Ehrenpreis, "is the mind of its author" (110). The narrator doesn't show the party's return to Abissinia because on the one hand they are almost already there, brooding on the vast Abyss of the rising inundation, and on the other hand their state once they cross that bourne from which none has ever returned is not accessible to language.

In the memorable association of *Paradise Lost*, chaos is first made "pregnant," and then, as the "wilde Abyss," imagined as "the Womb of Nature and perhaps her Grave" (2.910–11). Edward Young's *Night Thoughts* registers the impact of Milton's description in imagining that "the Almighty FATHER . . . / Impregnated the Womb of distant *Space*," "that *Abyss of Horror*" (9.1538–39, 1547). These conceptions can return us to *Rasselas's* beginning in the happy valley, a location some confident critics find to refer to "foetal existence" (Joost 166, Reed 61), though Milton's Edenic "happy . . . seat" and "flourie lap / Of som irriguous Valley" (PL 4.247, 254–55) seems more sexual than prenatal ("Nor those mysterious parts were then conceald, / Then was not guiltie shame" [4.312–13]). Certainly "gynecomorphic significance" (Meyer, "Application" 158) abounds in the happy valley, whose only entrance is by "a cavern that passed under a rock," the outlet of which "was concealed by a thick wood" and the mouth closed with iron gates "so massy that no man could, without the help of engines, open or shut them," and whose lake discharges "its superfluities by a stream which entered a dark cleft of the mountains" (R 39–40). The gates (sometimes gate) form a memorable feature of the happy-valley psychography: Johnson four times describes them (or it) as "iron" (39, 40, 49) and once even has the prince, "whose thoughts were always on the wing [Lt. *penna*], as he passed by the gate," address it intimately: "Why are thou so strong, and why is man so weak?" (R 70). The prince's accompanying "countenance of sorrow," however, changes to joy on observing some "conies" and their upwards tending "holes," which give him and Imlac the hint for effecting a "mine"—and they soon find "a small cavern, concealed by a thicket, where they resolved to make their experiment" (R 71).[4] Although Imlac states that he could "burst the gate, but cannot do it secretly" (R 70), the fact that the party avoids the iron gates makes an ironic comment on one "choice of life":

> Let us roll all our strength and all
> Our sweetness up into one ball,
> And tear our pleasures with rough strife
> Thorough the iron gates of life.
> (Marvell, "To His Coy Mistress" 41–44)

The distinction between "foetal" and "gynecomorphic" interpretations of the happy valley resolves into different stages in individual (here, male) psychosexual development—according to Rasselas, "none that once had passed [the gate] were ever able to return" (48–49), yet his father, the mighty "emperour," consummates an eight-day visit annually (40).

All this foregrounds the question of sex and the little death, the apparent absence of which, in an ostensibly systematic search for happiness, might raise some eyebrows. Arthur Murphy, after all, reported on David Garrick's authority "that when it was asked what was the greatest pleasure, Johnson answered f——g" (Campbell 68), and Boswell reports it as "well known" that Johnson's "amorous inclinations were uncommonly strong and impetuous" (*Life* 1375). One anecdote has Johnson telling Garrick, "I'll come no more behind your scenes, David; for the silk stockings and white bosoms ['bubbies,' in another account] of your actresses excite my amorous propensities ['genitals,' alternatively]" (Boswell, *Life* 143 [Pearson 48n.]). One can see Johnson wrestling with sexual fantasies in his personal writings; between 1758 and 1765, for example, come "frequent pleas to the Almighty to 'purify my thoughts from pollutions,' 'grant me chaste in thoughts, words and actions,' 'reject or expel sensual images.' He asks that 'all corrupt desires may be extinguished,' there are repeated sad comments: 'I have lived totally useless, more sensual in thought. . . . ' 'My thoughts have been clouded with sensuality'" (Clifford 315). Such evidence leads Jean Hagstrum to write of Johnson's "clamorous physicality" and to suggest that "his private being was constantly invaded if not by overt incitements to lasciviousness, then certainly by sensual imagery welling up from within" (46–47).

Perhaps more than chance, then, brings Rasselas on stage "in the twenty-sixth year of his age," when he is just a few months older than his author at his marriage to the forty-six-year-old widow Elizabeth Porter. In his first action, the prince fixes "his eyes upon the goats that were browsing among the rocks" and begins "to compare their condition with his own" (*R* 42).

The object of his comparison, Johnson's *Dictionary* attests, traditionally evokes "a lecherous animal," known for its "rankness" and "lust," and a dictionary of slang fifty years later defines "goat" simply as a "lascivious person" (cf. Cleland's Fanny Hill, ten years before *Rasselas*, whose defloration is contracted to a "liquorish old goat" [54]). The memorable heading of the following chapter—"The wants of him that wants nothing"—in effect offers as one of Rasselas's obscure objects of desire the big O, Hamlet's "nothing" or "fair thought to lie between maids' legs" and the subject in general about which the world makes "Much Ado."[5] Imlac's observation that "he whose real wants are supplied, must admit those of fancy" (R 56) puts "nothing" on a par with "fancy," that "parent of passion" (79) which with "transitory lustre" (80) leads one to "riot in scenes of folly" (86). The text risks the bawdy truth of "nothing" confident in its massive repression of erotic concerns;[6] the "desires" distinct from the senses Rasselas mentions "which must be satisfied before he can be happy" (43) are those that, according to *Idler* 52 (14 April 1759), near the publication of *Rasselas*, "by timely caution and suspicious vigilance . . . may be repressed." The sidestepping of sexual pleasure in *Rasselas* (despite the recognition that "celibacy has no pleasures" [95]), like the *Dictionary*'s avoidance of sexual denotations, can be related to Johnson's own observation that "no man talks of that which he is desirous to conceal, and every man desires to conceal that of which he is ashamed [Lt. *pudendum*]" (Boswell, *Life* 1048). When he associates with "young men of spirit and gaiety," the prince finds that "their pleasures were gross and sensual" and "he was ashamed" (78); and in *Idler* 52, just mentioned, "sensuality" occasions "dread of . . . shameful captivity."

The extended discussion in *Rasselas* concerning marriage, which several times approaches acrimony the better to make its point, bears witness to the pressure to resolve "the ardour" and "importunities of desire" (100, 119, 88). Perhaps the major consideration for "the choice of life" will be what Johnson describes as the "irrevocable choice" of a partner (R 101), but any thinking on this must lead to the idea of divorce and the nature and origin of irrevocability. Precisely the ongoing inability to resolve this question of the Other (whether woman or body or unconscious) and how even it should be considered leads Rasselas for the first time to the brink of the abyss as he argues to his sister, "You surely conclude too hastily from the infelicity of marriage against its institution; will not the misery of life prove equally that life cannot be the gift of heaven?" (99).[7] That life perhaps may not be "the gift of heaven," that it may be, as Marlow puts it in *Heart of Darkness*, "a greater riddle than some of us think it to be," seems one of the burdens of Johnson's self-described "little story book." Rasselas's recourse in the face of such possibilities is the surly assertion of his "surely"—just as in the second chapter he argues, "Surely the equity of providence has balanced peculiar sufferings with peculiar enjoyments" and that "man has surely some latent sense for which [the happy valley] affords no gratification" (and on at least six other occasions as well).

Comparing himself to the goat, Rasselas marks their differences and gives, in passing, one version of his name: unlike the animal, he says, "when thirst and hunger cease I am not at rest; I am, like him, pained with want, but am not, like him, satisfied with fulness" (43). Indeed, Rasselas later explicitly identifies himself as "restless" and "unsatisfied with those pleasures which I seem most to court" (76). Evidently he wishes "to court" elsewhere, perhaps finding himself—as did Boswell on 13 April 1763— "so much in the lewd humour that I felt myself restless, and took a little girl into a court" (*London Journal* 241). Like Johnson, Rasselas is restless: a near relation, it would seem, to the Idler's friend, "Tom Restless," who appears while *Rasselas* is in press (no. 48, 17 March 1759; "Tom has long had a mind to be a man of knowledge")—or to "Sober," Johnson's avowed self-portrait in an earlier issue of a man whose "strong desires and quick imagination . . . will not suffer him to lie quite at rest" (no. 31, 18 November 1758), or to "Omar," in a later *Idler*, possessed by "restless desire" (no. 101, 22 March 1760). A quotation from Bishop Atterbury that the *Dictionary* supplies to illustrate the sense of the word is pertinent here: "We find our souls disordered and *restless*, tossed and disquieted by passions, ever seeking happiness in the enjoyments of this world, and ever missing what they seek."[8] Or again, to illustrate the meaning of *phantom*, but keying as always on the idea of happiness, consider this quotation from John Rogers that Johnson chose for his *Dictionary*: "Restless and impatient to try every scheme and overture of present happiness, he hunts a phantom he can never overtake." "Still to new heights his restless wishes tower," says "The Vanity of Human Wishes" (line 105) of Wolsey. *Restless*, too, repeatedly describes a character who must have assured the "overmatch" Johnson encountered at nineteen in reading William Law's *A Serious Call to a Devout and Holy Life*: the allegorically named Flatus "is satisfied with nothing," "was a great student for one whole year," "loses several days in considering which of his cast-off ways he shall try again," and, in short, exhibits the "anxieties, delusions, and restless desires" of a "restless life" (134–38). A contemporary review of *Rasselas* picks up its theme word to criticize the book's tendency "to conclude too much from the restless disposition of mankind" (*Monthly Review* 20 [1759]: 429).

Even in the happy valley, where "every desire was immediately granted," Rasselas does not "feel [him]self delighted" (40, 43) and seems always without "rest": the "erect penis in its desired place of rest" (F. Rubinstein 219). The possible puns in his name may seem unlikely at first, but Rasselas's exemplifying "the wants of him that wants nothing" suggests that whatever Johnson may have written against puns or quibbles, he could on occasion use them as well as the next person in giving voice to the restless unconscious.[9] In the heading for chapter 3, the denotation of *want* vacillates between the principal definitions in the *Dictionary*, "need" and "deficiency." The term *nothing* becomes complicated beyond the passing Elizabethan sexual reference as one pursues it through the etymology *no* and *thing* and the *Dictionary* entries "negation of being," "nonentity," and finally "nonexistence" (cf. Young's *Night Thoughts*: "Non-Existence? NOTHING'S strange Abode!" [9.1522]). All these terms lead to the noun and verb *lack*, which Johnson defines as "[to] want," "[to] need," "to be without." The reciprocal implication of wanting and lacking shows up neatly in translations of Psalm 23:1, a verse singularly inappropriate for Rasselas at this juncture; in Coverdale's version, "The Lord is my shepherd, I can want nothing," but in the Great Bible, four years later (1539), "therefore can I lack nothing." Rasselas, however, wants more than anyone, desiring, in effect, to be a god: "That he who wants least is most like the gods who want nothing," was, according to Hester Thrale Piozzi, "a favorite sentence with Dr. Johnson" (150). It may be worth noting that nothing is also the object of the other famous and self-reflexive chapter heading, the conclusion "in which nothing is concluded"—a title that on one level, defensively, preemptively judges the "little story book" and its author as nugatory.

The chain of lack seems at work in chapter 7, where, as the lake (*le lac*) overflows its banks and the level of the valley is covered with the inundation, the text materializes a figure who could announce, "I'm Imlac." Johnson commented to Boswell regarding the name, "Imlac in *Rasselas* I spelt with a *c* at the end, because it is less like English, which should always have the Saxon *k* added to the *c*" (Boswell, *Life* 1088)—but perhaps, as well, a projection named "Imlack" comes too close to weird personification.[10] As the first model of "a man of learning" (the description is also applied to the astronomer at the book's end), Imlac suggests a self-conscious acceptance of lack, of want, of "the vanity of human wishes," or, heroically, "the tragic sense of life" (Krutch 176). On another level, "lack" denotes a felt inability to achieve viable, secure ego satisfaction: lack, then, of potency or, à la Lacan, "the phallus." In this dark and muffled realm, "happiness" might be to "have penis." Rasselas wants his "happiness" to be "something solid and permanent, without fear and without uncertainty" (78), and attends to the argument that with the "happiness" of conquered "passion," he cannot be "emasculated by tenderness" (80). However, for the narrator of *Rambler* 18, just such "command over [his] passions" correlates to his considering himself "a kind of neutral being between the sexes" who perceives, even without possessing it, that "happiness . . . is to be found only with a woman of virtue" (cf. *Rambler* 167, which finds "happiness only in the arms of virtue"). Mixed feelings about such female virility perhaps figure in Johnson's practice of taking "women of the town to taverns" to "hear them relate their history" (Boswell, *Life* 1375), or his comment that, barring "duties" and "reference to futurity, I would spend my life in driving briskly in a post-chaise with a pretty woman; but she would be one who could understand me, and would add something to the conversation" (Boswell, *Life* 845). The mad astronomer at the end of *Rasselas*, waking from his heavenly obsessions, can only regret the choice of life that has led him to miss "the endearing elegance of female friendship, and the happy commerce of domestick tenderness" (140). But the conflict between desires for verbal conversation and for physical "conversation"—between desire and guilt—furthers rooted depression, which in turn prompts desperate self-lacerating fantasies. On one occasion, "sighing, groaning, talking to himself, and restlessly walking from room to room," Johnson "used this emphatic expression of the misery which he felt: 'I would consent to have a limb amputated to recover my spirits'" (Boswell, *Life* 342).

Given the pervasiveness of lack, it seems in fact for nothing that the Nile—*le Nil* in the French version of Lobo's *A Voyage to Abyssinia*, which

Johnson translated—is ever present in the background of *Rasselas* as "a recurring symbol in the story" (Greene 811), "a repeated point of narrative reference" (Wasserman 12). Both Imlac and Rasselas were born near "the fountain of the Nile" (55), *caput Nili*, as if to suggest some privileged proximity to the void, the Other, the "secret to so many generations" (Lobo 169), "the fountains of knowledge" (R 57)—indeed, for Lucan's Caesar, quoted in Lobo, "Nihil est quod noscere malim / Quam . . . Niliacos fontes" (169). The restless pilgrimage begins in the abyss of Abissinia—"la source du Nil"—as the party beholds "the Nile, yet a narrow current, wandering beneath them" (R 14) and ends with "the inundation of the Nile" (149) and the intention to return to Abissinia or, Johnson's phrase elsewhere, "sink into nihility" ("Review" 531). Wordsworth uses much the same association in *The Prelude*, seeing Imagination as an "awful Power [risen] from the mind's abyss" and proceeding to liken it to "the mighty flood of Nile / Poured from his fount of Abyssinian clouds" (6.594, 614–15 [1850 version]). This flooding river of nothing, of nihil, appears as "the stream of time . . . the current of the world" (R 115), "the stream of life" (150) or "flux of life" (48) and exemplifies Johnson's "realization of the imagery latent in even the most abstract philosophic word" (Wimsatt, *Words* 66).

The emphasis on the Nile reminds one again how little *Rasselas* owes to Lobo's account, where Egypt and the lower reaches of the Nile hardly appear. But Rasselas and his party have their overdetermined mission to suffer the air of Cairo (Cair-o, a pronunciation still met with) and the world of care or (the *Dictionary* again) "solicitude; anxiety; perturbation of mind" (cf. Pekuah's train of association from Cairo to "cared so" [R 126]). Samuel Garth's "The Dispensary" (1699) joins "restless Anxiety, forlorn Despair, / And all the faded family of Care," to suggest how at home in Cairo one might suppose Rasselas to feel. Though it can appear a region "inaccessible to care or sorrow," yet among its inhabitants "there was not one who did not dread the moment when solitude should deliver him to the tyranny of reflection" (R 77).

"A man would be a blockhead who did not write for money," Johnson said, and, the story goes, he wrote *Rasselas* to raise funds for expenses associated with his mother's death (rather, one might suggest, to raise funds against his own psychic expenditure). The topic of money may lead, however, to the fourth and last-named character, Pekuah. As the one figure who has actual cash value ("two hundred ounces of gold" [R 121]) and who experiences firsthand "desire of money" (R 121), it is tempting to see Pekuah as related on some level to the Latin *pecua*, "money" (more commonly, *pecunia*—as in Coleridge's remark that he writes "compelled by the God Pecunia" [*Letters* 1.631]). So a Latinist of Johnson's order might formulate an overdetermined sentence to read: "Finding that his predominant passion was desire of money [*pecunia/pecua*], I began now to think my danger less, for I knew that no sum [*pecunia*] would be thought too great for the release of Pekuah" (R 121). With this secret passage sounded out, one can imagine a work founded literally in restlessness, lack, the recall of the dead, pecuniary concerns, the abyss, nihil and denial ("To deny early and inflexibly is the only art of checking the importunity of desire" [*Idler* 52]). With Bernard Einbond, we may perhaps not find in *Rasselas* "the allegorical punning and diction so characteristic of Johnson's short allegories" (83), but if, as Lacan holds, the unconscious is structured like a language, then for Johnson the lexes introduced above may crystallize some of its complexes.

The object of the pilgrimage is to be able to determine "the choice of life," the phrase initially envisioned as the title of *Rasselas*. But considering the abyss of nihilism and restless care to be found in the book's subterranean passages, one might begin to hear "the choice of life" as announcing not some *desideratum*—the possibility of deciding among lifestyles—but rather a more hard-won choice already made and according with Deuteronomy 30:19: "I have set before you life and death, blessing and cursing: therefore choose life, that both thou and thy seed may live." Nekayah, at any rate, appears to echo this verse when she says, "Of the blessings set before you make your choice, and be content" (103). He who wants nothing has, no doubt, like Johnson according to his old friend John Taylor, "at one time strongly entertained thoughts of Suicide" (Bate, *Johnson* 116); such thoughts and a remedy surface in Johnson's advice to Mrs. Thrale: "Get your Children into habits of loving a Book by every possible means; You do not know but it may one Day save them from Suicide" (in Irwin 60). George Irwin, however, quotes *Rambler* 110 to argue that "he who considered himself as 'suspended over the abyss of eternal perdition by the thread of life' never seriously considered breaking that thread" (60). Having chosen life, Johnson judges emphatically the alternative even in defining it: "the horrid crime of destroying one's self" (*Dictionary*).

Wittgenstein, who expressed admiration for Johnson's *Sermons*, concludes his early notebooks with the following:

> If suicide is allowed then everything is allowed.
> If anything is not allowed then suicide is not allowed.
> This throws a light on the nature of ethics, for suicide is, so to speak, the elementary sin.
> And when one investigates it it is like investigating mercury vapour in order to comprehend the nature of vapours.
> Or is even suicide in itself neither good nor evil? (91)

That is to say, Is life then ultimately lacking value or meaning, lacking any ground on which to judge? One answer should be evident given the terms stressed here: the tragic sense of life is the sense of its meaninglessness when one so wants it to have meaning. Johnson's "spiritual anxiety," for Max Byrd, turns on just such an "anguished demand for meaning from a world that absurdly refused to disclose it" (369; one might recall here Samuel Beckett's surprising disclosure: "It's Johnson, always Johnson who is with me. And if I follow any tradition, it is his" [in Davis 3]). Anyone familiar with Johnson's writing can imagine a dismissive response to all this considerably more vehement than the "Choose, and pursue your choice" by which he answered Boswell in 1763 (8 December, L 166). Johnson himself, however, just after completing *The Prince of Abissinia*, tries to give up the restless questioning he has broached: "A man who has duly considered the condition of his being, will contentedly yield to the course of things" (*Idler* 51).

Yet *Rasselas* toward its inconclusive conclusion raises the question of ultimates and in particular the religious outlook of that divided subject, Samuel Johnson. As Patrick O'Flaherty notes, though Johnson's "powerful empirical intellect was rarely at ease with the Christian faith, yet he could not bear the thought which rejection of Christianity would have entailed: the thought of annihilation"; and he quotes Samuel Rogers's observation that Johnson was "'literally afraid to examine his own thoughts on religious matters'" (207–8). The lack of reference to Christianity in *Rasselas* is striking, the more so as Abyssinia's Christian tradition was of particular interest and as Johnson's memory of "Rassela Christos" in Lobo's *Voyage to Abyssinia* seems one more determinant for the name of Rasselas. At the same time, the book offers recurring invocations of "the equity of providence" (43), "the unsearchable will of the Supreme Being" (64), and "him by whose laws our actions are governed, and who will suffer none to be finally punished by obedience" (112); and, significantly for someone who defines death as "the departure of the soul from the body" (*Dictionary*), in the penultimate chapter "Imlac discourses on the nature of the soul." Imlac's discourse at this important juncture deserves to be considered without its double negatives to appreciate better its rhetorical structure: "It is ~~no~~ limitation of omnipotence . . . to suppose that one thing is ~~not~~ consistent with another, that the same proposition can~~not~~ be at once true and false, that the same number can~~not~~ be even and odd, that cogitation can~~not~~ be conferred on that which is created [by 'omnipotence'!] incapable of cogitation" (147–48). One may wonder if Soame Jenyns, at least, recalled Johnson's scorn of two years before: "Surely a man who seems not completely master of his own opinion should have spoken more cautiously of omnipotence, nor have presumed to say what it could perform, or what it could prevent" ("Review" 532). The only sure point of Imlac's self-deconstructing (omnipotence ≠ omnipotence) discourse seems to be his contention that "we must humbly learn from *higher authority*" (148; italics added). At which "the whole assembly stood a while silent and collected." Indeed, what's left to say?—either you take it (perhaps with the help of a "collect" or "short prayer" [*Dictionary*]), or you don't. For as Johnson writes in his sermon on his wife's death, the doctrine that the soul exists "exempt from dissolution and corruption" is, for Christians, not "learned" but "*believed* upon . . . higher authority" (*Sermons* 264; italics added). *Rasselas*, however, doesn't stop with the silent assembly, and a brief coda to the scene signals impending demise *en abîme*.

After the lengthy detailing of the prevalence of imagination in the case of the astronomer and the demonstrating of fancy's obsessive dedication to the narcissistic phantom, how can one not weep with laughter (like Johnson over young Bennet Langton's making a will [Boswell, *Life* 548]) at the grandiosity of Rasselas's conclusion, "How gloomy would be these mansions of the dead to him who did not know that he shall never die; that what now acts shall continue its agency, and what now thinks shall think on for ever?" (149) The comedy of "a man of learning" (the astronomer) offering "a man of learning" (Imlac) "the inheritance of the sun" (132) seems reason itself beside Rasselas's oblique invocation of the Christian's inheritance of life everlasting from the Son.[11] But despite his gloom-dispelling belief, it is an evidently subdued prince who urges the group's departure from the "scene of mortality," leaving his sister to utter "what is *surely*, in one sense, Johnson's conclusion" (Hardy xxi; italics added) as she trumps "the choice of life" with "the choice of eternity." The narrator's chapter-closing comment that "under the protection of their guard" they "returned to Cairo" suggests that such belief or imagining of the "higher authority" of "*God*" (a word the text, like Nekayah, "fear[s] to name" [148]) is the most credible "guard" (i.e., *gawd*) one can trust in. Their "guard" is that hired authority ("They hired a guard" [145]: or, in the words of Isaac Watts's great hymn, "Our God, our Help in Ages past . . . Be thou our Guard"). The unconscious aspect of the hypothesized transcendental signifier suggests itself as well in Johnson's writing his stepdaughter of his regret at not having visited his mother but concluding that "God suffered it not" (23 January 1759, *L* 119). It wasn't just God that kept a mother's "dutiful son" (13, 16, 18, 20 January 1759) away from her house for her last nineteen years (in 1755 Johnson noted how his mother was "counting the days" to the publication of the *Dictionary* "in hopes of seeing me" [Boswell, *Life* 206]). Johnson's plight and his text cry out for some acknowledgment of the unconscious, inevitably vague though our picturing of it must be.[12]

The last comment on the pilgrimage, chapter 49, comes from an author himself in the forty-ninth year of his life's journey, who could report to Bennet Langton less than two weeks before selling the copyright to *Rasselas*, "When I was as you are now, towering in the confidence of twenty one, little did I suspect that I should be at forty nine what I now am" (9 January 1759, *L* 113). This last chapter concludes that "of these wishes that they had formed they well knew that none could be obtained. They deliberated a while what was to be done, and resolved, when the inundation should cease, to return to Abissinia. / FINIS." At the very least, these parting lines can confirm suspicion of the divided subject of the book—one which can wish and yet *well* know that wish's impossibility.

Rasselas is in part the interior dialogue of that divided subject, Samuel Johnson; a dialogue itself undertaken to ward off the "hunger of imagination which preys incessantly upon life" (R 108). In chapter 22 Rasselas relates the story of the hermit who abandoned his second choice of life, and after various comments an unidentified subject comes forward:

> One, who appeared more affected with the narrative than the rest, thought it likely, that the hermit would, in a few years, go back to his retreat, and perhaps, if shame did not restrain, or death intercept him, return once more from his retreat into the world: "For the hope of happiness, said he, is so strongly impressed, that the longest experience is not able to efface it. Of the present state, whatever it be, we feel, and are forced to confess, the misery, yet, when the same state is again at a distance, imagination paints it as desirable. But the time will surely come, when desire will be no longer our torment, and no man shall be wretched but by his own fault." (87)

The desired state, evidently, is complete self-control: the anonymous voice tropes Rasselas's desire to desire nothing, or to be like a god, completely self-determining. One echo hints that this time surely to come is identical with "the time [that] will come when you will acquit your father" (55), but another echo hints that freedom from desire comes only with death: "Desire shall fail: because man goeth to his long home, and the mourners go about the streets" (Ecclesiastes 12:5). The reality behind the fantasy of control is, naturally, that death cannot be controlled: "There is none who does not . . . hope another year for his parent or his friend; but the fallacy will be in time detected; the last year, the last day must come. It has come and is past" (*Idler* 41, 27 January 1759). The affected, anonymous "one" is in fact answered by a self-satisfied philosopher that "the time is already come, when none are wretched but by their own fault" (R 87). The problem is how our nature can be our fault, but from his consideration neither of psychology nor of religion can Johnson formulate an adequate response.

So he is left with an expanding collection of guilt-evoking ghosts: dead father, dead brother, dead wife, dead mother, and his own dead, inadequately loved childhood, which he cannot escape. According to Boswell,

> Johnson observed, that the force of our early habits was so great, that though reason approved, nay, though our sense relished a different course, almost every man returned to them. I do not believe there is

any observation upon human nature better founded than this; and in many cases, it is a very painful truth; for where early habits have been mean and wretched, the joy and elevation resulting from better modes of life must be damped by the gloomy consciousness of being under an almost inevitable doom to sink back into a situation which we recollect with disgust. (*Life* 628)

All this past is buried in the words of a "little story book" with its open and secret passages, its columns, unsuspected cavities and "reposited . . . treasures" (R 41), a book that thus offers a kind of crypt, like "the catacombs, or ancient repositories" toward which it tends: "Books are faithful repositories," Johnson wrote (*Journey* 83). Ehrenpreis complains that though the first chapter "ends with a detailed account of the internal plans of the palace and the storage of the imperial treasure, . . . we never return to the palace, and the treasure remains untouched" (111). But, exchanging the open passage and upper stories for the "labyrinth of subterraneous passages, where the bodies were laid in rows" (145), perhaps we never leave. In this "habitation of the dead" are lodged "the bodies of the earliest generations," where, "by the virtue of the gums which embalmed them, they yet remain without corruption" (145). The text thus points to and shrouds in silence the infantile desire for "mummy"—the word whose pertinence to this passage is made clear by the *Dictionary*: "A dead body preserved by the Egyptian art of embalming."[13] Shadowing the author "in the utmost exigencies" of his psychic kingdom, we watch dimly as he embalms himself in a little repository whose "private galleries" and "subterranean passages" make it "so large as to be fully known to none" (R 41).

4
Mary Godwin's Remonstrance

> *The mature man seldom retains the faintest recollections of the incidents of the two first years of his life. Is it to be supposed that that which has left no trace upon the memory can be in an eminent degree powerful in its associated effects?*
> —WILLIAM GODWIN, *Political Justice*

> *Our infantine dispositions . . . however much they may be afterwards modified, are never eradicated.*
> —MARY WOLLSTONECRAFT GODWIN SHELLEY, *Frankenstein*

Phantasmagoria has become a term frequently to be met with in criticism of *Frankenstein* (Moers 87; Knoepflmacher 91; Sherwin 885). The word, fittingly enough, entered English vocabulary in Mary Godwin's fourth year when, during the winter of 1801–2, Londoners received it as the name of a magic-lantern spectacle featuring moving, merging, size-changing ghostly projections (Altick 217–19).[1] This same winter completed the staging of Mary Godwin's core phantasmal assembly ("-agora") with her father's marriage to Mary Jane Clairmont, and the addition to the family of Mrs. Clairmont's two children, including a daughter very nearly Mary's age. The earlier marriage of William Godwin and Mary Wollstonecraft had joined the celebrated enquirer into political justice with the renowned vindicator of the rights of woman, making Mary the offspring of England's most (in)famous radical couple. Wollstonecraft, however, died of puerperal fever eleven days after the August 30, 1797, birth of their daughter, so that Godwin was left with the infant and a stepdaughter, three-year-old Fanny. In marrying Mrs. Clairmont, Godwin hoped to find at last the helpmeet he sorely needed and to supply the children with a mother's guidance—but with his young daughter's insecure bonding to him already set by her four longest years, the disruptive transition to a refashioned household, and his new wife's partiality for her own children, Godwin's remarriage instead "helped activate in Mary a lifelong desire to compensate her father for the loss of his exquisite first wife and their short-lived marital happiness" (Knoepflmacher 92). Godwin, for his part, remained genuinely fond of his spouse (St. Clair 243–44)—but that's another story.

There is no such thing as a baby, D. W. Winnicott proposes; there is only the unit of dependent infant and good or bad mother (so to denominate the primary caretaker). By this definition every child that survives has been mothered. And while many critics have written about Mary Shelley's need to recover the lost mother, the fact of the matter would seem to be that her father was her mother. Mary Godwin's involvement with her biological mother was necessarily imaginary, textual, and relatively late: Mary Wollstonecraft was present as a portrait in the study, some books on the shelf, a character made scandalous in public reception of the *Memoirs* published by Godwin the year after her death. Little Mary's reality was her father's assistant, Mr. Marshall; "Cooper, the nursemaid"; a devoted Louise Jones, who left before Mary was three (Mellor 4–7); and a socially active father preoccupied with his studies and writing. The absence of a reliable, constant, consistent human "object" (the infant's and child's relations are not to individuals) to lend sameness ("identity") to Mary Godwin's early formational experience of external relations can be read in her adolescent monster story, singularly notable for its "fluidity of relations . . . which converts each character into another's double" (Knoepflmacher 112) and for the way in which "all identities . . . are unstable and shifting" (Baldick 44). Like the projected images of the Phantasmagoria, *Frankenstein*'s fluid fragments of identity merge and split, beginning with the blending of addressor and addressee inherent in a frame situation of letters fictionally inscribed to MWS (Margaret Walton Saville, the narrator Robert Walton's sister) and published by MWS (Mary Wollstonecraft [Godwin] Shelley's signature for many communications, including the 1831 Introduction to the novel).

With no involving mothering in early childhood, Mary Godwin's focus on her father became correspondingly more intense. "Until I knew Shelley," she wrote of her father to a friend, "I may justly say that he was my God—& I remember many childish instances of the excess of attachment I bore for him" (5 December 1822, *Letters* 296). Godwin not surprisingly disapproved of his sixteen-year-old daughter's elopement with the already-married Percy Bysshe Shelley (not to mention their permitting Mrs. Godwin's daughter to run off along with them) and the weight of his rejection governs her self-pitying lines to Shelley in the months afterwards: "Hug your own Mary to your heart perhaps she will one day have a father *till then* be every thing to me love —& indeed I will be a good girl and never vex you any more" (28 October 1814, *Letters* 3; italics added). With the suicide of Percy's first wife and Mary's assumption of the vacant role very shortly thereafter, Godwin again admitted his daughter to his company, and Mary resumed her hopes of being still more valuable to him.[2] On 24 September 1817, for example, she wrote to Shelley in London: "A letter came from Godwin today—very short—You will see him tell me how he is—You are loaded with business [raising money]—the event of most of which I am very anxious to learn and none so much as whether you can do any thing for my father—" (*Letters* 42). Four days later, she again asked if anything could be done for her father and added, in a postscript, "Give my love to Godwin—when Mrs. G is not by or you must give it to her too and I do not *love* her" (*Letters* 47).

In the transparently autobiographical projection *Mathilda*, written three years after *Frankenstein*, the narrator recalls how she "clung to the memory of my parents; my mother I should never see, she was dead: but the idea of [my] unhappy, wandering father was the idol of my imagination" (11). The idolizing of the father perhaps originates in the need or lack occasioned by the actual father's physically undemonstrative behavior: several of Mary Shelley's narrators specifically remark how they were "never caressed" (*Mathilda* 8; *Tales* 244). Bound up in what one of his biographers, Don Locke, calls "a fantasy of reason," Godwin was passionately dedicated to envisioning a future when absolute truth, the "moral arithmetic" of political justice, would supersede emotional bias—when, in a notorious example from the first edition of *Political Justice* (1793), one would for the common good from a burning building choose rather to save the philosopher Fenelon than a chambermaid (1:42). So also, argues *Political Justice* (in the third edition published in Mary's infancy), "it is of no consequence that I am the parent of a child when it has once been ascertained that the child will live with greater benefit under the superintendence of a stranger" (233). The anxieties such obsessive rationalism might raise appeared in short order, as when Godwin, away in Ireland for the summer, instructed his three-year-old's caretaker, Mr. Marshall, to "tell Mary I will not give her away" (Dunn 20). Eighteen months later, however, the child was turned over to the strange new Mrs. Godwin, and ten years after that, as a result of never-ceasing tensions in that relationship, Mary found herself shipped off for seven months to a family of complete strangers to her and "mere acquaintance" to her father (Mellor 15). *Political Justice* urges that "we must divulge our sentiments with the utmost frankness" ([1791] 2:292), and *Frankenstein*'s monster does just that in declaring: "Still I desired love and fellowship, and I was still spurned. Was there no injustice in this?" (219).

One can easily imagine Mary Godwin, in part, angry with a father who did not in return recognize or validate that anger because of inability to deal with his own threatening ambivalence. "Let us compare the urgency of your wants and mine," he wrote, "and let justice decide" (*Political Justice* [1791] 2:278). Denied her right to express anger, the little girl internalized ("swallowed") it and continued the attempt to read her father through—and see herself in—the spontaneous reflectors of his eyes: "His eyes only seemed to speak, and as he turned their black, full lustre towards me they expressed a living sadness. There was somthing [sic] in those dark deep orbs so liquid, and intense that even in happiness I could never meet their full gaze that mine did not overflow" (*Mathilda* 24). The child intuited but could not understand the parent's conflicted projection, and the resulting melancholy became part of her personality, as evident in Mary's admission, "I know not whether it is early habit or affection but the idea of his silent quiet disapprobation makes me weep as it did in the days of my childhood" (18 October 1817, *Letters* 57).

Keeping quiet was an attitude internalized early on: Coleridge noted in December 1799 (when Mary was less than two and a half) that "the cadaverous Silence of Godwin's Children is to me quite catacomb-ish"—and six months later his wife, who had been *"lectured"* by Godwin for *her* son's "boisterousness," still recalled "dear meek little Mary" (*Letters* 553, 589). Such early inhibition culminated in the solitary, cold persona of Mary

Shelley; the "icy region" she felt her "cold heart" to encircle (11 November 1822, *Journal* 185) has one materialization in the "icy climes" where the telling of *Frankenstein* takes place. But the original ambivalence of Mary Godwin's relation to her father, though often deferrable through self-deprecating teariness, could break down in phantasy with catastrophic power: "He began to answer with violence: 'Yes, yes, I hate you! You are my bane, my poison, my disgust! Oh! No[!]' And then his manner changed, and fixing his eyes on me with an expression that convulsed every nerve and member of my frame—'you are none of all these; you are my light, my only one, my life.—My daughter, I love you!'" (*Mathilda* 30).[3] The projected incestuous desire of the father makes him a "monster" (31) with "monstrous passion" (37) which in turn makes his daughter a self-described "monster with whom none might mingle in converse and love" (71).[4]

The father's (projected) desire in effect castrates the girl by forcing her to accede to her culturally gendered identity as object of male desire. She who wanted to be the paternal phallus (his little pal) has instead to confront her lack—as she does in a scene several times repeated in Mary Shelley's work. Having been left the message from her now suicidal father that her "hopes are blasted" (37), Mathilda sets out after him. On the stormy way she encounters "a magnificent oak," the continuing existence of which she no sooner capriciously equates with the survival of her father "than a flash instantly followed by a tremendous peal of thunder descended on it; and when my eyes recovered their sight after the dazzling light, the oak no longer stood in the meadow" (44). In a similar scene the adolescent Victor Frankenstein sees in the midst of a storm "a stream of fire issue from an old and beautiful oak, which stood about twenty yards from our house; and so soon as the dazzling light vanished, the oak had disappeared, and nothing remained but a blasted stump" (35). The pertinence of this image for Victor is emphasized when he later describes himself as "a blasted tree; the bolt had entered my soul" (158): he who had wished to "penetrate into the recesses of nature" (42) is himself entered and devastated, though when the "sudden light" of discovery first "broke in" (47), he had experienced "delight," "rapture," and "gratifying consummation" (47). Lionel Verney, Mary Shelley's self-characterization and protagonist in *The Last Man*, written some eight years later after *Frankenstein*, similarly imagines that he is "a tree rent by lightning; never will the bark close over the bared fibres—never will their quivering life, torn by the winds, receive the opiate of a moment's calm" (329). Preoccupation with the "blasted stump . . . the tree shattered in a singular manner" may be related to the anxieties Mary Shelley expressed over assuming the pen and "composing" in the ghost-story competition with Shelley, Lord Byron, and John William Polidori ([1831] Introduction). Like his creator, Frankenstein finds that he "could not compose a female" (147), so the resulting "being like myself" (48) possesses a "detested form" (96, cf. 126). In this moment of the phantasmagoria, Mary Godwin's pen is the torn-off, monstrous penis disseminating its quivering life upon the page.

The inadequacies in infantile (preoedipal) and childhood-pubescent (oedipal) mirroring posited above constitute narcissistic injuries and occasion the rage that fills *Frankenstein*. "But where were my friends and relations?" the monster wonders. "No father had watched my infant days, no mother had blessed me with smiles and caresses; or if they had, all my past life was now a blot" (117). The monster experiences family only vicariously, watching the De Lacys for months through a chink in the wall and assuaging his lack in imagination. His attempt to disclose himself to the old, blind father De Lacy ends with horrified rejection by all those he pathetically terms his "protectors" (134, 128), and then, "for the first time feelings of *revenge and hatred* filled my bosom, and I did not strive to controul them" (134; italics added). "My *hatred and revenge* burst all bounds of moderation," says Victor (87; italics added), thinking of his double. The monster's "insatiate revenge" (166) and "insatiable thirst for vengeance" stem from "impotent envy and bitter indignation" (218) and desire to "compensate for . . . outrages and anguish" (138). Victor's revenge "is the devouring and only passion of [his] soul" (198), which alone keeps him from suicide (200).

Revenge—or, as he referred to it, "retribution"—had no place in Godwin's system of political justice. Alphonse Frankenstein reflects such sanctimonious reasoning when he writes his son, after William's murder, "Come, Victor; not brooding thoughts of vengeance against the assassin, but with feelings of peace and gentleness" (68). Shortly after the completion of *Frankenstein*, Mary Shelley echoed her father as she argued that the reformer William Cobbett "encourages in the multitude the worst possible human passion *revenge* or as he would probably give it that abominable *Christian* name retribution" (30 September 1817, *Letters* 49). In the novel Victor's cousin and destined wife, Elizabeth, attributes the judicial murder of the innocent Justine to "*retribution*. Hateful name! When that word is pronounced, I know greater and more horrid punishments are going to be inflicted than the gloomiest tyrant has ever invented to satiate his utmost revenge" (83). We might, however, pause over Elizabeth's own last name, Lavenza, and its indication of *la vendicanza* (Veeder 167), as well as the inscription of *venge*ance in Frankenstein's birthplace, Geneva (a setting that glances also at Godwin's Calvinist background, Rousseau, and the race—*gens*—of Eve). In a kind of ultimate rebuttal to Godwin's dismissal of retribution, the monster's vengeance culminates in Victor's fantasy of his father "writhing under his grasp" (195), a projection realized in somewhat less disturbing guise as an "apoplectic fit" that kills off the father in Victor's arms. "Alas! my father," laments Mary Godwin's protagonist, "how little do you know me" (182).

Gerhard Joseph suggests that "there are few characters in *Frankenstein* . . . only a succession of family relationships which counter and duplicate one another" (107). Different aspects of the author's conflicting relations with her father certainly seem to inform the interaction of both the monster and Victor, Victor and his father. The novel as a whole constitutes an attempted communication "to William Godwin" (dedication) that bares, writ large, the request of Victor—"Listen to my tale," "Listen to my history" (24)—and the monster: "Listen to my tale," "Hear me," "Listen to me," "Listen to me" (96), and anticipates Mathilda's injunction to her father, "Listen to me," "Listen to me, dearest friend" (28). For example, Victor recalls "an incident which took place when I was four years of age," or the age of the author when Godwin's remarriage brought a stepsister into her life. Victor's aunt has died, leaving an infant girl, and his father is asked whether he might not prefer " 'educating your niece yourself to her being brought up by a stepmother' " (29). "My father did not hesitate," Victor reports, fulfilling what must have been a recurrent phantasy of Mary Godwin's. In *Political Justice* William Godwin contends that "the very impression which, if not counteracted, shall decide upon the fortune of an entire life" can, by the "skillful parent," "be reduced to complete inefficiency in half an hour" ([1798] 105). Victor's father, though in principle "devoted . . . to the education of his children" (29), shows that practice will inevitably stumble when, after his child comes to him one day "bounding with joy" to communicate a discovery, he responds, "Do not waste your time upon this;

it is sad trash" (32). William Hazlitt remembered how in the mid-1790s Godwin incarnated "the metaphysician engrafted on the Dissenting Minister" and exhibited "a dictatorial, captious, quibbling pettiness of manner" (193), which must have affected his daughter as much as any matter he tried to offer.

Frankenstein; or, The Modern Prometheus embodies a critique of Godwin's rationalist-humanist beliefs by one who suffered their deprivations even as she was taught how "we are wrapped up in ourselves, and do not observe, as we ought, step by step the sensations that pass in the mind of our hearer" (*Political Justice* [1798] 109–10). The crucial name in the novel may offer another oblique comment, for Godwin reports with approbation how "the celebrated Franklin conjectured that 'mind would one day become omnipotent over matter'" (*Political Justice* [1791] 2:268). Franklin was an image of a modern, "new Prometheus" (so Kant labeled him [Seed 330]) who had brought fire down from the heavens, as Victor's father reminds us in repeating the famous, often lethal, kite-in-the-thunderstorm demonstration (35). But the deeper connection between Godwin, Franklin, and *Frankenstein* emerges in D. H. Lawrence's sense that "if on the one hand Benjamin Franklin is the perfect human being of Godwin, on the other hand he is a monster, not exactly as the monster in *Frankenstein*, but for the same reason, viz., that he is the production or fabrication of the human will, which projects itself upon a living being and automatizes that being according to a given precept" (in Levine 29).[5]

For Mary, two of Percy Shelley's principal attractions must have been his initial "real respect and veneration" for her father, whom he at first considered "the regulator and former of my mind" (16 January 1812, *Letters* 229) and his very considerable entailed inheritance, which might serve to end her father's perpetual financial distress. Through Shelley, Mary Godwin could both appropriate for herself ("your own Mary") a surrogate, nontaboo image of her father and hope to prove a more effectual provider to her real father than his second wife. Godwin's complete rejection of her during the two and a half years between her July 1814 elopement and December 1816 marriage was a monstrous outcome to the phantasy. Percy Shelley was to prove as inadequate as William Godwin in supplying Mary with what her monster craves, "the interchange of those sympathies necessary for my being" (*Frankenstein* 140), but for her own part, like her avatar in *The Last Man,* the adolescent Mary Godwin could not "throw off the habits of sixteen years" (338) and so fell to her overdetermined isolated and melancholy lot. As several critics have observed, the character of Victor Frankenstein draws considerably on Mary Godwin's knowledge of Shelley's circumstances:

> Victor was Percy Shelley's pen-name for his first publication, *Original Poetry; by Victor and Cazire* (1810). Victor Frankenstein's family resembles Percy Shelley's: in both, the father is married to a woman young enough to be his daughter; in both the oldest son has a favorite sister (adopted sister, or cousin, in Frankenstein's case) named Elizabeth. Frankenstein's education is based on Percy Shelley's: both were avid students of Albertus Magnus, Paraclesus, Pliny, and Buffon; both were fascinated by alchemy and chemistry; both were excellent linguists, acquiring fluency in Latin, Greek, German, French, English, and Italian. (Mellor 72–73)

Perhaps in a darker, more ambivalent mood she thought of Percy Shelley's 1816 "The Daemon of the World" with its opening picture of Ianthe, the name of his daughter by the wife he abandoned, and of Harriet Shelley's recent suicide, to put into Victor's mouth this subliminal, curiously pointed comment about Shelley: "*Shall I,* in cold blood, set loose upon the earth a daemon, whose delight is in death and wretchedness" (165; italics added).

No sooner does Victor see "the dull yellow eye" of his creation open and "a convulsive movement agitate its limbs" than he rushes off to fall asleep, though "disturbed by the wildest dreams" (53). In the only dream he proceeds to relate, Victor sees his fiancée, Elizabeth, "in the bloom of health, walking in the streets of Ingolstadt. Delighted and surprised, I embraced her; but as I imprinted the first kiss on her lips, they became livid with the hue of death; her features appeared to change, and I thought that I held the corpse of my dead mother in my arms; a shroud enveloped her form, and I saw the grave-worms crawling in the folds of the flannel" (*Frankenstein* 53). The phantasmagoria of identifications continues as one recalls the story that Percy Shelley and Mary Wollstonecraft Godwin consummated their infatuation at Mary's special retreat, the grave of her dead mother,

Mary Wollstonecraft Godwin (Veeder 114), in then secluded Saint Pancras churchyard. The necrotizing lips of the mother link her with the monster and its "black lips" (52), as does Victor's immediately following description of the monster as "the demoniacal corpse" (53). When Victor starts from his nightmare in a setting that will return and return, he meets the gaze of the monster as it "muttered some inarticulate sounds" (53). But while the other mothers of Ingolstadt are praising their infants' efforts with the *Muttersprache*, Victor reflects on his mutterer with this "significant pun" (Gilbert and Gubar 245): "Oh! no mortal could support the horror of that countenance. A mummy [even 'my mum'] again endued with animation could not be so hideous as that wretch" (53). Victor next meets his monster on "the sea of ice" with its implied French pun, "La Mer de Glace"/"La Mère [mother] de Glace" (Rubenstein 176), and there he hears the monster's story, which occupies most of the central volume of the novel. Mary Shelley avoids the actual name of the glacier (masculinized as "le Mer de Glace" in her journal, 25 July 1816), perhaps to emphasize a connection between the sea of ice at the heart of the story and the icy sea on which the novel opens and closes. On La Mer de Glace the reanimated mummy tells Victor, "Do your duty towards me," or, it threatens, "I will glut the maw of death" (94; cf. Milton's maw/ma pun, below). "I conceive it to be the duty of every rational creature to attend to its offspring," Mary Godwin read at the beginning of her dead mother's *Thoughts on the Education of Daughters* (7).

In the 1831 Introduction to *Frankenstein*, the author relates her conception of the story, and how she imagined "the artist" fleeing the work "which had received such imperfect animation" with the hope that it "would subside into dead matter" (*mater*) and that "the silence of the grave would quench forever [i.e., *hide*] the transient existence of the hideous corpse which he had looked upon as the cradle of life" (228). Recapitulating the primal scene of the novel, she continues, "He sleeps; but he is awakened; he opens his eyes; behold the horrid thing stands at his bedside, opening his curtains, and looking on him with yellow, watery, but speculative eyes" (228). The vision turns uncanny as it expands to involve the narrator, who recalls opening her eyes in terror: "I see them still; the very room, the dark *parquet*, the closed shutters, with the moonlight struggling through, and the sense I had that the glassy lake and the white high Alps were beyond"

(228). "Everywhere I turn I see the same figure," says Victor of his nightmare image (193). To "get rid" of "my hideous phantom," the author hides herself in "my ghost story," announcing at the same time, "'I have found it!'" (228). Subtracting nine months from her August birthdate, she begins the next day "with the words, *It was on a dreary night of November*" (228). This choice, and the awkward plot device that gives the monster fortuitous access to Frankenstein's journal of the months preceding its creation, points to Mary Godwin's fascination with her own conception (Rubenstein 169–70). Looking into her father's methodically kept journals after she had learned, like the monster, "to decypher the characters in which they were written," Mary Godwin could have followed "the whole detail of that series of disgusting circumstances" (e.g., 25 November 1796; "chez elle; ———") which led to "my accursed origin" (126; see St. Clair, ill. 6, for a photograph of two pertinent pages from Godwin's journal, and his appendix 1). The date of the eye-opening phantasied primal scene marks a key moment in Mary Godwin's phantasmagoria, for it entails the emerging recognition that her father loved ("really," sexually) someone other than herself. *Frankenstein* records the shock, pain, and anger of an adolescent discovering the extent of her loss and the massive imperfections of an idealization (father) she cannot afford to renounce because there is no other. In William Godwin's *Memoirs of the Author of "The Rights of Woman,"* Mary read that "no two persons ever found in each other's society, a satisfaction more pure and refined" than had her parents, and that "what it was in itself, can now only be known, in its full extent, to the survivor" (262). Mary also was "the survivor," but she knew nothing of that satisfaction.

The novel's originating phrase, "It was on a dreary night of November," came to stand at the beginning of chapter 4 (chapter 5 in the third edition), and within two sentences Victor sees "the dull yellow eye of the creature open; it breathed hard, and a convulsive motion agitated its limbs" (52). Two paragraphs later, waking from the *cauchemar* of his *mère cachée*, Victor reports that now *his* "every limb became convulsed," and he remains "in the greatest agitation" (53). "Unable to endure the aspect" of the monster's "yellow," "watery" and "speculative" eyes (52), Victor rushes from the room to dream the nightmare of his dead mother. He then starts from the dream into the scene of the novel's conception specified in the 1831 Introduction:

"By the dim and yellow light of the moon, as it forced its way through the window-shutters, I beheld the wretch—the miserable monster whom I had created. He held up the curtain of the bed; and his eyes, if eyes they may be called, were fixed on me" (53). This fascination with gaze and gazing recurs throughout the book, particularly in two later scenes that reassemble the moon, the monster, the female corpse (the maternal body), and the window.

In the midst of the monster's creation, Victor reports, "the moon gazed on my midnight labours" (49). Three fictional years later, Victor is meditating upon the monster's mate, which he has nearly completed, "when, on looking up, I saw, by the light of the moon, the daemon at the casement. A ghastly grin wrinkled his lips as he gazed on me" (163–64). The monster, framed by the window, stands in place of the moon (dae mon in dae moon), his "yellow eye" condensing the "yellow light" of the moon's eye. The gaze drives Victor, now officially engaged to Elizabeth, to tear "to pieces the thing on which I was engaged" (164), and the potentially integral, sexually viable female creature is scattered into fragments. Mary Godwin terminates the possibility of female sexuality not because of an absent mother, but at the instigation of the father conveyed in the monster's gaze. As Mathilda's father explains to her, reflecting what Mary Godwin had herself felt long before at her father's remarriage, "When I saw you become the object of another's love . . . then the fiend awoke within me" (39). The gaze becomes a kind of irresistible trigger reactivating the phantasy of a preoedipal, dyadic, exclusive relation: what makes *Frankenstein* so extraordinary, in part, is that this earliest, foundational relationship is imaged in what was traditionally its rarest form, the male-male (father-son) dyad.

Victor's wedding night realizes his nightmare as he again "embraces" Elizabeth only to find that he holds in his arms the corpse of his beloved. While he continues to "hang over" the dead body, he "happened to look up. The windows of the room had before been darkened; and I felt a kind of panic on seeing the pale yellow light of the moon illuminate the chamber. The shutters had been thrown back; and . . . I saw at the open window a figure the most hideous and abhorred" (193–94). "Every where I turn I see the same figure," were Victor's words two paragraphs before. Now he sees a "grin" on the face of the monster as it points toward the corpse before "plunging" (194) into the same lake that earlier had tempted Victor "to plunge" (87) in suicide. As with Johnson's *Rasselas*, the lake (the appropriately named Lac Léman in this case) can perhaps image the lack generating the story. Hours later, put to bed "hardly conscious of what had happened," Victor reports that "my eyes wandered round the room, as if to seek something that I had lost" (194). To heighten the element of maternal search, Mary Shelley added in the 1831 edition that Victor "as if by instinct, crawled into the room where the corpse of [his] beloved lay" (257). If repetition is the mark of the unconscious, and the unconscious is timeless (which is why it doesn't remark compulsive repetition), then perhaps one might see the figure of Victor crawling toward Elizabeth's body as the phantasy image of a baby seeking again a breast for comfort. What seems to happen, however, is that the sought-for breast transforms into the monster's threatening eye, doubled by a yellow moon behind it. Indeed, shortly after listening to the German *Fantasmagoriana* and being challenged to give birth to a ghost story of her own, Mary Godwin saw such a hallucinatory transformation enacted when, in the scene recounted by Polidori that we have already detailed (chapter 2), Percy Shelley fled from his *Christabel*-inspired vision of Mary Godwin with "eyes instead of nipples." The moon can join the association of eye and breast via the word *orb*; Erasmus Darwin, for instance, whose experiments as recounted by Byron and Percy Shelley encouraged Mary Godwin's reanimation fantasies (227), detailed in his poetry and scientific digressions a prescient object-relational sense of the infant's consuming interest in "the pearly orbs" or "the bosoms velvet orbs" (*Botanic Garden; Part I* 3:356; *Temple of Nature* 3:169). Percy Shelley's hallucination, like Victor's repeated vision described by Mary Godwin, suggests the residual effect of problematic early nurturing as an anxious projection of parental reproach, itself the imagined consequence of infantile anger and frustration over oral deprivation.[6]

The reiterated primal scene of the novel encodes this reproach through the monster's fixed gaze and recurrent grin: "His eyes, if eyes they may be called, were fixed on me. . . . while a grin wrinkled his cheeks" (53); "A ghastly grin wrinkled his lips as he gazed on me" (163–64); "I happened to look up. . . . I felt a kind of panic. . . . A grin was on the face of the monster" (193–94). Though today grins express amusement or laughter, an earlier and less dentally attended age saw anger or scorn in the showing of teeth; so Milton, in a passage which continues to a pun noted above, imagines that Death

> Grinned horrible a gastly smile, to hear
> His famine should be fill'd, and blest his *maw*
> Destin'd to that good hour: no less rejoyc'd
> His *mother* bad . . .
>
> (*Paradise Lost* 2.845–49; italics added)

The gaze, on the other hand, directs us back to the infant and its attempt to make sense of the eyes of an Other that solicit its attention. How are they not mine? What do they (want to) see? Why am "I" being watched? Lacan argues that "from the moment that this gaze appears, the subject tries to adapt himself to it," one result being the experience of "primal separation" that is confused with "self-mutilation" and "failure" (*Concepts* 83). Without the compensation of good-enough nurturing and mirroring/modeling feedback, negative internalizations become foundational. Regardless of the outcome, the gaze of an other becomes permanently invested with the power to access the unconscious and the timeless time of its constitution: "The gaze I encounter . . . is, not a seen gaze, but a gaze imagined by me in the field of the Other" (*Concepts* 84). Any particular gaze, then, is not actually seen so much as recalled in the kind of "afterglow" effect Percy Shelley's spectral "Wanderer" imprints in "the infant" who

>   would conceal
> His troubled visage in his mother's robe
> In terror at the glare of those wild eyes,
> To remember their strange light in many a dream
> Of after-times . . .
>
> (*Alastor* 262–66)

After the monster has killed the creator's angelic double, Henry Clerval, the imprisoned Victor sees "nothing but a dense and frightful darkness, penetrated by no light but the glimmer of two eyes that glared upon me. Sometimes they were the expressive eyes of Henry, languishing in death, the dark orbs nearly covered by the lids, and the long black lashes that fringed them; sometimes it was the watery clouded eyes of the monster, as I first saw them in my chamber at Ingolstadt" (179–80). To these haunting eyes one might add the Godwinian, liquid, "dark deep orbs" of Mathilda's father with "the long lashes that fringed them," and Victor's mother's "dark eyes, fringed by deep lashes."

Frankenstein's author could not escape ("I see them still," she wrote in the 1831 Introduction, fifteen years afterward [228]) a fearful—because undefined, unrecognized—sense of being observed by "the dull yellow eye of the creature," "the dim and yellow light of the moon," which "forced its way through the window-shutters" (52, 53) through her "shut eyes" (227). The eye of her father was the breast she suckled at, and grasping that, what she saw gazing back in her moment of vision is the imagined projection of herself, terrifying in its inescapable fixation on her own aborted development, and for the same reason enraging: "I, the miserable and the abandoned, am an abortion, to be spurned at, and kicked, and trampled on. Even now my blood boils at the recollection of this injustice" (219). The novel's pervasive concern with injustice returns the focus to the author of *Political Justice*, the father who could not mother enough and who principally inscribed his daughter's weak sense of self. For the child, according to Bruno Bettelheim, "worries not whether there is justice for individual man, but whether *he* will be treated justly" (47). The monster's language here (notably the now much remarked description, "an abortion") owes something to Percy Shelley, who was writing for Mary and himself to remonstrate with Godwin's "harshness and cruelty" some three months before *Frankenstein* was begun: "My blood boils in my veins, and my gall rises against all that bears human form, when I think of what I, their benefactor and ardent lover, have endured of enmity and contempt from you" (6 March 1816, *Letters* 324).

In "My Monster/My Self," Barbara Johnson invokes Nancy Friday's *My Mother/My Self* to offer astute speculations about the "repression of autobiography" in Shelley's novel. For Johnson, "what is at stake in Mary's introduction as well as in the novel is the description of a *primal scene of creation. Frankenstein* combines a monstrous answer to two of the most fundamental questions one can ask: where do babies come from? and where do stories come from?" (7). Such questions reformulate the monster's queries, "Who was I? What was I? Whence did I come?" (124), "I" being both myself, a once-upon infant, and a present story. Regarding her question, Johnson writes, "In both cases, the scene of creation is described, but the answer to these questions is still withheld" (7). These scenes, the reiterated configuration re-presented above might suggest, are one and the same. In a book that offers "a psychology without explanation" (Levine 20), perhaps the scene of overlapping moon, eye, and monster is as close as one gets to some answer: "I" came from and now am what eye saw in another's eye, though that "I" is not me. Blake suggests in his consideration of Mary Wollstonecraft Shelley's mother, "The eye sees more than the heart knows" (*VISIONS of the Daughters of Albion*). A cold heart knows no reasoning for its emptiness, and the explanation it tries to see must, as per Freud's formulation in "The Uncanny," be resumed again and again in the futile attempt to de-monstrate the past—what "really" happened—to its restless and lacking self. "Political justice" cannot redress psychological injuries of the first years of life.

5

Keats, Teats, and the Fane of Poesy

I am not strong enough to be weaned—
—LETTER FROM JOHN KEATS TO FANNY BRAWNE,
FEBRUARY(?) 1820

Detailed data for Keats's early life, as for most any life, are unavailable, so we make fictions of the little that is recorded and the less to be evoked here. The eldest son of young parents, displaced by a first brother at age sixteen months and by a second at age four, he "used to say," according to his friend Joseph Severn, "that his great misfortune had been that from his infancy he had no mother" (cited in Gittings, *Keats* 25). A window on Keats's sense of his past opens in this comment to his sister-in-law: "If I were your Son I shouldn't mind you, though you rapt me with the Scissars—But lord! I should be out of favor sin the little un be comm'd."[1] The death of a one-and-a-half-year-old third brother when Keats was seven harrowed his psyche for the ensuing trauma of his father's accidental death somewhat over a year later, and, to conclude the disastrous end to the young boy's first year away at school, the rash remarriage of his mother, like Hamlet's, two months after his father's death. This was not to be the end of unhappiness, for the following year saw the death of his mother's father, the strong paterfamilias whose first name John bore, a dispute over the will, and the three boys and toddler sister suddenly parked with the widowed grandmother while their mother, evidently troubled in her relationships, left her new husband for another fancy. Four years later, distressed and sick, she rejoined her children under her mother's care, to be nursed "with devoted attachment" by her favorite eldest son (as B. R. Haydon was told seven years afterward

[Haydon 2:107]), and to linger over a year until abandoning him forever in March of 1810. When told of her death, the fourteen-and-a-half-year-old student "gave way to 'impassioned and prolonged grief'; which overcame him so violently that even in the school-room he had to hide himself in an alcove under the master's high desk" (Gittings, *Keats* 29). The ensuing death of his "granny good," when he was nineteen, and the departure, four years later, of his brother George to America, followed by the wasting away of younger Tom, kept the experience of loss continually before the emerging poet. "I have never known any unalloy'd Happiness for many days together," he wrote in 1819; "the death or sickness of someone has always spoilt my hours" (2:123).

Keats's "burden of the past" is thus acutely personal as well as cultural, and the inescapable mourning of that past that both strives for and resists acknowledgment can be seen as one of the determinations directing Keats to puns and poetry.[2] Appropriately for this formulation, what often appears as his first poem, "Imitation of Spenser," opens with the line "Now Morning from her orient chamber came," whose double suggestion anticipates later images of "dewdrops of morning" ("On Receiving a Curious Shell" 32) as "the tears / That fill'd the eyes of morn" ("To My Brother George [sonnet]" 2–3) or "the early sobbing of the morn" ("I stood tip-toe" 7) and is fully realized in the injunction to "glut thy sorrow on a morning rose" ("Ode on Melancholy" 15). A section of *Endymion* continues this troping as it describes the hero "vex'd like a mourning eagle" in a "mournful place" and then carries him (via an eagle) to a bower where he imagines being "so sad, so melancholy, so bereft!" without his love, whom, despite her dancing "before the morning gates of heaven," he thinks to rescue "from the morning" (all in the space of sixty lines: 2.635, 650, 685, 688, 697). Keats knows, as well as Freud in "Mourning and Melancholia," that the mourning that cannot be spoken and worked through ends in the "morbid fancy" ("To Hope" 21) of melancholy:

> In melancholy realms big tears are shed,
> More sorrow like to this, and such-like woe,
> Too huge for mortal tongue, or pen of scribe.
>   (*The Fall of Hyperion* [FH] 2.7–9;
>   cf. *Hyperion* [H] 1.158–60)

But he knows too that his knowledge and fine language cannot finally help him: our own misfortunes "touch us too nearly for words," he writes his brother (19 March 1819, 2:79), and the image of the "full weight of utterless thought" in *Hyperion* bears testimony to the saturation of pining desire as it groans bleakly in "the roar of bleak-grown pines" (*H* 2.120, 122). So, toward the end of his life, he notes, "I am afraid to speak of what I would the fainest dwell upon" (1 November 1820, 2:351), and earlier, "How frequently I forget to speak of things, which I think of & feel most" (12 March 1819, 2:71). Still earlier he writes in verse to a friend that he has "a mysterious tale" that he "cannot speak": evidently a vision following his nightly "wonted thread / Of Shapes, and Shadows and Remembrances," and embodying the "flaw / In happiness to see beyond our bourn" that "forces us in Summer skies to mourn" ("Dear Reynolds" 2–3, 86–87, 82–83; 25 March 1818, 1:263).

Keats's poetry enacts the desperate double attempt at once to communicate and to circumvent personal history. "Tongues" are "loos'd in poesy. / Therefore no lover did of anguish die" ("I stood tip-toe" 235–36), but at the same time the writer announces with prophetic prescience that

> If I do hide myself, it sure shall be
> In the very fane, the light of Poesy.
>   ("Sleep and Poetry" 275–76)

Here the temple or "fane" perhaps would fain feign its alteration of "Fanny" (for Frances), the name of the poet's mother, sister, and intended wife—veiling already the foreknowledge that "in the very temple of Delight" (the fane of fain) "veil'd Melancholy has her sovran shrine" ("Ode on Melancholy" 25–26). The drive to hide in poetry must be related to some difficulty in facing directly, or even conceiving, what preoccupies his emotional life, the poet thus exemplifying D. W. Winnicott's sense of the artist's "urgent need to communicate and . . . still more urgent need not to be found" (in Phillips 151; cf. Freud's remark that Goethe "was not only, as a poet, a great self-revealer, but also, in spite of the abundance of autobiographical records, a careful concealer" ["Address" 212]).

Reading the poems chronologically, one senses that the better Keats writes, the more he realizes or intuits the depressive inability of his writing to right the void it would fill. The contradictions become better coordinated because they are more articulated, but the hole widens.³ For all the rhetoric of disinterestedness, he is so bound up with his feigning that he cannot escape the inevitable reflection of his motive for escape: "The fancy cannot cheat so well / As she is fam'd to do" ("Ode on a Nightingale," 73–74). Always with him will be his receptivity to something that can trigger unresolvable ambivalence. "Or" forms his poetic "ore" and underlies his advice to Shelley to "be more of an artist, and 'load every rift' of your subject with ore" (16 August 1820, 2:323). The affecting association and doubled "or" of "Forlorn! the very word" reveals the rift, breaking the "fine spell of words" of "Ode to a Nightingale" and, like the "passing-bell"'s evocation of death, "tolls" or unsouls the speaker to a "sole self" itself so ambivalent as not to know it if wakes or sleeps. One option, then, in the words of *Hyperion* just before it breaks off, is to "Die into life" (3.130)—a possibility that anticipates Keats's concluding speculation, recorded by Joseph Severn less than two months before the poet's death, that "were he to recover he could not write another line" (Rollins 1:85). In this context the "Ode on Melancholy"—the final destination of this essay—offers the starkest picture of the dynamic that looms behind the odes.

Keats's celebrated letters are, to be sure, sometimes put forward to exemplify candor and true feeling—to show, as Lionel Trilling imagines, "The Poet as Hero." But Trilling's "last image of health" in European culture can pick disturbing scripts—like the passage from William Hazlitt on Godwin's *St. Leon* that Keats transcribed for his brother. Lest any suspect self-reference, he prefaced his quotation by stating that it was selected "only on account of its being a specimen" of Hazlitt's style. But given an author never "free from speculating" (27 October 1818, 1:387), who claims not to feel "the influence of a Passion or Affection during a whole week" (22 November 1817, 1:186), who lives an "abstract careless and restless Life" (14 October 1818, 1:391), and whose brother with expectant wife is off in the woody solitude of Kentucky, this choice gives pause:

> He says of St. Leon "He is a limb torn off from Society. In possession of eternal youth and beauty, he can feel no love; surrounded, tantalized and tormented with riches, he can do no good. The faces of men

pass before him as in a speculum; but he is attached to them by no common tie of sympathy or suffering. He is thrown back into himself and his own thoughts. He lives in the solitude of his own breast,—without wife or child or friend or Enemy in the world. *His is the solitude of the Soul, not of woods, or trees or mountains*—but the desert of society—the waste and oblivi[on] of the heart. He is himself alone. His existence is purely intellectual, and is therefore intolerable to one who has felt the rapture of affection or the anguish of woe." (2 January 1819, 2.24–25).

This description well suits one, like Keats, familiar with "the feel of not to feel it" ("In drear nighted December" 21), with "sensations . . . deadened for weeks together" (13 July 1818, 1:325), and with "continual 'agonie ennuiyeuse'" (10 January 1819, 2:32)—one, that is, who exhibited the paralyzing, depressive ambivalence of unresolvable deep-seated conflicts. Such psychological disturbance perhaps forced Keats to be, like the clergymen he hated, "continually acting" (19 February 1819, 2:63). At least, despite the idea of their sincerity, one may sometimes read in the letters an obsessively scripted self-presentation and audience manipulation, at moments too cute by half: "Good bye I've an appoantment—can't stop pon word—good bye—now dont get up—open the door myself—go-o-o d bye—see ye Monday" (1 May 1819, 2:57). One feels him acting as he told the brother and sister-in-law who had abandoned him and dying Tom ("who looks upon me as his only comfort") not to feel sorry, since he kept himself cheerful for their sakes (14 October 1818, 1:391), or when he scripted out in narcissistic detail the process of their reading his letter (20 September 1819, 2:205–6). Little wonder all the effort at epistolary control and anticipation should end with the exertion becoming "so irksome" that "a great aversion to letter writing . . . grows more and more upon me" (24 August 1819, 2:147; 3 October 1819, 2:219).

The power and centrality of ambivalence in Keats is exemplified and thematized in the apostrophe that opens the second book of *Endymion*:

O sovereign power of love! O grief! O balm!
All records, saving thine, come cool, and calm,
And shadowy, through the mist of passed years:

> For others, good or bad, hatred and tears
> Have become indolent; but touching thine,
> One sigh doth echo, one poor sob doth pine,
> One kiss brings honey-dew from buried days.

The conflicting evaluations of love as grief and as balm point to an unresolved ambivalence about the identity of the object, "love," hence its significance and existence for the subject (cf. 2.773: "O bliss! O pain!"). Such a split itself occasions mist in and out of the missed past—the divided subject's present—and all its "cloudy phantasms" (*Endymion* 4.651), "thousand images" (16 August 1819, 2:140), "Shapes, and Shadows and Remembrances" ("Dear Reynolds," above). More particularly, the split expresses itself in contradictory signs, like the "sigh" that earlier in *Endymion* "grief itself embalms" (1.402) or the indirect allusion of the "honey-dew" that summons up Coleridge's "Kubla Khan" and its less-censored double, the "milk of paradise" (Keats's "sovereign power of love" is manifest after seven hundred lines as the "tenderest, milky sovereignties" on the "known Unknown" body of Endymion's "soft embrace" [2.759, 739, 756]). And the image of the honey-dewed "buried days" must contend with the later

>   tombs
> Of buried griefs the spirit sees, but scarce
> One hour doth linger weeping, for the pierce
> Of new-born woe it feels more inly smart.
>   (4.516–19)

The "grievous feud" reflected by such conceptions constantly generates new ones; the "native hell" of the buried griefs, for instance, transforms into the "Cave of Quietude," a new synthesis attempting to regain a fix on at least static depression—here "woe-hurricanes" beat at the gate, "yet all is still ['continuing' as well as 'quiet'] within and desolate" (4.547, 523, 548, 527–28). One curious line of association of the many that are *Endymion* suggests what sudden access to this still-existing cave is like:

> Just when the sufferer begins to burn,
> Then it is free to him; and from an urn,
> Still fed by melting ice, he takes a draught—
> Young Semele such richness never quaft

> In her maternal longing! Happy gloom!
> Dark paradise!
>
> (4.533–38)

When six months pregnant by Zeus, Semele was tricked into gaining and insisting on her lover's promise to appear to her in all his glory, and as a result not only began to burn but suffered complete incineration; one would, however, be hard-pressed to describe her legendary, misguided desire as "maternal longing." Keats could, of course, on his own be supplying her with feelings toward getting pregnant, or toward her fetus (rescued from her consummation to become Dionysus/Bacchus), but one might also imagine a dynamic in which Keats's imagination, caught up with its own "maternal longing" as the burning cause of suffering, jumped to "young Semele" as the antitype of a good-enough mother: one whose pursuit of fancy deprives her child by her resulting death. The earlier refrain "We follow Bacchus!" (4.222, 235) indicates the narrator's allegiance to Semele's infant, and Keats's mother's "inordinate Appetites" were the subject of at least some contemporary speculation.[4]

Maternal longing and its consequent "hyp" or low spirits pervade the world of Keats's words, perhaps most evidently in the cavernous hollows of the two *Hyperion* fragments. There, "in the shady sadness of a vale," the narrator struggles to say good-bye ("Aeternumque vale," in the Virgil Keats translated) to obsessive mourning, although he remains "far sunken from the healthy breath of morn" (*H* 1.1, 2) in "that sad place / Where Cebele and the bruised Titans mourn'd" (*H* 2.3–4), "ending in mist / Of nothing" (*FH* 1.84–85). Some sort of resolution appears through the vision of Moneta in *The Fall of Hyperion*, but even there, after he hears words "as near as an immortal's . . . Could to a mother's soften" and sees "that face," the narrator finds his consolation "like the mild moon, / Who comforts those she sees not" (1.249–50, 263, 269–70). That neither poetic effort with *Hyperion* was completed stands as a final, negative comment on the narrator's pose that "poesy" with "the fine spell of words" can save "imagination" from "dumb enchantment" or that he has been "well nurtured in his mother tongue" (*FH* 1.9, 10, 11, 14–15). So, just as the hymn to Venus in *Endymion* breaks off after the words "And by thy Mother's lips—" and is "heard no more" (3.990), the last word on the two *Hyperions* is mum. The double associations in the word were suggested when Keats wrote, "And yet does not the word mum! go for ones finger beside the nose—I hope it does. I have to make use of the word Mum! before I tell you that Severn has got a little Baby—all his own let us hope—" (20 September 1819, 2:205). Only if the mum is all Severn's own could Severn hope the same for his child—evidently there are other alternatives, but one must keep mum (to keep Mum). Keats's fealty to the *real mum* took him from the "realms of gold" to the knowledge of "sunk realms" (*FH* 68) and of the way the frozen figure of melancholy Saturn sat "when he had lost his realms" (302), his "realmless eyes" closed as he seemed "listening to the Earth, / His antient mother, for some comfort yet" (324–26). "I fear there is no one can give me any comfort," wrote Keats in one of his last letters (1 November 1820, 2:352).

A sense of déjà vu, replacing Mum, haunts Keats's poetry and appears in one of his very early poems, written—he told a friend—after briefly catching sight of an unknown woman at the Vauxhall pleasure gardens (Allott 6). Here the speaker seeks "some drug" or "a draught . . . from Lethe's waves" to banish from his mind "the image of the fairest form" that ever his "wand'ring fancy spell'd." But, he laments,

> 'Tis vain—away I cannot chace
> The melting softness of that face—
> The beaminess of those bright eyes—
> That breast, earth's only paradise!
> ("Fill for me a brimming bowl" 13–16)

The hyperbole—especially regarding the unknown breast—asks us to cast about for some more familiar referent, as does the easy (melting) transition from "that face" and its pair-of-eyes to "that breast" and its paradise. One possible repetition prompting the image goes back to the archaic depths of the nursing infant's equation of face and breast, eye and nipple that we have already noted in chapter 2. The speaker concludes with the fantasy that "had she but known how beat my heart" and smiled, he would have "felt 'the joy of grief'!" But exiled from her bosom he feels like someone in the snow of (e.g., mother's) "Lapland" whose unknown "she" is to be hailed as "the halo of my memory" (thus a version of the moon that is responsible for the other three halos in Keats's verse).

Almost from the beginning Keats puts the moon in a special relation to those who mourn and moan and seek comfort. "To Hope," for example, repeats the "bright eyes" of his Vauxhall vision as it asks Hope to "peep with the moon-beams through the leafy roof" and ward off "the fiend Despondence":

> Whene'er the fate of those I hold most dear
>   Tells to my fearful breast a tale of sorrow,
> O bright-eyed Hope, my morbid fancy cheer;
>   Let me awhile thy sweetest comforts borrow:
>   Thy heaven-born radiance around me shed,
>   And wave thy silver pinions o'er my head!
>   (19–24)

And the smile missed at Vauxhall was evidently later compensated by the moon, as Endymion, in Keats's story of his moony love, asks

> What is there in thee, Moon! that thou shouldst move
> My heart so potently? When yet a child
> I oft have dried my tears when thou hast smil'd.
> Thou seem'dst my sister . . .
>   (3.142–45)

Indeed, Keats became a poet so that he could continue talking to the moon, that "maker of sweet poets, dear delight" ("I stood tip-toe" 116), which he can imagine "waxing warm / To hear what I shall say" (" 'Tis the 'witching time of night' " 9–10) and addresses as

> Lover of loneliness, and wandering,
> Of upcast eye, and tender pondering!
> Thee must I praise above all other glories
> That smile us on to tell delightful stories.
>   ("I stood tip-toe" 121–24)

The isolation of the moon images the poet's sense of himself as a solitary being: "the moon in ether, all alone" ("Calidore" 157), "most meek and most alone" (*Endymion* 3.46). The rhyming linkages of "alone"/"moan" ("Isabella" 236, 238), "alone"/"boon" (*Lamia* 1.110–11), and "boon"/ "moon" (*Endymion* 1.13–14) suggest not only that being alone is a lunar experience, but also that "the moon / The passion poesy" (*Endymion* 1.28–29) is the lonely one's boon, a melodious form of moan. To complicate matters further, the moon reflects aspects of an idealized (or phantasized) maternal figure: "The Moon is now shining full and brilliant—she is the same to me in Matter, what you are to me in Spirit—If you were here my dear Sister[-in-law] I could not pronounce the words which I can write to you from a distance: I have a tenderness for you, and an admiration which I feel to be as great and more chaste than I can have for any woman in the world" (14 October 1818, 1:392). Of a self-assured young woman—"a Charmian"—encountered at a party, he wrote with characteristic verbal two-step, "I dont cry to take the moon home with me in my Pocket not [i.e., nor] do I fret to leave her behind me. I like her and her like because one has no *sensations*—" (14 October 1818, 1:395). "O Moon!" (*Endymion* 3.52, 54, 70) can thus suggest an invocation of "*ooman*" (a dialectical form of *woman*, also in Shakespeare, which Keats twice used in a letter [24 January 1819, 2:35]); at any rate, argues Endymion, "Thou wast the charm of woman, lovely Moon!" (3.169).

As "the charm of woman," the moon presents a singular image of the mammae that so fascinated Keats (like the other popular euphemism, *beauties, charm* is usually plural—but Erasmus Darwin's 1803 *Temple of Nature* imagines the "hundred breasts" of Nature unveiled "charm after charm, succession bright" (1.170), and Keats's Alpheus longs to "warm / Between [Arethusa's] kissing breasts, and every charm / Touch raptur'd!" [*Endymion* 2.946–48]). When the moon goddess Cynthia relocates a desolate Endymion, she "sooth'd her light / Against his pallid face: he felt the charm / To breathlessness"; he lays his head down "to taste the gentle moon" (*Endymion* 3.104–6, 110), like, one supposes, the clouds that "suck their fill of light" in *The Fall of Hyperion* (1.421). Shortly afterward Endymion tells this "gentle Orb!" (recalling Darwin's "velvet orbs" and "pearly orbs") how he "prest / Nature's soft pillow in a wakeful rest" (3.173–74), a description anticipating the lover's desire in "Bright star" to be

> Pillow'd upon my fair love's ripening breast,
> To feel for ever its soft swell and fall,
> Awake for ever in a sweet unrest . . .
> (10–12)

This charged association of breast and moon colors Porphyro's titillating vision of "the wintry moon" throwing "warm gules on Madeline's fair breast" ("Eve" 217–18)—"gules" ostensibly denoting the tint from heraldic red bars in the stained window (a physical impossibility in moonlight), but touching as well the phantasy of a "thirsty gule" or throat, gullet (*OED*, S.V. "gule," 1750).

Such archaic and regressive phantasy appears explicitly in Glaucus's account of his first days with a new love:

> She took me like a child of suckling time,
> And cradled me in roses.
> (*Endymion* 3.456–57)

One morning, however, evidently seeking the "creamy breast" ("Woman! when I behold thee" 16) or "breasts of cream" ("To Charles Cowden Clarke" 34), Glaucus sought "to slake / My greedy thirst with nectarous cameldraughts; / But she was gone" (*Endymion* 3.478–80). Endymion also invokes such precious nourishment when he swears by the "tenderest, milky sovereignties— / These tenderest, and by the nectar-wine" (2.759–60), and both images gloss Keats's own investment in "nectarine-sucking" (28 August 1819, 2:149): "Talking of Pleasure, this moment I was writing with one hand, and with the other holding to my Mouth a Nectarine—good god how fine—It went down soft pulpy, slushy, oozy—all its delicious embonpoint melted down my throat like a large beatified strawberry. I shall certainly breed" (22 September 1819, 2:179). An even more satisfying feed or phantasy looms behind the narrator's report that Endymion "had swoon'd / Drunken from pleasure's nipple; and his love / Henceforth was dove-like" (2.868–70)—like the "dove-like breast."

As for Glaucus, whose mourning begins with deprivation, after witnessing secretly his beloved's identity-altering power and realizing that she is the merciless witch Circe (*Endymion* 3.554, 567), he flees. But on the third day she stands before him and with scornful curse mocks his self-enthralling breast phantasy:

> Ha! ha! Sir Dainty! there must be a nurse
> Made of rose leaves and thistledown, express,

> To cradle thee, my sweet, and lull thee: yes,
> I am too flinty hard for thy nice touch.
>
> (3.570–73)

The awkward reference in "Isabella" to the lady's breasts as "those dainties made to still an infant's cries" (374) can help explain the epithet "Sir Dainty." Circe's curse continues, promising, with heavy irony, that Glaucus "shall still [his] cries / Upon some breast more lily-feminine" (3.576–77), an apparently negative image to be kept in mind when the moon goddess, the good witch Cynthia, promises Endymion command of "our sad fate" and swears "by the lily truth / Of my own breast" (4.980–81). The contrast between, as it were, good and bad breasts figures explicitly in book 2 of *Endymion*, where a nymph ("uprisen to the breast," not surprisingly) tells the protagonist that he must wander "past the scanty bar / To mortal steps" before he can be taken "into the gentle bosom of thy love" (2.98, 123–24, 127).

Here one might invoke again Melanie Klein's ideas concerning the nursing infant's splitting of the mother into a good, available, nourishing breast and a bad, absent, or frustrating one.[5] These "objects" are drunk up by the mind or "introjected" to become almost ontological feelings of happy reassurance or of persecuting, destructive anxiety. With time (i.e., months) the infant sees that these good and bad qualities are in fact related to a single (external, physical) object, but though this realization represents a necessary step toward integration and identity, the bounce-back or projection of the phantasized, split qualities onto the single object establishes ambivalence within the subject. With this ambivalence comes depression, for the subject imagines that past negative feelings and aggressive anger against the "bad" breast are responsible for impairment or emptying of the—as now perceived—only breast (mother) there evidently is, and hence at fault for the subject's own insecure, hungry identity. "Love and hunger," Freud remarks, "meet at a woman's breast" (*Interpretation* 238). An ongoing concern with ingestion—feeding, tasting, drinking—marks one possible response to such lack, and this Keats shows to excess, as in the phantasized teat that at one point figured in *Lamia*'s banquet scene—"saith Glutton 'Mum' / Then makes his shiny mouth a napkin for his thumb" (5 September 1819, 2:159)—or in the "jellies soother than the creamy curd" and myriad other cloying "dainties" Porphyro collects for Madeline ("The Eve of St. Agnes" 266, 269). Words themselves, in their sensuous, sonorous, mouth- and eye-filling materiality, can be as much the object of the poet's consuming as the phantasies constructed with them—the word *moon*'s two orbs, for instance (oo), graphically overdetermine its association with the female bosom. But given inadequately resolved ambivalence, ingestion turns into wasting consumption:

> 'Tis the pest
> Of love, that fairest joys give most unrest;
> That things of delicate and tenderest worth
> Are swallow'd all, and made a seared dearth,
> By one consuming flame: it doth immerse
> And suffocate true blessings in a curse.
> (*Endymion* 2.365–70).

The one poem addressed "To Fanny," coming amid associated evocations of the beloved's "softer breast," "dazzling breast," "warm, white, lucent, million-pleasured breast" ("The day is gone" 2; "What can I do" 49; "I cry your mercy" 8), expresses similar anxieties as it expands the meaning of Fanny:

> "Who now, with greedy looks, eats up my feast?
> What stare outfaces now my silver moon!"
> (17–18)[6]

Deep-seated ambivalence disrupts the achievement of identity, in part because the option of regression to the familiar, still more schizoid position is so available—"in passions of tears or outrageous fits of laughter always in extremes," one schoolfellow described Keats (Bate, *Keats* 17). And Keats at twenty-two reported, "I carry all matters to an extreme—so that when I have any little vexation it grows in five Minutes into a theme for Sophocles—then and in that temper if I write to any friend I have so little self-possession that I give him matter for grieving at the very time perhaps when I am laughing at a Pun" (18 July 1818, 1:340). Perhaps because he is primed by his coming mention of "a Pun," Keats at this moment for once writes correctly the word that, Gittings tells us, "he almost invariably wrote 'perpaps'" (Gittings, *Letters* xxi). As the sign of mastery over ambivalence by the articulating of it in one word, a pun seems here to represent escape from vexation and extremes. In any event, an author "especially liable to puns and to portmanteaux" (Ricks, *Keats* 69) and also dazzled, like Keats, by teats, is not likely to glom onto the word *identity* for its philosophical heritage alone. A poet "has no identity," runs his oft-cited argument of 27 October 1818, though later in the same letter and in others of that time Keats worried over how the "identity of every one" had begun—in a repeated description—to "press upon" him (27 October 1818, 1:387; 21 September 1818, 1:368–69; 14 October 1818, 1:392; 17 March 1819, 2:77). Half a year later, in the context of imagining the world as "the vale of Soul-making," identity had become a positive good, and its pressing association emerges in his description of the heart as "the teat from which the Mind or Intelligence sucks its identity" (21 April 1819, 2:103; see also H 1.123–24, where "bosom" equals "identity").

As if to compensate for the identity difficulties he raises, Keats concludes the letter of 27 October 1818 by invoking "the mere yearning and fondness I have for the Beautiful" (1:388), reaffirming his description, three days before, of "the yearning Passion I have for the beautiful" (1:404). Earlier, giving full vent to his abstract speculation, he argues jejunely that "with a great poet the sense of Beauty overcomes every other consideration, or rather obliterates all consideration" (27 December 1817, 1:194). In effect, he identifies beauty and the breast, as in the ego-obliterating response to "a dove-like bosom. In truth there is no freeing / One's thoughts from such a beauty" ("Woman! when I behold thee" 36–37), from which one might infer, given that "what the imagination seizes as Beauty must be truth" (22 November 1817, 1:187), that a beautiful titty is truth.[7] Such beautiful preoccupation earns Keats Aubrey de Vere's 1849 judgment that, while "Shelley admired the beautiful, Keats was absorbed in it; and admired it no more than an infant admires the mother at whose breast he feeds" (in Ricks, *Keats* 102)—and yearned after it, one might add, no more than the psyche denied adequate nurture (hence, "I have no nature" [27 October 1818, 1:387]). Here one might recall Erasmus Darwin's associationalist argument in *The Temple of Nature* (1803) that the infant learns "IDEAL BEAUTY from its Mother's breast" (3:176) and that in later life when one sees forms with "the nice curves, which swell the female breast" (216)—forms such as "the smooth surface of Etrurian urns" (214)—the originating association is revived, "in lively trains of unextinct delight" (219), and

> Fond Fancy's eye recalls the form divine,
> And TASTE sits smiling upon Beauty's shrine.
> (221–22)

And according to Robert Burton, in *The Anatomy of Melancholy*, "Beauty alone is a sovereign remedy against fear, grief, and all melancholy fits" (2.120).

But given an inability to realize a confident relation with the good breast (or internalized self-image) as opposed to the bad, the idealized abstraction of Beauty becomes itself contaminated with ambivalence. "A thing of beauty is a joy for ever," runs the memorable first line of *Endymion*, and by the end of the stanza it is associated with the beautiful bounty of "an endless fountain of immortal drink" (1.23). Beauty can, however, be "drunk... up" (*Lamia* 1.251) and "swallow'd all" (*Endymion* 2.368); hence the conclusion of *Endymion*'s second stanza already addresses underlying anxiety about the essences of beauty: "They alway must be with us, or we die" (1.33). For the reality of loss will out, as in the déjà vu the speaker experiences in "On Visiting the Tomb of Burns," where the churchyard locale, down to the last detail of its "rounded hills," seems "Though beautiful, cold—strange—as in a dream / I dreamed long ago" (3–4). Keats—who early on fantasized at length about standing "tip-toe on a little hill"—knew that some rounded hills were called "paps" (as at *Lamia* 1.176 before revision by Woodhouse). The "rounded hills" of the dream's vision that "all is cold beauty" (8) might thus adjoin the psychic geography and mammary-memory behind

> The latest dream I ever dream'd
> On the cold hill's side

in "La Belle Dame sans Merci."[8] The "full beautiful" dame has for some time been labeled a "bad-breast mother" (Williams), and as a bewitching *beldam* or "death-pale" "mother Cybele" (*Endymion* 2.642, 640) she certainly does seem, like Circe with Glaucus, to work some terrible and unexpected deprivation on her knight-at-/babe-in-arms and his "death pale"

(38) peers. As often in Keats, the poem turns on ambivalence, in this instance most dramatically in the unsure assurance of "And sure in language strange she said— / I love thee true" (27–28). Similarly in "Isabella," when the eidolon of the beloved appears, "strange sound it was, when the pale shadow spake" (281).

The strange language of "La Belle Dame sans Merci" centers on its neologism *gloam*, a back-formation from *gloaming*, or twilight: "I saw their starv'd lips in the gloam" (41). One might however see the word as an attempt to censor (through the secondary revision of a *g*) a dream vision of starved lips in the *loam*, as in "Isabella"'s graphic picture of the beloved's buried body "loamed" and, again, with "smeared loam" (279, 405). That poem also offers the rationale for "loitering." The knight's presenting symptom is his solitary "loitering" on the cold hill's side, and he in effect gives most of "La Belle Dame" as his explanation; "Isabella" offers, more impartially, the image of one who has

> loiter'd in a green church-yard,
> And let his spirit, like a demon-mole,
> Work through the clayey soil and gravel hard,
> To see scull, coffin'd bones, and funeral stole;
> Pitying each form that hungry Death hath marr'd,
> And filling it once more with human soul.
> (353–58)

Speculations like these underlie Keats's various scenes of reanimation in which the dead "each their old love found," or where dear friends wonder at the recovery of the "languid sick" and "feel their arms, and breasts, and kiss and stare" (*Endymion* 3.824; "I stood tip-toe" 229).

Such wish fulfillments help account for the "high commission" of "fancy," which can restore "beauties that the earth hath lost" ("Fancy" 30). Recalling the moon's "completed form of all completeness," with "a paradise of lips and eyes" and "faintest sighs," Endymion says that

> when I think thereon, my spirit clings
> And plays about its fancy, till the stings
> Of human neighbourhood envenom all.

> Unto what awful power shall I call?
> To what high fane?
>
> (1.620–24)

"Ah! see her hovering feet," he continues directly after the caesura, offering a momentary feminine personification of the "fane" as the "awful power." In the unfinished book 3 of *Hyperion* the "awful Goddess," "ancient Power," "supreme shape" appears to a dimly recollecting Apollo as Mnemosyne, soliciting him to explain his griefs and asserting that she has watched over him since his infancy. Apollo's complaint of numbing melancholy and mourning inability to know "wherefore I am so sad" (3.88) offers a kind of last resistance before the acknowledgment of "beauty that must die" ("Ode on Melancholy") in the great odes. In the "Ode to Psyche" the speaker proposes to be Psyche's "priest, and build a fane" that will be dressed "with all the gardener Fancy e'er could feign" (50, 62). His punning structure will have "branched thoughts . . . / Instead of pines"—that is, thoughts instead of pining desires, and these, "new grown with pleasant pain," shall "murmur" not groan anew; but ambivalence triumphs as one sees that the "happy happy dove" for whom he will "make a moan" (22, 44) is also, shifting odes, "mournful Psyche" ("Ode on Melancholy" 7).

Psyche's "fane" leads to the images of temple, altar, and sacrifice, and to the drive for psychic at-one-ment or identity that occasions them. Ideal poesy is itself a temple, like the "living fane of sounds" to be found in Milton ("Lines on Seeing a Lock of Milton's Hair" 12 [early draft]) and contrasted with the author's own "burnt sacrifice of verse / And melody" (9–10). But Keats's classic picture of "the sacrifice" includes, as in "Ode on a Grecian Urn," an "altar," the "mysterious priest," and "that heifer lowing at the skies." These projections first appear in the verse epistle to Reynolds and its recollection of a landscape of Claude's in which

> The sacrifice goes on; the pontif knife
> Gleams in the sun, the milk-white heifer lows,
> The pipes go shrilly, the libation flows.
>
> (20–22)

Perhaps the image impressed Keats in part owing to the colloquial use of *heifer* for woman (stemming from Samson's "ploughed with my heifer" metaphor in Judges 14:18). Another early poem, already quoted for its fixation on the unforgettable beauty of the dovelike breast, compares a fair woman not to a heifer but "a milk-white lamb that bleats / For man's protection" ("Woman! when I behold thee" 31–32), and according to a contemporary account the poet once burst into tears over this image, "overpowered by the tenderness of his own imagination" (G. F. Mathew, in Gittings, *Keats* 46). As for the heifer's characteristic sound, in Keats "to low" is also to "sound mournfully" and "moan" ("Isabella" 445, 441). These indications of investment with the sacrificial victim are furthered by their dramatic reversal at the end of *Otho the Great* where the lover, bemoaning his faithless bride and that "the extremest beauty of the world / Should so entrench herself away from me," announces

> She is in the temple-stall
> Being garnish'd for the sacrifice, and I,
> The priest of justice, will immolate her
> Upon the altar of wrath!
> (5.5.154–57)

But Auranthe dies on her own, and the lover follows directly, holding his father's hand—his tenuously achieved oedipal identification at the self-destructive cost of "the sacrifice" of beauty acting out again Keats's tragic ambivalence.

Making the sacrificial fane (/Fan[ni]e) poetic includes fashioning some beautiful artifice out of ambiguous marble. On the one hand the heros of Thermopylae are seen "not yet dead, / But in old marbles ever beautiful," but then within the space of ninety lines the hero Endymion is "as dead-still as a marble man, / Frozen in that old tale Arabian" (*Endymion* 1.318–19, 405–6). The grandeur and decay of some sculpture "Bring round the heart an undescribable feud" ("On seeing the Elgin Marbles" 10), but other cultural monuments suggest that irresoluble ambivalence might end with forgetting oneself "to marble," or, like Niobe, turning to marble, petrified with grief (Milton, "Il Penseroso" 41; Dryden, "Threnodia in Augustalis" 2). It is hard to imagine that Porphyro, the protagonist of "The Eve of St. Agnes," does not tag that poem as a "fane / Of liny marble" ("Sleep and Poetry," 363–64) through his name's closeness to *porphyry*.[9] Right after he awakens his Madeline by playing "la belle dame sans mercy" no less, Porphyro sinks, "pale as smooth-sculptured stone" (297). So does he rejoin "The sculptur'd dead" of the poem's second stanza, "emprison'd in black, purgatorial rails" of typography with Keats's other "Shapes, and Shadows and Remembrances" seeking release in new-made lines. The marmoreal memorial of the "Grecian Urn" and the "yearning . . . for the Beautiful" it inurns similarly breed "marble men and maidens overwrought" and frozen generalizations concerning Art in a frieze that nothing frees.

Responding to the speaker's sense in "Ode to a Nightingale" that he "Lethe-wards had sunk," Melancholy's poet moans (in a tour de force of ode-initiating O's to prime the poem's underlying sorrowful or/ro music):

> No, no, go not to Lethe, neither twist
>   Wolf's-bane, tight-rooted, for its poisonous wine;
> Nor suffer thy pale forehead to be kiss'd
>   By nightshade, ruby grape of Proserpine.
>   (1–4)

Nightshade—the former apothecary's apprentice Keats doubtless knew—is another name for belladonna and—as a reader in the midst of Beaumont and Fletcher might have noted—archaic slang for a "night-walker" or prostitute: so much for a retrospective warning to the knight of "La Belle Dame sans Merci." Belladonna's being proscribed as the "ruby grape of Proserpine" glosses the "grape" burst at the poem's climax but also incorporates Keats's paradigm of loss and melancholy, the rape of Proserpine. The speaker continues, urging you to avoid "yew-berries" for your rosary and not to bury yourself in suicidal prayer to Our Lady of Melancholy:

> Make not your rosary of yew-berries;
>   Nor let the beetle, nor the death-moth be
>   Your mournful Psyche, nor the downy owl
> A partner in your sorrow's mysteries.
>   (5–8)

The would-be priest of the "Ode to Psyche" sees his "happy happy dove" here "mournful" and equated with "the beetle" or "the death-moth" if not the dead moth-er; and the "mysterious priest" of "Ode on a Grecian Urn" can be recalled as a better partner for "your sorrow's mysteries" and mist of tears. Most of the first stanza, then, enjoins against strange possibilities which could apply most probably only to a poet weighing images; but the mention of "your sorrow's mysteries" leads to the curious logic behind the poetic prohibitions:

> For shade to shade will come too drowsily,
>   And drown the wakeful anguish of the soul.
> (9–10)

The argument seems to run: no, no, don't do yourself in, because your w/akeful anguish will be drowned—and that illogicality doubles with the statement that whatever is to do the drowning will arrive "excessively drowsily." These perplexities might tease one into the more consoling thought that the (night) shades—as Keats could term the spirits of Hades—will awake or "come to" drowsily (as one might expect) and in their reviving quench the sole soul's anguish over its fill of wakes (for the previously departed but now present shades). If Lethe will come to you, no need to go to it.[10]

This relatively happy situation accounts for the contrast announced at the beginning of the second fit:

> But when the melancholy fit shall fall
>   Sudden from heaven like a weeping cloud,
> That fosters the droop-headed flowers all,
>   And hides the green hill in an April shroud.
> (11–14)

Milton's "pleasing fit of melancholy" ("Comus" 546) here becomes more intensely pathological in its sudden onset, yet its occurrence can hardly be unexpected, given its likeness to an English April shower. Such paradoxical oppositions seem melancholy's nature—on the one hand it "fosters" (a potent word for anyone effectively orphaned at age eight) flowers, yet on the other it enshrouds their true parent, the "green hill o'erspread with . . . flowers" ("Sleep and Poetry" 77–78). And given that the season is encouraging, one must suspect that, as in Shakespeare's "Venus and Adonis," these "fresh flowers . . . droop with grief and hang the head" (665–66)—and that melancholy particularly nourishes all such "droop-headed flowers."

The thought of nurture reflects the underlying hunger now urged to feed itself on flowers:

> Then glut thy sorrow on a morning rose,
>   Or on the rainbow of the salt sand-wave,
>   Or on the wealth of globed peonies.
>   (15–17)

The imperative *glut* marks a pressing need to "feed to repletion," but since *glut*'s preposition *on* (instead of the usual, incorporative *with*) offers this sorrow only visual options, one might imagine filling one's sorrow by weeping over images which happen to echo it (mo*rn*ing *ro*se, *Or on*, *Or on*). The "morning rose" recalls Keats's early pictures of "the dewy birth / Of morning roses" ("To the Ladies" 5–6) and "flowers with dew . . . yet drooping" ("To Some Ladies" 13), but a rose mourning the mist-shrouded mystery-morning might droop as well. The sequence of alternative images ("Or . . . Or . . .") on which to glut reiterates the lack of adequate stable object that occasions melancholy. Wordsworth's rainbow in the sky that "comes and goes" and causes that poet's heart to "leap up" here takes grains of salt unnumbered as Keats joins the "sad waves" of Spenser's Gardin of Proserpina (*Faerie Queene* 2.7.57) with Shakespeare's "salt-wave . . . a quick venue of wit" (*Love's Labour's Lost* 5.1.57). He must have enjoyed Aristotle's opinion, reported by Burton, that "melancholy men of all others are most witty" (1.3.1.3, 1.401).

The third consecutive verse beginning "Or" breaks the parallel construction it would at first indicate in order to introduce a new alternative altogether for the melancholy fit and sorrow-glutting response:

> Or if thy mistress some rich anger shows,
>   Emprison her soft hand, and let her rave,
>   And feed deep, deep upon her peerless eyes.
>   (18–20)

The new coordination links "thy mistress" with the "melancholy fit," while the opening syllable of her title links her to the misty weeping cloud and to sorrow's mysteries. Given that Keats elsewhere imagines "the mistress with a shine / Of anger in her eyes" (*The Jealousies* 66–67) and that the eyes are here fed upon, the adjective for melancholy's anger seems to render her emotion a choice food, one (as the *OED* says of *rich* in this sense) particularly "stimulative or nourishing." That the narrator may be thinking not of the mistress's anger but "of the pleasure to be found" in its display (Allott 540) only makes his implied attitude more crucial to his ode—as do the spuriously authoritative injunctions ("emprison," "let her," "feed"), and the disturbing closeness between her rage or rave and his ravening, and the one-way peering upon peerless eyes, and the immediate obsession with *es* (cf. "easeful Death" in "Ode to a Nightingale"). Striving to know why he is "so sad . . . melancholy," *Hyperion*'s Apollo "raves" in "aching ignorance" until he reads in Mnemosyne's "silent face" a "wondrous lesson" the effect of which he compares to that of drinking "bright elixir peerless" (3.88–89, 110, 107, 112, 119). *Mistress* is of course a richly polysemic word which can denote head of a household, goddess, teacher, concubine, and beloved, but also the "blessed moon" or "sovereign mistress of true melancholy" in Shakespeare's *Anthony and Cleopatra* (4.9.11), whose light, for Keats's other favorite, Milton, is "peerless" (*Paradise Lost* 4.608).

Journeying where "beauty dwells," Endymion finds himself with a 'moon-beam" in "the deep, deep, water-world" (3.93, 101); now, having experienced "deep, deep" the "eyes of melancholy" that recur in Keats (*H* 1.70; *Lamia* 1.84; "Isabella" 433), the later narrator finds that

> She dwells with Beauty—Beauty that must die;
>   And Joy, whose hand is ever at his lips
> Bidding adieu; and aching Pleasure nigh,
>   Turning to poison while the bee-mouth sips:
> Ay, in the very temple of Delight
>   Veil'd Melancholy has her sovran shrine,
>   Though seen of none save him whose strenuous tongue
> Can burst Joy's grape against his palate fine;
>   His soul shall taste the sadness of her might,
>   And be among her cloudy trophies hung.

"One could not expect a better picture of the 'depressive position' than this," comments Stephen Reid (411), invoking Klein's term for the state, originating in early infancy and persisting in the unconscious, marked by ambivalence and guilt over aggressive impulses toward the ("bad") breast. As before, in *Endymion*, the good-object "Queen of Beauty" overseeing "panting bosoms bare!" turns out also to be responsible for the "delicious poisoner" whose "venom'd goblet . . . we quaff until / We fill" (3.976,

985, 987–88). The blazoned Miltonism, "sovran" (e.g., "sovran Mistress" [*Paradise Lost* 9.532]), evokes Peerless Poetry of the sort Keats had already imagined as a "Live temple of sweet noise; . . . giving delight" ("Lines on Seeing" 12, 14). In the early, more sensuous tongue of "Sleep and Poetry," he recalls being in

> . . . a poet's house who keeps the keys
> Of pleasure's temple. Round about were hung
> The glorious features of the bards who sung
> In other ages . . .
>
> (354–57)

Now, however, "the very fane, the light of Poesy" (276) discloses, still deeper within, a secret altar, the veiled Holy of Melancholies, knowledge of which warrants the speaker's third-person description of his fate as the high priest of Psyche's fanciful mind-sanctuary. Long since he had thought to join the "great Bards" of Milton's melancholy "Il Penseroso" who "have sung . . . of Trophies hung" (116–18), and now he finds that in achieving that goal, given his inward subject (and subjection), he has hung himself and become one with the mist. Having worked beyond the "weak" or "mourning" or "feeble tongue" (*Endymion* 1.128; 4.160; H 1.49) of earlier poems, the speaker's exertion produces that notoriously hard nut or tough tit, "Joy's grape," to follow the unexpected picture of Joy's ever "bidding adieu" (a dew such as droops all).[11] Joy's grief [which we might bend to "grafe"; cf. "the joy of grief," above], already inscribed in and rued by the *grape* "of Proserpine," is in bidding adieu—"all things mourn awhile / At fleeting blisses" ("Think not of it" 17–18)—and the more strenuously the would-be(e) mouth sucks at Fan$^c/_n$y's teat for the burst of joy, the more sadly must its possessor poison himself acknowledging the might of what might have been (the uberous uva turns to a bursting uvula).[12] Helen Vendler's discomfort at the resemblance between "the tongue-burst grape" and "the fed-on eyes" (167) recalls the still more disturbing phantasy of eyes as nipples, a possibility underscored by the usually double-blooming "globed peonies" that rhyme the eyes and offer the nearest sips for the bee-mouth: melancholy sexuality is infantile not genital, as melancholy poetry well knows. The triangulation of eyes, grapes, and teats can be illustrated by an eighteenth-century image of Erigone (appoached by Bacchus in the

Fig. 6. Johan Gotthard Müller (after R. Jollain), "La nymphe Erigone" (1773). Edward Fuchs, *Illustrierte Sittengeschichte*, vol. 2, pt. 2 (*Die galante Zeit*). München: Albert Langen Verlag, n.d. [c. 1911], fig. 268.

form of a cluster or grapes, according to Ovid; fig. 6), or again by Hendrick Goltzius's 1593 pen work "Without Ceres or Bacchus [Venus Freezes]" (fig. 7).

But the "sovran shrine" of Melancholy's ode pales in comparison with the "old sanctuary" Keats discovers in *The Fall of Hyperion*. Here the saturnine psychic structure behind his temples and contemplations memorializes its internal doom in an "eternal domed monument" of unfathomable extent: "The silent massy range / Of columns north and south, ending in mist / Of nothing" (1.83–85). The space, characteristically, is entered by phantasizing about the maternal body, as the dreamer sees, before a "wreathed doorway, on a mound / Of moss" (1.28–29), a feast that seems the "refuse of

Fig. 7. Hendrick Goltzius, "Sine Cerere et Libero Friget Venus" (1593). Philadelphia Museum of Art. Purchased by the Walter H. Annenberg Fund for Major Aquisitions, the Henry P. McIlhenny Fund in memory of Frances P. McIlhenny, and other Museum funds.

a meal / By angel tasted, or our mother Eve" (1.30–31). As often, thought of the mother underground occasions a nod to her in the guise of "Proserpine return'd to her own fields, / Where the white heifers low" (1.37–38). A feeling of "appetite / More yearning than on earth I ever felt" (1.39–40) seems the source of the imaginary plenty, just as "after not long" the dreamer thirsts in order to imbibe his parent; returning also to "Ode on Melancholy" and its "bee-mouth sips," he

> thirsted, for thereby
> Stood a cool vessel of transparent juice,
> Sipp'd by the wander'd bee, the which I took,
> And, pledging all the mortals of the world,
> And all the dead whose names are in our lips,
> Drank. That full draught is parent of my theme.
> (1.41–46)

As before, when the bursting of Joy's grape turned the poet into one of melancholy's "cloudy trophies," here the full draught brings on a "cloudy swoon" (1.55) which links the dreamer to Endymion's "melancholy thought: O he had swoon'd / Drunken from pleasure's nipple" (2.868–69).

At the "fane" of this vast temple between the temples, veil'd Melancholy takes the form of a "veiled shadow" (1.141, cf. 194). She is the "shade of Memory!" (1.282) whose name, Moneta, is overdetermined by Keats's long investment in "mourn," "moon," and "moan"—not to mention teats and eats. The verses in which she first tells her name are described as "Moneta's mourn" (1.231) and the succeeding climactic passage describing her face dwells most on the eyes which "in blank splendor beam'd like the mild moon" (1.269). The "sole priestess" of Saturn's desolation, she falls silent "a whole moon" (1.392) so that her idol's "strange musings" are duly emphasized. And the word that saturates Saturn's lament is *moan*. That speech seems, according to the dreamer, like one of "some old man of the earth / Bewailing earthly loss"; but he then proceeds to remark its form as if on behalf of the author:

> nor could my eyes
> And ears act with that pleasant union of sense
> Which marries sweet sound with the grace of form,

> And dolorous accent from a tragic harp
> With large limb'd visions.
>
> (1.441–45)

The fanciful feigning of a nourishing, self-generated "poesy" that would "sooth the cares, and lift the thoughts of man" ("Sleep and Poetry" 247) ends in the unassimilable burden of "Moan, brethren, moan," "Moan and wail. / Moan, brethren, moan," "Moan, moan, / Moan, Cybele, moan," "Moan, brethren, moan," "Moan, moan" (1.412, 417–18, 424–25, 427, 430).

For Keats, "perpaps," the inmost fane of poesy is hidden, with him, without it.

6

Tears, Ay, Dull Tears: Tennyson's Idle Idol-Idyl

> *As when we dwell upon a word we know,*
> *Repeating, till the word we know so well*
> *Becomes a wonder, and we know not why* . . .
> —TENNYSON, *"Lancelot and Elaine"*

Tennyson's best editor and astute critic makes an unimportant but suggestive tiny slip in his fine study of the poet's life and works. In a discussion of the 1855 publication *Maud*, Christopher Ricks writes that "Tennyson at this stage of his life was haunted by the feeling that the dead are all too intimidatingly alive"; and, lending the poet the words of *Maud*'s narrator, Ricks continues: "He remembers his dead mother—'And that dead man at her heart and mine'" (*Tennyson* 242). In fact, however, Alfred Tennyson's mother, Elizabeth, was to live for ten years after *Maud* (indeed the date is reported by Ricks in an footnote [222]). Can the living be intimidatingly dead? Ricks's elision of Tennyson's mother is the more curious because he chooses as the epigraph for his first chapter these lines from "The Coming of Arthur":

> Moreover, always in my mind I hear
> A cry from out the dawning of my life,
> A mother weeping[1]

and writes that this cry and weeping "were the core of [the poet's] childhood and youth." But that first chapter, titled "Tennyson and His Father till 1827" (when the poet turned eighteen), is after more dramatic and accessible material than the "good and kind" mother (10), and we soon read that what Tennyson "deeply and experimentally felt from his earlier years" was "the plight of his father" (10). Certainly growing up as a younger son of an epileptic dipsomaniac locked in a struggle with *his* rejecting father ("the old man of the wolds") offers ample occasion for psychic traumata: "When the Rector's moods were at their worst, Alfred would run through the night to the churchyard and throw himself prostrate among the graves, wishing that he were dead" (Martin 25). Such a problematic paternal model might well lend a greater prominence to the mother's role in shaping the son's sensibilities, though to be sure, Tennyson, more than most, insists on our keeping in mind the inaccessibly complex interactions of genetic endowment (the all-too-evident "black blood" of the Tennysons) and family conflict across generations and bloodlines, not to mention intimate family dynamics.

Tennyson's few comments about his mother suggest some postadolescent idealization: in a letter written when he was twenty-three he referred to her as "one of the most angelick natures on God's earth, always doing good as it were by a sort of intuition" (*Letters* [L] 1:90), and at her funeral he told the officiating clergyman, rather fulsomely, "I hope you will not think that I have spoken in exaggerated terms of my beloved mother, but indeed she was the beautifullest thing God Almighty ever did make" (L 2:394n.).

These descriptions sit a bit awkwardly with the ludicrous picture a thirty-nine-year-old Tennyson related of his mother "grovelling on the floor in an extremity of fear" during a thunderstorm, and his following comment: "My mother is afraid if I go to town even for a night; how could they get on without me for months?" (L 1.171). So the narrator of *Maud* recalls

> . . . my dark-dawning youth,
> Darkened watching a mother decline
> And that dead man at her heart and mine:
> For who was left to watch but I?
> Yet so did I let my freshness die.
> (690–94, 2:557)

Alan Ker, one of the poet's in-laws, reported for Hallam Tennyson's memoir of his father that Elizabeth Tennyson was "so sensitive that touch her feelings ever so lightly and the tears rushed to her eyes" (H. Tennyson 220). This account continues with the remarkable information: "Then it was we used to hear your father say, 'Dam your eyes, mother, dam your eyes!' and then she smiled and applied the white pocket-handkerchief and shook her head at her son" (220). However improbable the suggestion of the poet's punning on the abusive expression "Damn your eyes!" the description seems drawn from life—or if not, adds strikingly to Ker's recollection of *Maud* and the narrator's memory of his mother:

> For how often I caught her with eyes all wet,
> Shaking her head at her son and sighing
> A world of trouble within!
> (706–8, 2:557)

These teary mother's eyes are far from those the poet earlier fantasized for the "trustful infant" who knows "Nothing beyond his mother's eyes. / They comfort him by night and day" ("Supposed Confession of a Second-Rate Sensitive Mind" 44–45, 1:218). These "mild deep eyes upraised" may manifest "The beauty and repose of faith, / And the clear spirit shining through" (75–76, 1:219), but in realizing that her faith is not faith in him, the boy soon experiences cognitive dissonance and ambivalence.

The piety of Tennyson's mother can be gauged from one of her few letters to him that survive, albeit one written when she was near eighty and her "Dearest Ally" fifty. "It does indeed" give her "the purest satisfaction," she writes, "to notice that a spirit of Christianity is perceptible" through her son's latest volume (*Idylls of the King*):

> O dearest Ally, how fervently have I prayed for years that our merciful Redeemer would intercede with our Heavenly Father, to grant thee His Holy Spirit to urge thee to employ the talents He has given thee, by taking every opportunity of endeavouring to impress the precepts of His Holy Word on the minds of others. My beloved son, words are too feeble to express the joy of my heart in perceiving that thou art earnestly endeavouring to do so. Dearest Ally, there is nothing for a moment to be compared to the favour of God: I need not ask thee if thou art of the same opinion. Thy writings are a convincive proof

that thou art. My beloved child, when our Heavenly Father summons us hence, may we meet, and all that are dear to us, in that blessed state where sorrow is unknown, never more to be separated. (In H. Tennyson 379–80)

Her son's contention that "There lives more faith in honest doubt, / Believe me, than in half the creeds" (*In Memoriam* 96.11–12, 2:415) evidently didn't warrant concern (Tennyson's feelings about religion included his punning "Te Deum" into "tedium" [Martin 480]).

But for Tennyson the disjuncture between his doubts and his mother's faith pointed to something more serious, and at twenty, in his "Supposed Confessions of a Second-Rate Sensitive Mind," he wondered "wherefore do we grow awry," and

> What Devil had the heart to scathe
> Flowers thou hadst reared—to brush the dew
> From thine own lily, when thy grave
> Was deep, my mother, in the clay?
> Myself? Is it thus? Myself? Had I
> So little love for thee? But why
> Prevailed not thy pure prayers?
> (83–89, 1:219)

As speaker moves to conclude his confession, he expresses his fear that "everywhere / Some must clasp Idols." "Yet, my God," he wonders, "Whom call I Idol?" (177–80, 1:222). Devotion to what Tennyson called "*mein liebes Ich*" (H. Tennyson 268) is the desperate defense against the second-rate sensitivity bequeathed by the mother:

> O weary life! O weary death!
> O spirit and heart made desolate!
> O damnéd vacillating state!
> (188–finis, 1:222)

"Perdidi Diem," whose title invokes the Emperor Titus's lament for a day lost to good action, is another early poem that suggests preoedipal phantasies. Here the speaker reports,

> I must needs pore upon the mysteries
> Of my own infinite Nature and torment
> My spirit with a fruitless discontent.
> (19–21, 1:294)

This self-wasting idleness is glossed by the ensuing extended simile, which tells of "young ravens fallen from their cherishing nest" (24). Though they cry continually and "trail and spoil / Their new plumes on the misty soil," still "not the more for this / Shall the loved mother minister" to them nor win them to their wonted rest "with sleep-compelling down of her most glossy breast":

> In chill discomfort still they cry:
> What is the death of life if this be not to die?
> (34–35, 1:294)

Once again "trustful infancy" with "no care of life or death" ("Supposed Confessions" 48) drops into hyperconsciousness of that opposition and attempts to escape in idle poring upon the self-idol and the idle—ineffectual for real change—outpouring of writing.

Tennyson's disciple and the famed anthologist of *The Golden Treasury*, F. T. Palgrave, reported the poet as saying, more than once, "that his poems sprang from a 'nucleus,' some one word, may be, or brief melodious phrase which had floated through the brain, as it were unbidden" (in Gillett 324). The most celebrated instance of this is Hallam Tennyson's story of how his father "wrote 'The Charge of the Light Brigade' in a few minutes, after reading the description in the *Times* in which occurred the phrase 'some one had blundered,' and this was the origin of the metre of his poem" (320). Edgar Shannon and Christopher Ricks make this account still more interesting by pointing out that the actual source phrase read "some hideous blunder" and that it appeared in the *Times* three weeks before the poem's composition (Ricks, *Tennyson* 325). "Far—Far—Away," written when Tennyson was seventy-nine, offers another example, the title (and refrain) being words that "had always a strange charm" for him (H. Tennyson 9). One wonders if the charm of the phrase owed anything to a context where Tennyson may have met (or remet) it and which it then served to condense: for in Coleridge's *Zapolya*, published in 1817, he would have read that "love's dreams prove seldom true" and hence, "We must away; / Far, far away!" (part 2, 2.2.75, 79–80).

As it happens, the single word *idle* of the quintessentially Tennysonian lyric known by its incipit, "Tears, idle tears," revises an earlier *foolish* ("Tears, foolish tears"), but the exponential increase in meaning that the revision achieves reveals an aural matrix of idols, idyls, and idleness, not to mention the repetition compulsion now incipient in the sounds ("Tears, idle tears, I . . ."). Idle, idol, and idyl each represent a different emphasis or interpretation or *hearing* of the poem; each reflects a different drive motivating the text. The poem presents a particularly successful compromise between the different voices that would claim it—that want to speak through it as a single voice. In the unconscious ongoing negotiation of composition and revision the seemingly unbidden, floating phonemes of the poem's "charged word," *idle* (Hartman 111), come together as a kind of *Knotenpunkt* or nodal point that binds up the text, ensuring that each conflicting, constituting element has the possibility of a hearing. The identical sound of the semes facilitates the plurality of themes. *Idle* can be imagined as first the catalyst and lastly the precipitate of the mix making up the text's authority, the trace of tension in whatever intention one imputes to the author.

The poem is not a hostage to language, to be liberated by deconstruction, but a new moment and monument of Tennyson's language, his mother tongue, participating in an orbit of associations the ideal display of which (were it ever accessible) would show something like the terms and structure of Tennyson's unconscious. As Ricks observes, "No poem of Tennyson compacts more of his deepest feelings with a more graceful fluency" (*Tennyson* 190). Hearing the different meanings broached by the mother word requires a sense of parallel (rather than serial) mental processing with which *one* will probably never be entirely at ease. The sound of the poem's second word, at any rate, activates several channels: the *OED* pronounces *idle*, *idol*, and *idyl* as [əid'l], [əi·d'l], and [əi·dil]; Daniel Jones's *English Pronouncing Dictionary* (12th ed., 1964) suggests ['aid l], ['aidl], and ['idil] or ['aid-l].

Tears, idle tears, I know not what they mean,
Tears from the depth of some divine despair
Rise in the heart, and gather to the eyes,
In looking on the happy Autumn-fields,
And thinking of the days that are no more.

Fresh as the first beam glittering on a sail,
That brings our friends up from the underworld,
Sad as the last which reddens over one
That sinks with all we love below the verge;
So sad, so fresh, the days that are no more.

Ah, sad and strange as in dark summer dawns
The earliest pipe of half-awakened birds
To dying ears, when unto dying eyes
The casement slowly grows a glimmering square;
So sad, so strange, the days that are no more.

Dear as remembered kisses after death,
And sweet as those by hopeless fancy feigned
On lips that are for others; deep as love,
Deep as first love, and wild with all regret;
O Death in Life, the days that are no more.
           (*The Princess* 4.21–40, 2:232–33)

The poem's conflicting voices come closest to the surface with the image of friends brought "up from the underworld." An audience concerned with physical reality and its mimesis might construe "the underworld" as "the Antipodes" or Australia ("down under"), and for this sense—as the first instance—the *OED* cites this passage. But since the publication of *The Well Wrought Urn* in 1947, readers have had the benefit of Cleanth Brooks's sense that the word would "necessarily suggest the underworld of Greek mythology" (170)—an argument for Tennysonian "paradox and ambiguity" now thoroughly assimilated. In "Ulysses" Tennyson joins Homer's account of Odysseus's sailing to the entrance of the underworld with Dante's vision of Ulysses' sea voyage to Purgatory, so that Tennyson's old wanderer says:

> It may be that the gulfs will wash us down,
> It may be we shall touch the Happy Isles,
> And see the great Achilles, whom we knew.
>
> (62–64)

But the hero of the *Odyssey*, as Tennyson could expect his readers to know, meets Achilles not in any "Happy Isles" or Elysian "happy Autumn-fields," but in the land of the dead, where dwell the "mere imitations of perished mortals": "broton eidola kamonton" (*Od.* 11.476). These dead are *idols* (*eidola*—images, literally, "things seen"), as, in turn, some readers suspect Tennyson's Ulysses himself to be, an "idle king" speaking in a kind of afterlife as a "gray spirit" to his "mariners, souls" who, according to the *Odyssey*, at least, have long since died. The big tears ("thalaron dakru," *Od.* 11.466) that Homer's dead share with mortal Odysseus are, literally, idol tears; Tennyson, too, can imagine "phantasms weeping tears" ("The Palace of Art" 249, 1:454). Still more common are mortal tears shed for the idol or image of a loved one, like those of Odysseus for his dead mother—an "idoll" in Chapman's 1616 translation—or Aeneas for the *imago* of his wife (*Od.* 11.84–87, *Aeneid* 2.771–91; the image becomes a commonplace). As the *OED* notes, *idol* functions as subjective and objective genitive, permitting "idol tears" that are both "tears of an idol" and "tears for an idol."

Odysseus's lament following the underworld interview with his mother—that embodiment of "first love"—can shade into that of the speaker of "Tears, Idle Tears," who ends "wild with all regret." Odysseus strives to embrace his mother's image, but, in the translation of Pope, which young Tennyson often imitated,

> Thrice through my arms she slipp'd like empty wind,
> Or dreams, the vain illusions of the mind.
> Wild with despair, I shed a copious tide
> Of flowing tears . . .
>
> (11.249–52)

Similarly, in *In Memoriam*:

> Tears of the widower, when he sees
>   A late-lost form that sleep reveals,

And moves his doubtful arms, and feels
Her place is empty, fall like these.
(13.1–4, 2:331)

So, also, section 10 of *In Memoriam* imagines the sailing ship conveying Arthur Hallam's body as bearing "dark freight, a vanish'd life" and comments, "We have idle dreams . . . home-bred fancies." The frequent collocation in English of *idle* and *fancy* must be in part encouraged by the semantic identity of *idol* (*eidolon*) and *phantom*, a power of association evident in a somewhat different way when Tennyson writes how, looking in a stream "with idle care . . . I saw your troubled image there" ("The Miller's Daughter" [1832 version] 73–76, 1.410n.). But vanity—the quality of being (in) vain—seems to be the underlying sense joining *idol* ("late-lost form") and *idle* ("empty"): Swift, for example, writes of "vain, idle, visionary thoughts" ("A Modest Proposal"), and Pope, in a poem partly memorized by Tennyson, describes Dulness's created image of "a Poet's form" (gifted with "empty words") as an "idol void and vain!" (*Dunciad* A 2.42). Blake, similarly, punningly mocks the vain, in vain "Idol Virtues of the Natural Heart" (*Milton* 38.46). And Joyce's "Araby" (*Dubliners*) has the narrator recall how, owing to his idolizing "adoration" of his first love, "my eyes were often full of tears (I could not tell why)"; at night and by day "her image came between me and the page," he relates, and the punning outcome is that his schoolmaster criticizes him for beginning "to idle."

Eidola, according to Cicero, figure in the system of Epicurus as the films given off by any object and conveying an impression to the eye: the exterior *eidola* give rise to interior *phantasia*, fancy or mental vision (*Epistulae ad familiares* 15.16). Lucretius develops this idea in *De rerum natura*, book 4, and, in Tennyson's poem about him, wonders, as he despairs of *his* "death-in-life," how he can be troubled by unbidden mental images: "How should the mind, except it loves them, clasp / These idols to herself?" ("Lucretius" 164–65, 2:715). So, "in looking," the image-films, the idol tears are torn from their source and, like the image of the happy Autumn-fields, "gather to the eyes" in some way that implicates "I." The poem, Tennyson said, "was written in the yellowing autumn-tide at Tintern Abbey, full for me of its bygone memories" (H. Tennyson 221). Those memories included Wordsworth's "Lines Written a Few Miles Above Tintern Abbey," and, more powerful for Tennyson, Keats's "To Autumn." But as Herbert F. Tucker notes, it is precisely at his greatest idol's most personal and self-referential moment that Tennyson tears away into his own inner space (366).[2] Keats asks, "Where are the songs of Spring? Ay, where are they?" only to enjoin, "Think not of them, thou hast thy music too" ("To Autumn" 23–24). Tennyson's music, however, rises in "thinking of the days that are no more" and is finally unconcerned whether autumn or summer waits outside.

The emphatic source of the eye-dulling tears echoes though the poem in the vocal signature carried by the shifting first-person *i* sounds: "*i*dle," "*I*," "r*i*se," "*ey*es," "p*i*pe," "d*y*ing," "w*i*ld," "l*i*fe." The speaker gives rise to the tears; indeed, "I" doles them out (like Tennyson's Ulysses, "an *idle* king . . . I mete and *dole*" [3]) as dole (as when Elaine dies and "there was dole in Astolat" ["Lancelot and Elaine" 1129, 3:454]). In doling (out) his condition the speaker makes the poem, like so many others of Tennyson's, an elegiac idyl; and one, moreover, evoking a recurrent theme of the 1842 *Poems* (initially titled *Morte d'Arthur; Dora, and Other Idyls*): "recollections of older men recalling their youth, in which the beloved had died" (Pattison 71). "Tears, Idle Tears" appears as a song in the volume that followed those idyls in 1847, *The Princess* (given Tennyson's habits of revision, publication dates give little indication of compositional chronology; *The Princess* was begun, evidently, in 1839, and "Tears, Idle Tears" perhaps dates from 1834 [Martin 194]). When *The Princess* appeared, Tennyson was already strongly associated with the word *idyl*; contemporary reviews remarked the volume's "idyllic manner," and later critics call it "a series of idylls," "a poem that seeks to evolve the idyll beyond its previous Tennysonian limits" (Kozicki 59; Ryals 23; Pattison 95). William Allingham reports Tennyson using a curiously possessive turn of phrase to express displeasure over the title of Browning's *Dramatic Idylls*: "I wish Browning had not taken my word Idyll" (291). After his name, then, *idyl* would perhaps best qualify as "the word that is the symbol of myself" ("The Ancient Sage" goes on to say that "idle gleams to thee are light to me"; 231, 246, 3:145).

In the framing context of *The Princess*, the "mournful song" of "Tears, Idle Tears" is sung by "a maid . . . with such passion that the tear, / She sang of, shook and fell" (4.41–42). The princess, however, condemns the song, using an association already noted to argue that women should stop their ears to such a siren song of "fancies hatched / In silken-folded idleness" (4.48–49). Following a revealing line of association, she urges that women "let the past be past" and not care though "the wild figtree split / [Men's] monstrous idols" (4.61–62). Tennyson names the princess Ida, and at one point permutates the name in the space of fifty-five lines from "sweet Ida" to "sweet dream" to another "sweet Idyl" set within the text (7.120, 134, 175). For Tennyson, the name Ida powerfully associates with the idea of mother and death of the I through the story and obsessive refrain of "Oenone" (first published in 1832):

> My eyes are full of tears, my heart of love,
> My heart is breaking, and my eyes are dim,
> And I am all aweary of my life.
>   "O mother Ida, many-fountained Ida,
> Dear mother Ida, hearken ere I die."
>   (30–34, 1:422)

The male protagonist of *The Princess*, whose presence in effect occasions "Tears, Idle Tears," is himself a kind of *eidolon*, as Tennyson made clear in revising the poem. Subject to recurrent "weird seizures," the prince often seems "to move among a world of ghosts," himself "the shadow of a dream" (1.14, 17–18; 3.188; 4.560–61; 5.481—some half-century later, "Akbar's Dream" will feature "The Shadow of a dream—an idle one" [5, 3:236]). Given the old proverb "after wyrd comes weird" and the poet's being possessed by "some one word, may be, or brief melodious phrase," one wonders whether the prince's trances might not be "seizures" by "words, / Themselves but shadows of a shadow-world" ("The Ancient Sage" 238–39, 3.145). Toward the end of *The Princess*, the action of which revolves around the prince's attempt to make Ida his own, the prince, near defeat, gives himself up to tears "all for langour and self-pity" and asks Ida only "to kiss me ere I die" (7.124, 135).

As the conclusion unfolds, the prince argues for a kind of mutual marriage—"The two-celled heart beating, with one full stroke" (7.289)—and Ida asks him from what woman he learned that idea. The response is a long encomium on his mother, concerning which the poet once evasively assented that it was indeed based on Elizabeth Tennyson (H. Tennyson 221):

> No Angel, but a dearer being, all dipt
> In Angel instincts, breathing Paradise,
> Interpreter between the Gods and men,
> Who looked all native to her place, and yet
> On tiptoe seemed to touch a sphere
> Too gross to tread, and all male minds perforce
> Swayed to her from their orbits as they moved,
> And girdled her with music. Happy he
> With such a mother! faith in womankind
> Beats with his blood, and trust in all things high
> Comes easy to him, and though he trip and fall
> He shall not blind his soul with clay.
>
> (7.301–12)

Despite such praise and professed importance of his mother, it is oddly "never clear whether she is alive or dead" (Ricks, *Tennyson* 184). Princess Ida immediately notes that this idealization doesn't suit her and marks her distance from it:

> It seems you love to cheat yourself with words:
> This mother is your model. I have heard
> Of your strange doubts.
>
> (7.315–17)

But the prince, swept up in his projection, denigrates his doubts with what for Tennyson would be a most fantastic possibility: "the past / Melts mist-like into this bright hour, and this / Is morn to more" (7.333–35).

According to its author, "Tears, Idle Tears" expresses "the passion of the past, the abiding in the transient" (H. Tennyson 211), which suggests that one might see its speaker as weeping over the little picture (*eidullion*, idyl) of his self-idolizing or idyllizing. Tennyson refers not to some antique passion *for* the past but raises the suggestion of a past suffering on in his present: suffering on and being suffered (Lt. *passus*, whence "passion," is the perfect participle of *patior*, "I suffer"). The speaker of "Tears, Idle Tears" might in this case be heard to recognize that the action in which he is engaged (idyl making) is potentially "idle"—that his very poetic spinning of wheels prevents the authentic experience of a different, transformed reality that is, at least on one level, desired. If the speaker knows he does not know what his tears mean and thus what he himself means and is ("Tears, idle tears, I know not what I mean"), then he is in one way admitting to "idle chatter" in the face of the gospel that "every idle word that men shall speak, they shall give an account thereof in the day of judgment" (Matthew 12:36). That day, says Revelation, "there should be time no longer" (10:6), or, as Tennyson preferred to translate it, "time should be no more" (H. Tennyson 233).

The ultimate dissatisfaction of "Tears, Idle Tears," then, is with "days that are no more" *than* a meaningless, inauthentic "Death in Life"—with, finally, itself. The poem cannot escape Shelley's earlier insight in *The Revolt of Islam* that

> It is the dark idolatry of self,
>   Which, when our thoughts and actions once are gone,
>   Demands that man should weep, and bleed, and groan;
> O vacant expiation!
>
> (8.22.3–6)

Grounds for the narcissistic avoidance of the reality-principle inherent in laboring such idleness (as well as in the long tradition of English literary melancholy) can be seen in George Meredith's dissection of Sir Willoughby Patterne's I-doll in *The Egoist* (1879). There, Patterne's "hatred of the world" stems from "an appalling fear on behalf of his naked eidolon, the tender infant self swaddled in his name before the world, for which he felt as the most highly civilized of men alone can feel, and which it was impossible for him to stretch out his hands to protect" (356).[3]

The self-idol or selfhood is the state that the individual enters as he or she grows, losing touch with an imagined original *eidos* or form: "I am not what I see, . . . / And other than the things I touch . . ." (*In Memoriam* 45.7–8). "I," in this reading, originates in the separation of "the baby" from "the circle of the breast" (1, 3), and despair over such unpairing seems the source of "Tears, Idle Tears" and much of Tennyson's work. Despair is the active link to that ancient break, hence "divine" or idolized in order that, as Odysseus says to the image of his mother, "We may delight ourselves with sorrow" (Pope's translation of *Od.* 11.212). The holding on to sorrow occurs unconsciously for the most part, following a dynamic Tennyson identified in dedicating his Arthurian cycle to the memory of the prince consort:

"since he held them dear, / Perchance as finding there unconsciously / Some image of himself" (so, he continues, "I dedicate, I consecrate with tears—/ These Idylls" ["Dedication" 1–5, 3:263]).

But the last half of "Tears, Idle Tears" offers the possibility of breaking the idle idol-idyl by dying to this world, not necessarily by physical death, since the poet proposes in the first section of *In Memoriam* that "men may rise on stepping stones / Of their dead selves" (3–4). The third stanza of "Tears, Idle Tears" calls up mythic imagery to set the scene for this death of the self. As the body "dies," the birds awaken and the spirit awakens to join them, like the soul of the speaker in Andrew Marvell's "The Garden" (51–60). The birds are, perhaps, a new form of the idols, "our friends," recognized as we change form of being. Here again, *In Memoriam*, section 13, supplies an apposite comment:

> For now so strange do these things seem,
> Mine eyes have leisure for their tears;
>
> My fancies time to rise on wing,
>   And glance about the approaching sails.
>   (15–18)

The fancies, or phantoms, idols, rise—like tears to the eyes and friends from the underworld—and take wing in bird form. In Tennyson's early "Remorse" the speaker feels himself condemned by "shadowy forms of guilt" to "living death" and proposes that his "soul shall wing her weary way" to underworld depths where "glow / The glimmerings of the boundless flame" (3, 22, 27, 30).

The casement that slowly turns into a glimmering square of window invokes one of Tennyson's favorite images in Keats, the "Charm'd magic casements, opening on the foam / Of perilous seas, in faery lands forlorn" of "Ode to a Nightingale" (69–70; Allingham records two instances of Tennyson's quoting this [296, 327]). As in Keats, the glimmering threshold—the "square of text," the "arch wherethrough / Gleams that untravelled world" ("Merlin and Vivien" 671; "Ulysses" 19–20)—is no sooner formulated than (and in consequence) the speaker is thrown back to his burden of loss, solitude, desperation, and his attempt to write a passage out of the world rendered idle:

> There he sat down gazing on all below;
> There did a thousand memories roll upon him,
> Unspeakable for sadness. By and by
> The ruddy square of comfortable light,
> Far-blazing from the rear of Philip's house,
> Allured him, as the beacon-blaze allures
> The bird of passage, till he madly strikes
> Against it, and beats out his weary life.
> ("Enoch Arden" 719–26, 2:644)

The polysemous line that opens the final stanza of "Tears, Idle Tears" establishes the possibility that the speaker himself is among the dead (remembering kisses during life), so confirming the silent presence of the poem's "idol" and giving one reason for its tears. "Hopeless fancy" can thus offer an instance of one idol's idle idyl hopes. The lack of such surplus of meaning in the words prompts the text's lament that there is "no more," but the "sweetness" attributed to "feigned"—imaginary—kisses reveals that real contact with others is not the surface speaker's only desire. "Hopeless" brings up its Latin equivalent from line 2, "despair" (*desperare*), and evidently both "hopeless fancy" and "divine despair" offer the speaker a certain pleasurable melancholy. Fancy and despair are false others, spurious formulations of the speaker's ground that in reality permit a narcissistic avoidance of the encounter with the other, particularly that other the self may become through change. Instead of a poem bemoaning inconsolable loss, we begin to see the outline of one that, like a young Rasselas, turns inward to lament its own regret (and regression). The succeeding characterization, "deep as first love," adds to this impression. First love, rooted in the preoedipal relation to the mother, is but another form of self-love, the intrinsic self-regard arising in infancy and then projected onto another. The artist-narrator of "The Gardener's Daughter" literally defines himself through the *eidolon* he has painted to keep his past before him; at the poem's climax he raises the veil from the picture of

> My first, last love; the idol of my youth,
> The darling of my manhood, and alas!
> Now the most blessed memory of mine age.
> (271–73, 1:569)

Here again the "idol" is a function of present memory, and the speaker's "first, last love" equates in effect with the self-imaged "memory of mine."

The speaker of "The Miller's Daughter" manifests a slightly less idolizing attitude toward the object of his memory as he recalls a song occasioned by a "blue Forget-me-not" and which recognizes the possibility that

> Love is made a vague regret.
> Eyes with idle tears are wet.
> Idle habit links us yet.
> (210–12, 1:416)

This same speaker as much as confesses to an earlier idle idol-idyl as he remembers lines from his "long and listless" youth that

> haunted me, the morning long,
>   With weary sameness in the rhymes,
> The phantom of a silent song.
> (69–71, 1:410)

Wordsworth's Matthew, somewhat similarly, finds

> My eyes are dim with childish tears,
> My heart is idly stirred,
> For the same sound is in my ears
> As in those days I heard.
> ("The Fountain" 29–32)

But in "Tears, Idle Tears" the speaker's wild emotions stem from the realization, as one critic observes of the (again, evidently male) speaker of Tennyson's "Break, Break, Break," that "not only will his friend never come back, but he will never be able to recapture his presence in memory" (Rackin 226). In "Tears, Idle Tears" the presence that cannot be recaptured is that of the speaker himself, who in the very act of articulation begins to slip away from, to tear himself from—and so, know more about—the days that are no more. We verge here on the poem's desperate yet trancelike, obsessive refrain and injunction, "No mor/e." But the speaker's superficial hope for no mortality, Revelation's promise of "no more death" ("*mors ultra non erit*") founders on an inability to accept that "the former things are passed away" (21:4). Tennyson's concern with the repeated phrase appears in a short poem written when he was seventeen and evidently the germ for "Tears, Idle Tears":

> Oh sad *No More!* Oh sweet *No More!*
>   Oh strange *No More!*
> By a mossed brookbank on a stone
> I smelt a wildweed-flower alone;
> There was a ringing in my ears,
> And both my eyes gushed out with tears.
>   Surely all pleasant things had gone before,
>   Lowburied fathomdeep beneath with thee, NO MORE!
>
> (1:175)

Memory (*me-mori*, so to speak) is the form of Death in Life, the idol, the past; though in the present of the poem (as in real time) even that is dying. The single, concluding exclamation mark inserted by some editors ("the days that are no more!") may serve to mark the sense (or hope!) that the speaker is entering into his future, a critical experience of self-awareness and the realization of change.[4] *At the same time* that he is filled with wild regret for the days past, he experiences anxious agitation that his days are no more than a memory-filled Death in Life. *At the same time* that he would fain live a fuller life to relieve the pressure of loss, he weeps for the impending change in psychic investment which such a fuller life implies ("O last regret, regret can die!" [*In Memoriam* 78.17]). So one might argue, as does Leo Spitzer, that the poem offers "two protagonists"; but while Spitzer limits these to "the poet who sheds idle tears" and a god named Death-in-Life, "wrapped in idle despair," his discussion suggests another possibility. The "impersonal supernal power" of which Spitzer sees the poet becoming aware at the end, "in a manner reminiscent of ancient tragedy" ("Tears" 194n.) is not despair but consciousness itself, a textual "I" verging on "the place where that was" (Lacan, *Ecrits* 171). But like a belated Peter Pan—like so many of Tennyson's characters young and old—the speaker suggests a powerful drive never to grow up, change, shift, or become conscious. "Memory [feeds] the soul of Love with tears," we learn in "The Lover's Tale" (810, 1:362), which is to say that memory, that fancy word for phantasized reconstruction of the past, offers an easy defense against the pain for what never was.

According to Tennyson, "Tears, Idle Tears" did not express real woe, but "rather the yearning that young people occasionally experience for that which *seems* to have passed away from them for ever" (2.232n.; italics added). Yet one might well wonder if this is only another one of Tennyson's "two voices," here defensively passing the poem off as "not real woe." Section 6 of *The Princess*, for instance, looks back to describe "Tears, Idle Tears," as "the mournful song" and also tells, for the first time, that it was sung by someone named Violet (298). In the 1832 song "Who Can Say," Tennyson finds that "The violet, recalls the dewy prime / Of youth and buried time" (6–7, 1:493). Similarly, the speaker of "A Dream of Fair Women" (1832), familiar with the "tearful glimmer of the languid dawn" (74), reports that "the smell of violets" pours

> back into my empty soul and frame
> The times when I remember to have been
> Joyful and free from blame.
> (78–80, 1:484)

Here, then, are "the days that are no more" and the attraction of a life free from guilt. "A Dream of Fair Women" concludes with an image of inviolate memory that belies the "not real woe" and "occasional yearning" that the author used to characterize his "Tears, Idle Tears":

> As when a soul laments, which hath been blest,
>   Desiring what is mingled with past years,
> In yearnings that can never be exprest
>   By signs or groans or tears;
>
> Because all words, though culled with choicest art,
>   Failing to give the bitter of the sweet,
> Wither beneath the palate, and the heart
>   Faints, faded by its heat.
> (281–88, 1:492)

"Melancholia" seems the appropriate description of this condition, which, as Freud defines it, "borrows some of its features from mourning, and others from the process of regression . . . to narcissism" ("Mourning and Melancholia" 250).

Still, one might claim for the poem the insight that, despite the narcissistic opposition of the surface speaker, the dying of the old self through change and growth is already under way, that the dynamic of "Tears, Idle Tears" connects with the "one basic action" Donald S. Hair identifies in his study of Tennyson's idyls, the process of "dying out of an unsatisfactory life and . . . a birth into a new and better one" (103, 104). As the speaker is dis-paired (tears tear him away) from the old days, from the dead, from idle language and "Melancholy's idol dreams" (Wordsworth, *Letters* 74), so— the poem begins painfully to divine—"rounds he to a separate mind . . . / His isolation grows defined" (*In Memoriam* 14.9, 12). Like the melancholic in Freud's analysis, the speaker begins to feel that "he himself has willed" the condition and so to feel anxiety as guilt. Guilt, here, for the idleness he has willed by wallowing in the continually asserted "fresh" and "so sad" quality of his emotions, "emotion" (as F. R. Leavis objected) "for its own sake without a justifying situation" (in Pattison 100). In such a case, the speaker "wild with all regret" would be only a few steps from "no longer caring to embalm / In dying songs a dead regret" (*In Memoriam*, "Epilogue" 13–14, 2:452). But the immediate and nearly universal affect-effect of the poem on readers testifies that an idyllic appeal to our narcissistic identification, our idol, is its own justification—however guilty our complicity in that idle thrill, whatever the account to be required in the day of judgment.

Ricks points out (2:232n.) that the "idle tears" can be compared with those Aeneas weeps on leaving Carthage and Dido: "Mens immota manet; lacrimae volvuntur inanes" (*Aeneid* 4.449). Many critics have noticed Virgilian parallels and sentiment in Tennyson's work, and one commentator even describes "Tears, Idle Tears" as "the century's most intense lyric distillation of the Vergilian 'tears of things'" (McSweeney 70). But where Aeneas serves the impersonal power of history, Tennyson's speaker is but a man emoting. The speaker himself is the victim, caught (*mens immota*) between the conflicting drives of an Other-seeking Eros and a narcissistic, stasis-seeking Thanatos. As the product of merely one moment of equilibrium in the history of those drives, the text has, finally, no one speaker, no "I" at all—at least, we know not what its "I" means (even arguing that whatever it meant it means no more). If we credit the presence of such unconscious authority, perhaps it is not surprising to find one of the central terms behind the poem, *idol*, making a cryptographic appearance in the variously identified "tortured cry," "loose appositive," or (and) "vocative" address of the poem's concluding line:

> O Death in Life, the days that are no more

so as to subjoin "idol, the days that are, know more."[5] As Blake has it, "The ratio of all we have already known. is not the same that it shall be when we know more" ("There Is No Natural Religion"). The "I" that comes to know more is that "I" no more, just as the "I" that grasps "no more," even unto "Death in Life," is an "I" that comes to know more. So does Tennyson's idle idol-idyl rise in the hearing as we gather in its "I"s.

7
Under Brontëan Thunder

> *A single word so seen at such a time*
> *Opens a hundred corridors in the heart.*
> —CHARLOTTE BRONTË, *Poems*

A survey of critics who contend to name a dominant psychodynamic in Charlotte Brontë's life and work encourages the suspicion that early object relations influence what a particular critical vision perceives, that one receives back one's own message in reverse, as Lacan has it (*Ecrits* 85). So for one scholar the "central figure in Brontë's imaginative confrontation with her own experience is . . . her father" (Sadoff 139), but for another "the single most important event . . . was the death of her mother" (Keefe xi), and for a third it was her brother's life that "profoundly affected Charlotte's personal and artistic development" (Moglen 39). But like her heroines who hold "two lives" or seem "double-existent" (*Villette* [V] 140, 464), one imagines that the author also, "to speak truth . . . compromised matters" and "served two masters" at least (V 334). Texts, like lives, are overdetermined. In her detailed study of Charlotte Brontë's style, Margot Peters notes how characters are frequently split so that they function at once as individuals and as parts of a personality; she finds that "ambivalence is the key to Brontë's themes and style" and suggests that such ambivalence results "from the continual but unresolved conflict of opposing drives" (128, 156). So characters, imitating their author, pace relentlessly backward and forward, and so we see the two-faced god explicitly invoked in *Jane Eyre* as the heroine makes a "true Janian reply" ("I have been with my aunt, sir, who is dead" [*JE* 215]). A word that looks two ways can offer a temporary respite from such conflict—or rather, the conflict is sublated into the effort to find words adequately ambivalent for it.

One of the interesting splits occasioned by ambivalence occurs as the author throws out or projects the text. The text, for Brontë as for Blake, is an "emanation" made up of other emanations, spectres, and powers. Scott's *Kenilworth*, she writes Ellen Nussey at sixteen, is "one of the most interesting works that ever emanated from the great Sir Walter's pen" (1 January 1833, Wise and Symington [WS] 1:109). Like Caroline in *Shirley*, "the whole time . . . talking inwardly" (S 191), the Brontë text carries on a dialogue with itself as well as with its hypothesized "Reader." In *Jane Eyre*, the emanation of an author whose early childhood passed at the village of Thornton finds in "the third story of Thornfield Hall the aspect of a home of the past: a shrine of memory" (92). Retreating into her foreknowledge of the plot and its impending mystery story, the narrator remarks: "My sole relief was to walk along the corridor of the third story, backwards and forwards, safe in the silence and solitude of the spot and allow my mind's eye to dwell on whatever bright visions rose before it . . . and, best of all, to open my inward ear to a tale . . . —a tale my imagination created" (95–96). Rochester disappears for "a visit to the third story" (132), which takes us, as it moves toward its disclosure, "here then . . . in the third story, fastened into one of its mystic cells" (184). Hearing "the snarling, canine noise" (as of a dog "worrying" something) that summarizes Bertha's story, the narrator reports that "my own thoughts worried me"—which "thoughts" are glossed on the next page by Dick's [Richard Mason's] comment that his sister Bertha "worried me like a tigress" (185, 186). Once this story is dislodged from its "secret inner cabinet," Bertha's lair literally changes to become merely "that *third*-storey room" (272; italic added).

Another instance of the text's internal dialogue takes the shape of one word at the novel's crucial juncture. Having left Thornfield by coach, Jane is set "down at a place called Whitcross" (283). Although many readers have felt that the last third of *Jane Eyre* represents an unfortunate turn into fantasy, one critic argues that this place "appropriately signals [Jane's] entry into a land of literalized dreams, because the name's meaning is as close to literal as any naming can be": "Whitcross names only itself" (Homans 94). But given the repeated "whispering to myself over and over again, 'What shall I do?'" "What am I to do?" and "What was I to do?" (33, 261, 284), we hear at this crossroad or word a crossed wit at her wit's end worrying over how to progress with her pilgrim: which story to explore with *Jane Eyre*. Whitcross names itself as an event in the unfolding of the text. The decision to "hold on to a hollow" (284) determines the novel's concluding, unsatisfying swerve into wish fulfillment (beginning with Jane's "nestling to the breast of the hill").

So close does Brontë seem to the shifting energy of the letter that one wonders whether any of her literal constructions could be found to name "only itself." The name Jane Eyre, to take a highly remarkable instance, suggests a vast complex of overdetermination and cryptonymy. Nicolas Abraham and Maria Torok introduce the term *cryptonymy* to describe the repression, burying, encrypting, or making taboo of words that would name or locate the traumatic origin of certain neuroses, and the displacing of those taboo words by other lexically contiguous ones.[1] Reanalyzing Freud's "Wolfman," they find the text of Serge Pankejeff's life as expressed through its particular vocabulary or "verbarium" to be structured by a network of interlingual puns that deflect attention from—even as they preserve—key words (*tieret* ["rub"], *goulfik* ["fly," "slit"], and *vidietz* ["witness"]) that frame his "impossible desire to occupy one or the other place in the scene [between father and sister] he saw, his genuine 'primal scene'" (*Magic Word* 40). Such a scene can no more be remembered than it can be erased, and so occasions the hollowing out for it of a crypt, an unconsciousness that must continually be maintained and that in being maintained continually impinges on the ego and its language and strength. One critic, joining these formulations to *Jane Eyre*'s wealth of "ere" sounds and inadequate maternal figures, has no difficulty in suggesting that the *mot tabou* Jane hides is *mère* (Rapaport 1099; to put it more economically, *her* mot: *mother*). That this method then produces from the heroine's first name "the immediate French equivalent . . . *haine*" ["hate," "hatred"] (Rapaport 1100) may seem "startling," excessive, or just inane, but undeniably Brontë's involvement with French went very deep, and the fact that she wrote only once of her mother in her copious correspondence and journals (Moglen 21) indicates some powerful psychodynamic.

Certainly the sounds and shapes of the letters that echo and chime through "Jane Eyre" make an eerie medley of the novel's concerns. First of all, in this story of Jane *before* she married and became a writer, *ere* frequently appears, often to introduce Jane herself (e.g., "Ere long I became aware," "Ere I had finished," "Ere I rose," "Ere I permitted myself" [15, 31, 85, 143]). *Ere* also becomes *where*, to pose the unanswerable question to the past: "Where was the Jane Eyre of yesterday [i.e., of 'ere']?—where was her life?—where were her prospects?" (260—the contemplation of these questions leads to Jane's "longing to be dead"). The "spiritual" or neurotic intensity Jane receives from times ere underlies her associations with *air* and *fairy*. So Jane's young, French-speaking charge stumbles over the name of her new governess, "Aire? Bah! I cannot say it" (89), and Rochester tells the "puzzled Miss Eyre" that "a puzzled air" becomes her (116). The difficulty of getting the invisible to speak (or the unconscious to stop speaking) generates this catalogue of synonyms: "Oh for some good *spirit* to suggest a judicious and satisfactory response! Vain *aspiration!* The west *wind* whispered in the ivy round me; but no gentle *Ariel* borrowed its *breath* as a medium of speech" (192; italics added)—here Eyre cannot answer. Other images, however, suggest that spirits not gentle would borrow the breath of the wind to communicate with Charlotte Brontë. Recovering from her first unconscious fit, Jane hears voices "speaking with a hollow sound, as if muffled by a rush of wind" (15), and on the night preceding her second, as the wind seems "to [her] ear to muffle a mournful under-sound," Jane finds the "'sullen, moaning sound' . . . eerie" (247). Invisible or not, the reality of spiritual being is never in question: "It is my spirit that addresses your spirit; just as if both had passed through the grave, and we stood at God's feet, equal,—as we are!" (222). "Are" is heard as "ayre" in V*illette* (127), and for Jane Eyre French begins with "the verb E*tre*" (65).

All this only begins to sound what "I am Jane Eyre" might mean. Jane's association with fire has long been seen as a means for showing her passionate nature, or, more specifically, her embittered rage, anger, and ire. Brontë's father, of course, came from Ireland (or Eire), and Brontë set her juvenile tales in a land she and her brother named Angria, where, on a fine day, one might encounter a woman who "flew into a most unimaginable fury—tore her hair from her head and shrieked like a rabbid [sic] wild cat. . . . 'I do hate you!—I abhor you!—I could kill you!' . . . grinding her teeth, and then, crying afresh, . . . 'But still, still—I love you till my heart aches as if it would break'" (in Chase 23).[2] Jane Eyre remembers "the embers" of her "ire" (13) and attributes her initial liberating expression of anger to a "sentiment of deep ire and desperate revolt" (22). Her uncle Eyre is placed on the island with the doubly irate-sounding name of Madeira, making it perhaps more appropriate that Jane should be made heir. But given her "habitual mood of humiliation, self-doubt, forlorn depression," Eyre usually regards expression of ire or anger as error; she knows that strong anger makes one the stranger she fears to become, and learns nothing new from Rochester's injunction, "Dread remorse when you are tempted to err, Miss Eyre" (120). With such intense conflicts and repressions, a recurrent term for Jane's condition is *misery* (Fr. *misère*). Little "Miss Jane Eyre" tells the apothecary that she cries "because I am miserable" (18–19), and much later Miss Eyre tries to conceal her identity though admitting, "Miserable I am" (306). *Eyre* also is an old word for a journey or errand, as in the ancient "justices in eyre" and the name of their court, the "justice eyre," was available to Brontë through her childhood favorite, Sir Walter Scott. Jane's life can be seen as a journey, to be sure, but more interesting is the word's connection to the "all-pervading legal language" (Peters 146) of the novel. Peters astutely relates *Jane Eyre*'s preoccupation with courtroom vocabulary to "the one word conspicuous by its absence in the novel—guilt" (152).

We may wonder what it would mean to be conscious, simultaneously, of all these airy nothings, much less (if it could be conceived) to intend them (if they could be intended). But perhaps the question is moot in the case of someone who discovers cues and guidance in language. *Shirley*'s Caroline, for instance, "mutely excited," finds "her own mind . . . too busy, teeming, wandering, to listen to the language of another mind" (S 189)—evidently "she," whatever this would refer to here, attends instead to "the language of her own mind." One aspect of the signature Brontëan split, then—as of every other poetic text in its way—is such a separation from language, even what seemed one's own. The split from language, which is a split from oneself inasmuch as that self is largely constituted by language, can be materialized by wordplay or pun. One laughs or groans at the momentary encounter of our fundamental repression, the knowledge that "one" is not a unified subject speaking a univocal language. Rather like an obverse to Lacan's "mirror stage," in which the infant laughs jubilantly at appropriating and imagining the *image* (only) of a nonfragmented self, the pun shows the "I" how it shifts among the invisible constituents of a single material image. As a kind of mirror, the pun shows not a surface that reflects back, but a depth which that draws one out of oneself: Brontë's "visionary hollow" (*JE* 11) of the looking glass hollows "I . . . myself" into "a faded, hollow-eyed vision" (V 96).

The Name of the Father

Puns and wordplay, at any rate, offer a symptom or index of a certain orientation toward language and overdetermination that, once established, may encourage further speculation. To take a simple example, in *Villette* Lucy Snowe thinks of "England . . . that dear land of mists" (196) with a touch of nostalgia for what's missed; but when she comes to consider expenses, the adjective takes additional bearing: " 'Living costs little,' said I to myself, 'in this economical town of Villette, where people are more sensible than I understand they are in dear old England' " (450).[3] *Jane Eyre* characterizes a socialite as loving "if not [Rochester's] person, at least his purse" (176), and when Brontë places us outside a Methodist service to overhear a "shout of 'I've found liberty!' 'Doad o' Bill's has fun' liberty!' " we share her fun in mocking the license of the enthusiastic "shouts, yells, ejaculations, frantic cries, agonized groans" (S 163–64). Taking liberty with the Word of her father requires more caution. "*Levit*ical" (italics added), the famous first chapter of *Shirley*, opens with the amusing image of the "shower of curates" who "lie very thick" (39) on the countryside, and though it proceeds to ridicule these "rods of Aaron" and their "gift of tongues," only after thirty chapters does the text risk recalling the joke in its initial chapter title: "No levity, Miss! This is not a laughing matter" (515). Some of Brontë's readers would surely not have been amused at the symmetry to be inferred between the "shower of curates" and their thick lies and the "shower of manna" or "Biblical promises" reserved for those like the humble spinster Miss Mann (i.e., Woman), forgotten by "all humanity" (196). When another religious spinster is praised as one who "with meek heart and due reverence, treads close in her Redeemer's steps," Brontë has one of the curates interject not the expected "Amen!" but "Ahem!" (285).

That biblical echo and allusion pervade the work of all the Brontës cannot be surprising in view of the strong Methodist heritage conveyed by their father and their environment: for and through his evangelical allegiances the Reverend Mr. Patrick Brontë was promoted to Haworth, the rugged Yorkshire parish formerly ministered to by Wesley's chosen successor, William Grimshaw (Harrison's engaging 1948 discussion of these matters deserves revival). The question is what to make of all the suggestiveness and influence: how to see, for instance, one of the Reverend's daughters as aspiring to an image of "the writer as apostle, serving that Master of all masters, the Word," that is, "the saving Word Himself" (Tayler 177, 302), while another "maintains the inheritance of the Bible . . . solely in order to protest it back against itself" (Davies 18). Brontë's punning shows her relation to the discourse of the institutionalized, patriarchal Christianity of her father to be problematic, as though she intuited, with Gass, that "the worship of the word must be pagan and polytheistic. It cannot endure one god" (20). Hence the curiously relativizing edge in *Shirley*'s argument that "Caroline was a Christian; therefore in trouble she framed many a prayer after the Christian creed" (342—Brontë must remember her Angrian Caroline, who worships a different idol and is told, "Crede Zamorna!" [*Novelettes* 353]); and hence, in *Villette*, the odd appropriation of Saint Paul to characterize Paulina as a child with "no mind or life of her own" who "must necessarily live, move, and have her being in another" (83; cf. Acts 17:28). Paul is a crucial figure and indeed can be considered as "the grand progenitor of Patrick Brontë as published author" according to identifications put forth in the prefaces to his three books (Tayler 276–77). Both, then, share responsibility for upholding the silence and subjection of women that the typical chauvinist Joe Scott urges upon Shirley (S 322–23). With his "great respect for the doctrines delivered in the second chapter of St. Paul's first Epistle to Timothy," Scott argues dogmatically that "Adam was first formed" and that "the woman, being deceived, was in the transgression." These remarks are no doubt introduced to illustrate Shirley's immediately preceding radical and rhetorical question that Milton—and with him the male ethos generally—"was great; but was he good?" and her conclusion that "Milton tried to see the first woman; but, Cary, he saw her not" (314–15). We are, perhaps, as did Blake a generation earlier, to see the patriarchal system as moving from Saint Paul to Milton and, most recently, to the appalling mill towns that *Shirley* sees darkening the landscape.

Saint Paul figures more largely in *Villette* through the submissive Paulina and the dominating Paul Emanuel. When Lucy Snowe finally takes off on her own and passes her first night in the greater world of London, she finds herself overcome by "a terrible oppression": "A deep, low, mighty tone swung through the night. At first I knew it not; but it was uttered twelve times, and at the twelfth colossal hum and trembling knell, I said: 'I lie in the shadow of St. Paul's'" (107). We think of the cathedral, no doubt, but the author of the epistle to the Colossians casts a deep shadow over the heroine's struggle for self-determination and mutual respect. And while St. John Rivers can propose marriage saying, "With St. Paul, I acknowledge myself the chiefest of sinners" (354), Jane Eyre's saving grace before this "man, erring as I" (358) is her realization that even the seemingly noblest ideology merely serves the ends of those it empowers (St. John, for instance, sees himself as not subject to the "erring control of my feeble fellow-worms" and grandiosely authorized "to offer . . . direct from God, a place in the ranks of His chosen" [353]).

Brontë's most scandalous wordplay in this vein comes when Lucy, having no acquaintance, must spend "the long vacation" at the Pensionnat: "The house was left quite empty, but for me, a servant, and a poor deformed and imbecile pupil, a sort of crétin" (227). What sort? Cretins are dwarfish, which might remind one of Charlotte Brontë's tiny frame ("the smallest creature I had ever seen (except at a fair)," wrote Harriet Martineau [Gérin, *Charlotte Brontë* 411]), and the word is indeed cognate with *Christian* or, in French, *chrétien* (the idea perhaps being that such afflicted individuals were also Christians, that is, human beings). Lucy makes the crétin a double by feeding her and by other unspecified "personal attentions." This double's name, Marie Broc, takes her more than halfway into the *Brontë* family with the icons of its Marias, the dead mother and eldest daughter (one notes also *Broc*'s expansion in the "father" who arranges Jane's/Charlotte's transfer to Lowood/Cowan Bridge, Mr. Brocklehurst). Owing to the crétin's presence, Lucy prays "to Heaven for consolation and support," though she concludes that God's "great plan" entails "that some must deeply suffer while they live, and . . . of this number, I was one" (229). Later she refers more realistically to depressed "imbecile extravagances of self-accusation" (349), but her struggle with cretinism reflects the past of one who had to grapple, at age eight, for instance, with a father's preaching that "whatever may tend to give you unworthy notions of Christ; whatever may be calculated to make you think highly of yourselves, or to look down with discontentment upon your lot; whatever would aim at inflaming your natural passions, which are already much too fiery and ungovernable, is bad, and ought carefully to be avoided" (P. Brontë 202).[4]

The Name of the Mother

The phonemes of imbecile Marie Broc can direct us to another of Brontë's split-off phantasms in *Villette*, Madame Modeste Maria Beck. Indeed, *Villette* increasingly reveals itself as one of literature's most complicated artifices of splitting and projection. The text, like the narrator, seems "to hold two lives," one of which is "nourished with a sufficiency of the strange necromantic joys of fancy" (140) or imagined communication with the dead. The author even has the narrator overhear a personal letter and observe that "several of these passages appeared to comprise family secrets, and bore special reference to one 'Charlotte'" (112). The book opens with a description of the narrator's good "godmother," Mrs. Bretton of Bretton, and the first chapter is titled with that family name, as if to flaunt the author's anagram (Bretton/Brontë). Then, immediately following a letter erroneously supposed by the heroine,[5] Lucy Snowe, to come "from home," a young avatar arrives in the form of "Missy" Home; at the age of six, she has, like the author before her, "recently lost her mother" (62), though "the loss was not so great" because Mrs. Home "had neglected her child" (62–63). Madame Beck, so long seen as a bitter fictionalization of Madame Heger from Charlotte's Brussels experience, seems an unlikely addition to the family manes, but perhaps images nearly ten years old (as were Charlotte's memories of the Pensionnat when she wrote *Villette*) are maintained to the extent that they screen—both conceal and express—more formative and enduring images constructed in childhood. Madame Beck, for instance, was "née Kint," or, to draw on the German that Lucy studies throughout, "born Child" (*Kind*).[6] She suddenly appears to Lucy in a sentence that also illustrates the author's denial, word recombination, and interlingual amplification: "*No* ghost stood beside me, *nor* anything of *spec*tral a*spect*; *mere*ly a *mother*ly, dumpy little woman" (127; italics added). While the image of Madame Beck's "dumpy, motherly little body" (185) persists, she quickly becomes for Lucy a "white figure" seen "in the dead of night" with a "face of stone (for of stone in its present night-aspect it looked: it had been human and, as I said before, motherly, in the salon)" (132) who glides about "ghost-like" on "souliers de silence" (136). This stone mother of the narrator's "spectral and intolerable memories" (548) "never seemed to know the wish to take her little children upon her lap, to press their rosy lips with her own, to gather them in a genial embrace, to shower on them softly the benignant caress, the loving word" (157). In short, she embodies what Brontë calls "the hollow system" (158).

Up until a week before its completion, Brontë evidently thought that her second published novel should be titled *Hollow's Mill* (letters of 21, 24, and 29 August 1849, WS 3:12–15), so emphasizing a crucial site and agent of the social tensions that concern *Shirley*. Once the haunt of fairies (242, 599) and "green, and lone, and wild," "a bonnie spot" (599), the joys of the Hollow have been hollowed out by men—beginning with Shirley's father, who first built the mill there. As the novel opens, Hollow's mill has become "the place held most abominable" (62) by the local working class; the present owner, Robert Moore, receives an anonymous note addressed "to the Divil of Hollow's miln" (64). By the concluding paragraphs the dominating Moore (subsuming the Angrian Caroline's Zamorna amour, the Moor of Venice, and the hero of Friedrich Schiller's *The Robbers*, Karl Moor) wants still more and promises to turn the "barren Hollow" into a mill-town hell: "The rough pebbled track shall be an even, firm, broad, black, sooty road, bedded with the cinders from my mill: and my mill, Caroline—my mill shall fill its present yard" (597). Preoccupied with their own power of action, men like Moore are oblivious to the "terrible hollowness, mockery, want, craving" (190) in an existence with no object of its own, such as that lived by "Low Persons" (chapter 18, title) like laborers, children, and women in particular. *Shirley*'s social vision of "the whole enginery of this human mill" (496) initiates what emerges in *Villette* as the "hollow unreal" (594).

Villette knows that "the starved hollow" (334) exists because something unassimilable is put within it and sealed away. When Lucy decides to dispose of her precious letters from Graham she goes to "a hole, or rather a deep hollow" in the pear tree she has named Methusaleh: "I knew there was such a hollow, hidden partly by ivy and creepers," she says, and there she intends "to hide a treasure" and "bury a grief." Finding the hole large enough to receive the hermetically sealed "casket" of letters, she "thrust[ed] it deep in"; this done, she put a "slate on the hollow, secured it with cement, covered the whole with black mould, and, finally, replaced the ivy." Then she rests, "like any other mourner, beside a newly-sodded grave" (380–81). Lucy here reenacts a fantasy of "non-introjection," or a *rejection* of loss and mourning the goal of which is the "reinforced strength" Lucy temporarily obtains (Abraham and Torok, "Introjection" 381), but whose cost is another extension of the internal crypt or hollow. That Lucy's letter grave repeats the past is marked by its exact duplication of another, earlier offering to Methusaleh's patriarchy, for another "slab, smooth, hard, and black" visible between its roots is said to be "the portal of a vault" containing "the bones of a girl . . . buried alive, for some sin against her vow" (172).[7] The girl Lucy wants most to repress, by holding her "in catalepsy and a dead trance," lives in her feelings and thoughts "of past days" (175). "Oh, my childhood!" constitutes for her "the being I was always lulling" but which certain signifiers, including "accidents of the weather," can rouse to "a craving cry I could not satisfy" (175–76). For most of the novel, Lucy's problem is that she remains pent up at Pensionnat Rue Fossette—ruing her little "fosse" or "hole in the ground, grave."

The fault line linking hollows, graves, and craving may help to gloss one of the most striking elements in Lucy's "strange vision of Villette" toward the novel's end. Given a "strong opiate," Lucy sees in imagination the city's "summer park, with its long alleys all silent, lone and safe; among these lay a huge stone-basin—that basin I knew, and beside which I had often stood—deep-set in the tree-shadows, brimming with cool water, clear, with a green, leafy, rushy bed" (547). The sound of distant music engenders in her the desire "to listen to it alone by the rushy basin" (548), and so she sets off "to find the stone-basin, with its clear depth and green lining," thinking of its "coolness and verdure" with "the passionate thirst of unconscious fever" and longing "to come on that circular mirror of crystal, and surprise the moon glassing therein her pearly front" (551). Instead, her quest for this visionary reflection of the maternal breast leads her into a dreamlike review of past acquaintance—including the Brettons, Becks, and de Bassompierres. De Bassompierre is the new name of the narrator's first double, Missy (Polly/Paulina) Home, now ennobled and, through the machinations of a plot probable only psychologically, engaged to marry Mrs. Bretton's son; it is as close as one could ask for a French version of "stone-basin" ("bassin de pierre"). *Beck* in English can mean "basin" (*OED* has a citation from

1828), but in any event brings up the common German *Becker,* or basin. Each of these terms—*basin, bassin, Becker*—is used to denominate the pelvis, and so might evoke Charlotte's mother's death from the "stomach cancer" of the early biographers, which has been appraised more recently as "some chronic disorder consequent upon her rapid childbearing, probably pelvic sepsis" (Rhodes in Moglen 21n.). "Look unto the rock whence ye are hewn, and to the hole of the pit whence ye are digged," counsels Isaiah (51:1), and in *Villette* Brontë attempts just that. Indeed, the phantom mother, dead before Charlotte was five and a half, precedes the conception of *Villette* in the form of her courtship letters, made available to Charlotte for the first time. "The records of a mind whence my own sprang," Brontë calls them, noting the "modesty" in the letters and concluding, "I wish she had lived, and that I had known her" (WS 3:18). But as the figure of "Modeste Maria Beck" suggests, the author still wrestles with Jane Eyre's realization about such revenants—that "this idea, consolatory in theory, I felt would be terrible if realised" (13). Every dream has a "navel," Freud writes, "a tangle of dream-thoughts" marking "the spot where it reaches down into the unknown" (*Interpretation* 564)—or the hollow, the crypt, the pelvic cavity. The "stone-basin" offers such a spot for *Villette*'s dream text; Lucy, after all, never actually reaches it, becoming fascinated instead with the "shadow-world" (185) conjured up out of her hollow.[8]

Yet another trace of the mother in the kaleidoscope of *Villette* dominates the novel's structurally rather awkward chapter 4. Here—sandwiched between images of childhood and adolescence in Bretton and her decision at twenty-two to seek a wider world—Lucy Snowe for a few pages and unspecified but correspondingly short fictional time serves as nurse and companion to Miss Marchmont. That Marchmont offers a kind of guide or mentor or spirit mother (as against Lucy's actual godmother, Mrs. Bretton) is suggested by the reappearance of her name, joined to a tangible legacy, at the novel's end. Her surname in fact serves as a kind of double imperative: the narrator writes of her longing for something "to fetch me out of my present existence, and lead me *upwards* and *onwards*" (176; italics added) and again links the name's components together in describing her fear that some beetles might "steal on me a *march, mount* my throne" (205; italics added). Miss Marchmont is, moreover, the first Maria of the novel, and though invalid, she gives Lucy "the power of her passions to admire, the truth of her feelings to trust" (97).[9]

Maria Marchmont's tragedy is the inexplicable, accidental, Christmas Eve death, thirty years before, of the lover whose name she quite emphasizes: "My heart lived with Frank's heart. O my noble Frank—my faithful Frank—my *good* Frank!" (99). One might note that if, as seems likely, Charlotte Brontë wrote this in the year following September 1851, the elapsed thirty years also commemorates the death in 1821 of her mother, Maria Brontë. Maria Marchmont, in the climax of the short, obtrusive chapter that ends with her death, sees herself as a "woe-struck and selfish woman," but one now ready to prepare "for reunion with Frank" (101) because she can say "with sincerity, what I never tried to say before—Inscrutable God, Thy will be done!" (99). The desired's name seems set as an emblem of this text's ostensible desire to be frank, to eschew the lies and falsehoods Lucy equates with everyday life in Villette. One can see the slide of this particular signifier in Brontë's letter to W. S. Williams of 6 November 1851, which reports that a "frank kind answer" from Mrs. Gaskell permits the enclosure "for your Son Frank" of a requested letter of introduction (WS 3:286).

Graham Bretton has a "frank tread" which Lucy believes she would follow "to the world's end" (125), but the word is more strongly associated with the "fierce and frank, dark and candid, testy and fearless" M. Paul (396). With his "frank fashion, which knew not secretiveness," Paul encourages Lucy—usually *en français*—to "speak frankly" (513, 512), and by the novel's close Lucy can relate to him her "whole history . . . truthful, literal, ardent, bitter," including, in particular, her jealousy regarding his "goddaughter and ward, Justine Marie Saveur." Like her namesake, Paul's first beloved who "gave herself to God" (484), like the crétin chrétienne, and like Miss Marchmont, this Marie Saveur is also linked problematically to the Savior; together with Modeste Maria Beck, these five versions of Maria/e exemplify how for the author, as for her double in *Shirley*, "memory kept harping on the name . . . an elegy over the past still rung constantly in her ear; a funereal inward cry haunted and harassed her" (199). Still grappling with whatever Christian consolation was given after the deaths of Maria when the author was five (mother Maria) and nine (eldest sister, mother surrogate Maria), the narrator of *Villette* wishes to speak frankly about lies, and especially against the notion that "as to what lies below"—in the hollow ground or in the unconscious—"leave that with God" (252). But her frank wish is another disguise.

The Brother's Keepers

Although the many Marias in Charlotte Brontë's last novel indicate some kind of conscious acknowledgment of their namesakes' formative role in her psyche, the complete repression of another principal object of her relations suggests its greater importance in the text. The collapse and death of Charlotte's brother, Patrick Branwell, one can surmise, made the black hole that distorts the space-time of *Villette*'s universe. There are, to be sure, biographical connections available for the two male protagonists. Dr. John Graham Bretton (nicknamed Isidore by one character to supply an additional miscue) is linked to George Smith of Brontë's publishers, Smith Elder, several times Brontë's host in London and like Graham an aging mama's boy; Paul Carl David Emanuel is seen, naturally, as a version of the idolized Professor Heger the author encountered in Brussels. Without questioning the pertinence of these associations, one might imagine that they are also themselves screens for others deeper and more repressed.

A character is a bundle of relations and associations, some of which may be strong enough to relay considerable jolts of affect. The most striking aspect of the relationship between Charlotte and her only brother, one year younger, comes in the complete reversal of Charlotte's attitude toward him beginning with her return from Brussels when she was twenty-seven. Their decade-long, mutual preoccupation in the creation and elaboration of Angria is well known, and Charlotte's residual if ambivalent allegiance to him in spite of already evident transgression can be seen in her 1837 story of "Henry Hastings" (one of Branwell's Angrian pseudonyms).[10] In 1843 she writes from Brussels to say how "very much" she wants to hear from him, displaces her anger at his neglect into berating her companions, and closes by reminding him of their shared past: "I always recur as fanatically as ever to the old ideas, the old faces, and the old scenes in the world below. Give my love to Ann and believe me // YOURN!" (WS 1:297). But by 1844 Charlotte had been forced to confront and introject her idealized fantasy for the married Professor Heger, while Branwell was constructing his fantasy relationship with the married Mrs. Robinson, seventeen years his senior, mistress of the household where he and Anne Brontë were employed as tutor and governess. Rather than outrage over the public infamy, Charlotte perhaps experienced more the anger of a jealous lover scorned. When Branwell's fantasy burst and he spent the next three years giving up to his inability to cope, she retreated into icy observation. A few days after his death she writes W. S. Williams, "It is not permitted us to grieve for him who is gone as others grieve;" there is, she continues, "no dear companion lost," and "nothing remains of him but a memory of errors and sufferings." "I trust time will allay these feelings," she writes (2 October 1848, WS 2:261), unaware that she will have first to deal with the deaths of Emily and Anne and their memorial in *Shirley* before her unconscious can reconsider Branwell.

The narrator of *Villette* reports, "Certainly, at some hour, though perhaps not *your* hour, the waiting waters will stir; in *some* shape, though perhaps not the shape you dreamed, which your heart loved, and for which it bled, the healing herald will descend" (252). Yet for most, the passage concludes, the first and sole visitant is the one whom the "easterns call Azrael"—the Mohammedan angel of death but also Branwell's persona in one of his longest poems and a name to which Charlotte and Branwell often refer in their early coproductions (C. Brontë, *Early Writings* 347n.). By the time Brontë was writing *Villette* she had returned to Branwell via an effective transitional object in the form of James Taylor, one of her correspondents at the firm of Smith, Elder. Taylor's resemblance to Branwell struck Brontë "forcibly"—"it is marked," she writes; he had her brother's physiognomy and red hair, and already in late 1849, Brontë writes of the "determined, dreadful nose in the middle of his face which when poked into my countenance cuts into my soul like iron" (WS 3:220, 53).

At the same time as James Taylor becomes a Branwell signifier, Brontë confronts the spectacle of her old friend Mary Taylor's brother, Joe Taylor, in a state of mind like "that which was so appalling exhibited in poor Branwell during the last few years of his life" (31 January 1850, WS 3:72). Two months later, ostensibly responding to the recent death of an acquaintance's mother, Brontë swerves from the maternal realm to dwell on "the oblivion of faults which succeeds to Death. No sooner are the eyes grown dim, no sooner is the pulse stilled than we forget what anxiety, what anguish, what shame the frailties and vices of *that poor unconscious mould of clay* once caused us; yearning love and bitter pity are the only sentiments the heart admits" (italics added). The repetition of "poor" in the next paragraph to describe "my poor brother" points to Branwell's heavy presence (31 March 1850, WS 3:91–92). Six months later, she writes to praise Sydney Dobell's poetry, especially "a certain brief lyric . . . a sort of dirge over a dead brother—*that* not only charmed the ear and brain—it smote the heart" (25 October 1850, WS 3:175).[11] In April 1851 James Taylor passed through Haworth on his way to five years in India and proposed marriage. Brontë's consequent behavior acts out her ambivalent feelings about Branwell: "Each moment he came near me—and that I could see his eyes fastened on me—my veins ran ice. Now that he is away, I feel far more gently towards him—it is only close by that I grow rigid—stiffening with a strange mixture of apprehension and anger—which nothing softens but his retreat" (9 April 1851, WS 3:222). That "Papa" took "a decided liking" to Taylor only complicated matters. Then he was gone overseas, nothing resolved, and the fitful and evaporating correspondence of the following year left Brontë in "that anxiety which is inseparable from a state of absolute uncertainty about a somewhat momentous matter" (4 March 1852, WS 3:319), with "the saddest memories my only company" (12 April 1852, WS 3:331). Finally, in the summer of 1852, she answers her friend's query "about India": "Let us dismiss the subject in a few words and not recur to it. All is silent as the grave" (1 July 1852, WS 3:341) and ready, judging by the completion of the manuscript in November, for burial in *Villette*.

All of this context can be brought to bear on one of the most remarkable images in Brontë's novel. Sometime after having sealed her Graham-grams into the tree hollow, Lucy finds herself at the spot and recalls her "faith in his excellence" and "warm affection" for Dr. John ("Dr. Graham," besides making it more difficult to play with his identity, would perhaps risk a connection with the Dr. Graham whose *Domestic Medicine* the family used to track Branwell's decline [Gérin, *Branwell Brontë* 133]). "What was become," she wonders, "of that curious one-sided friendship? . . ." "Was this feeling dead? I do not know, but it was buried. Sometimes I thought the tomb unquiet, and dreamed strangely of disturbed earth, and of hair, still golden and living, obtruded through coffin-chinks" (451). (Graham's hair, like Branwell's, is variously "auburn," "orange-red," "golden" [73, 217, 531;

cf. Gérin, *Branwell Brontë* 254, 292, 19]). The underlying concern with Branwell helps to account for some of the strange displacements of *Villette*'s narrative—the older Lucy Snowe, for instance, looking back to her adolescent investment with Graham but distancing the affect onto the still younger Paulina. As for Graham's "mama's boy" aspect that deflects attention to (and surely takes material from) George Smith, one notes that Charlotte's only recorded memory of her mother recalls Mrs. Brontë "playing with her little boy at twilight in the parlour" (Gérin, *Branwell Brontë* 2). The narrator's sense of the different memories, times, people, and feelings making up her character lead her to attempt to head off objections by announcing that "the reader is requested to note a seeming contraction in the two views which have been given of Graham Bretton—the public and the private" (273). "Both portraits are correct," she states, and the need to affirm these contradictions, or to suggest that someone buried may not be dead, seems an important dynamic of Brontë's fiction.

But the yearning of "YOURN!" can never be filled,[12] and another of the novel's remarkable moments looks at Graham while seeming to recall a shared love of *Arabian Nights* and the old world of the Genii and its co-creator Patrick, "Little Bany" (Gérin, *Branwell Brontë* 170): "I kept a place for him, too—a place of which I never took the measure . . . I think it was like the tent of *Peri-Banou*. All my life long I carried it folded in the hollow of my hand—yet, released from that hold and constriction, I know not but its innate capacity for expanse might have magnified it into a tabernacle for a host" (555; italics added). Here again we come upon the navel of the novel, for the hollow of Charlotte Brontë's hand in fact holds the pen milling out its capacity for expanse in the overdetermined letters that let her live and by which she can "let live" in *Villette*. As for Peri-Banou, Brontë knows the word actually signifies a female genie, and the context suggests that she recalls from her childhood reading the fairy's anguished reproach to Prince Ahmed, "Is it possible that you should have forgot that you have pledged your faith to me, and that you no longer love one who is passionately fond of you?" (*Tales of the East* [1812] 1:442, in Allott 635).

If, as Edward Chitham concludes, "the matrix of *Wuthering Heights* is a return to the intense and absorbing feelings of childhood and early adolescence" (249), then we might expect to sense in Emily Brontë's novel, as in Charlotte Brontë's text, the shadow, among others, of Branwell and the Glass Town world shared at first by all the children. One can, for instance, relate the personification of the moor, the "dark" (38, 260), "black villain" (97) Heathcliff to Branwell's longstanding blackamoor villain, Quashia Quamina. Mr. Earnshaw's trip to Liverpool (itself a near anagram of "Verdopolis" or Glass Town) where he finds Heathcliff matches curiously with one of Charlotte's parodies of Branwell. Earnshaw says he will "walk there and back; sixty miles each way" (38) and yet is absent only for three days. Charlotte's Patrick Benjamin Wiggins, however, seems to satirize some similar, fraternal trait with his claim to have walked between two towns, the distance being "forty miles and I did it all in twelve hours,—indeed it's more than forty, nearer fifty. O yes, and above sixty I daresay, or sixty-five. Now sir, what do you say to a man's walking sixty-five miles in a day?" (Gérin, *Branwell Brontë* 70).

A more intriguing shadow comes in Catherine's report of an early visit to her ill-fated, ineffectual—Branwellian—"sweet, darling cousin," "pretty Linton": "He consented to play at ball with me. We found two in a cupboard, among a heap of old toys: tops, and hoops, and battledores, and shuttlecocks. One was marked C., and the other H.; I wished to have the C., because that stood for Catherine, and the H. might be for Heathcliff, his name; but the bran came out of H., and Linton didn't like it" (199). The narrator imagines Catherine as wishing to appropriate what seems her fitting signifier and to impose on Linton, via his unfamiliar surname, a signifier which also suits Hareton and Hindley. In contrast to these ambiguous possibilities, however, the shifting, masculine "H." evidently stands in some special relation to "the bran" that comes out of it (a bran well, then; and regarding "the bran," note "the Varens" in *JE* 126). That Linton does not like "the bran," and/or its "coming out," and/or his proposed signifier without "the bran" hints at some more personal involvement the reciprocal of which would be Branwell's dislike in seeing that Linton came out of him. As for the possibility of a bran-filled H. for Heathcliff, we might ponder one of the most enigmatical remarks in this mysterious book, Lockwood's post-nightmare, manic, vatic, never-answered challenge to Heathcliff, "Was not the Reverend Jabes Branderham akin to you on the mother's side?" (31). It does seem that Branwell's namesake mother and her sister, Aunt Branwell, who took over the mother's role, permanently branded him with a religious jabber and imagery and sense of guilt which, with at times Heathcliffian bravado and language, he tried vainly to undo (as in his occasionally quite amusing prose fragment, "And the weary are at rest").

In thinking about possible "sources" for Emily Brontë's fiction, one has to recall that "apart from their father, Branwell was practically the only man she was ever to know with any degree of closeness and intimacy" (Rees 47). The father, nearing seventy as *Wuthering Heights* was being written, seems to shade into the comic figure of Joseph. In his own heavy brogue, the Reverend Brontë was ever using already-anachronistic Methodist jargon (Harrison 94); owing to his dyspepsia he took his meals alone, and Lockwood's "charitable conjecture" that old Joseph "must have need of divine aid to digest his dinner" (14) perhaps reflects the joke at the other dinner table. Lockwood, in this attributing schema, does not need a male model if one imagines Emily Brontë's perspective on her sister's authorial impersonation and her urbane pretensions as "Captain Tree," "Charles Wellesley," "Charles Townsend," or "Charles Thunder" (punning on the Greek signification of the family name). But that Branwell might inform or even govern the figure of Heathcliff offers a possibility still capable of surprising. One crucial connection in this regard is Branwell's devotion to the figure of the dead sister, Maria, who obsessively occupies his poetry, usually under the name not of Catherine but of Caroline (which as a feminine form of Charles also kept Charlotte in reference). Branwell's tormented, inverted religiosity, too, looms in the extraordinary picture Emily Brontë has Nelly Dean relate of Heathcliff "praying like a Methodist; only the deity he implored is senseless dust and ashes; and God, when addressed, was curiously confounded with his own black father!" (144). The question of Branwell's language during the drinking bouts that marked his long breakdown to death raises other considerations.

Even by modern standards, the scope and intensity of the abusive terms that reach liminal, typographic representation in *Wuthering Heights* are striking. Heathcliff, Nelly learns from little Hareton, is the "Devil Daddy" who teaches the boy "a string of curses, which, whether he comprehended them or not, were delivered with practiced emphasis, and distorted his baby features into a shocking expression of malignity" (95). Considering that "those fine words" that Nelly reports include "Damn the curate, and thee!" one can only wonder at what she omits from Hareton's report of Heathcliff's promise that "'the curate should have his —— teeth dashed down his —— throat, if he stepped over the threshold." In light of Nelly's move from the quoted "damn" to the expletive-deleting dash, one might note the OED's observation that *fuck* is "used profanely in imprecations and exclamations as the coarsest equivalent of Damn," and that *fucking* is cited in a like sense. It appears that Heathcliff's blasphemous vocabulary approaches verbalization, while the sexual and scatological obscenities go uncited—Lockwood, for example, overhears "a brutal curse" from Hareton but comments, "I took care not to notice" (21).

But the text, in the guise of the shocked Mrs. Linton on hearing Heathcliff, reiterates, "Did you notice his language?" (49). Heathcliff says that Isabella "degenerates into a mere slut!" (126) and refers to Catherine as an "insolent slut" (252). Isabella finds herself labeled a "pitiful, slavish, mean-minded brach," or bitch, and herself relates Heathcliff's earlier threat: "'You'd better open the door, you ——' he answered, addressing me by some elegant term that I don't care to repeat" (146). Her choice of "elegant" perhaps points by alliteration to the term. In this vein one might recall the vehement language of Anne Brontë's censorious version of Branwell in decline, Arthur Huntingdon (in *The Tenant of Wildfell Hall*). Considering that she reports his expressions "G—— d——n him!" (198) and "that old bitch, Rachel" (371), one can only suspect the worst of the "bad language," "dreadful language" (316, 445) used in assaulting his wife with "a volley of the vilest and grossest abuse it was possible for the imagination to conceive or the tongue to utter" (365) or the "cursing and abusing . . . epithets" that his wife "will not defile this paper with repeating" (373).

In her preface to *Wuthering Heights*, Charlotte Brontë anticipates that the language of her sister's novel offers a problem for "a large class of readers" who will "suffer greatly from the introduction into the pages of this work of words printed with all their letters, which it has become the custom to represent by the initial and final letter only—a blank line filling the interval" (9). One may feel, indeed, that Charlotte fully appreciated the extent to which her more uncompromising sister admitted a "language" Brontë knew would appear to many readers "unintelligible, and—where intelligible—repulsive": that Emily might hint by single words, rather than by single letters, at what the preface terms "those expletives with which profane and violent persons are wont to garnish their discourse" (9). With this context one can reconsider the dream-traumatized Lockwood's account of a brief predawn scene between Heathcliff and Catherine: "'And you, you worthless ———' he broke out as I entered, turning to his daughter-in-law, and employing an epithet as harmless as duck, or sheep, but generally represented by a dash" (34). Here we have a specific instance to support Margaret Homan's contention that "according to Lockwood . . . literal meaning must be . . . replaced by substitutes that resemble the original but without its threatening power" (72). Charlotte Brontë's comment, in the preface, that "men and women who, perhaps, naturally very calm . . . have been trained from their cradle to observe the utmost evenness of manner and guardedness of language, will hardly know what to make of the rough, strong utterance" (9) would itself be exemplified in advance by Lockwood's choice of "duck, or sheep" to displace "fuck, or shit." The reader who has finished *Wuthering Heights* and can imagine Heathcliff "swearing his tongue out" (34) with harmless execrations like "worthless duck" or "worthless sheep" will hardly know what to make of Emily Brontë's unreliable narrators, much less the "bracing ventilation" (14) they cannot confront.

This last suggestion raises the topic of sexual reference in a novel the language of which one recent critic describes as "pure *jeu d'esprit*" (Davies 89). The theme opens with Lockwood's characterization of what he calls "shameless little boys" (14) in the "grotesque carving" over the front door—which sets up the contrast, several paragraphs on, where he confesses "with shame" his own sexual avoidance (15). Pushing into "the penetralium," Lockwood—whom one might imagine, like his author, to be conversant with French idiom—focuses on what "the huge fire-place" does not disclose: "*cul*inary utensils," "*cul*lenders" (14; italics added). Similarly, to his way of seeing and saying things, while the room possesses a "dresser, to the roof," the latter "had never been underdrawn [the place lacked underdrawers, by one construction]: its entire anatomy lay bare to an inquiring eye" except where "legs . . . concealed it" (14). "In an arch under the dresser," he concludes, "reposed a huge, liver-coloured bitch pointer" (15). Lockwood proceeds to tell how his "dear mother used to say" he was unworthy of feminine attention, and how he had just proved her right. At the seacoast he had admired "a most fascinating creature, a real goddess in my eyes, as long as she took no notice of me" (15). When, however, she "looked a return," he confesses "with shame" that he shrank "like a snail" and the girl "persuaded *her* mamma to decamp" (15; italics added). This told, he returns us to the hearthstone, where he "fills up an interval of silence by attempting to caress the canine mother, who . . . was sneaking wolfishly to the back of my legs, her lip curled up, and her white teeth watering for a snatch" (15). That the dog is named Juno and so suggests "a real goddess" in our eyes helps support a vision of its mocking of Lockwood's feeble copulatory urge—for as Partridge's *Dictionary of Slang* confirms, *snatch* denotes "a hasty or illicit or mercenary copulation" and was, in particular, Yorkshire dialect for "the female pudend."[13] So, considering the function names of some other dogs (e.g., Gnasher, 24), one pauses over the information that even those with whom "the ruffianly bitch" (16) owns acquaintance (like Lockwood, 18) are to avoid the house at night, since "Juno mounts sentinel there" (33). Lockwood, however, contents himself with relishing Cathy's "whole figure" and "admirable form" (19); as a "vain weather-cock," he thinks "to hold [him]self independent of all social intercourse" (35). "Miss Cathy," however, has already had "the mysteries of the Fairy Cave, and twenty other queer places" "opened" for her by Hareton on their trip to Penistone Craggs.

The novel's syntax bears out the playful multiple combinational possibilities of such verbal atoms. In the first sentence, Lockwood describes his landlord as "the solitary neighbour that I shall be troubled with," leaving the reader who would lock on a reading to decide whether he means "only" or "lonely" neighbor, and "troubled" idiomatically or precisely. Confusion heightens at the first introduction:

> I announced my name.
> "Mr. Heathcliff?" I said.
> A nod was the answer.
> "Mr. Lockwood, your new tenant, sir." (13)

Heathcliff's "'walk in,'" Lockwood writes, "was uttered with closed teeth [this should be attempted to be appreciated] and expressed the sentiment, 'Go to the Deuce!'" (13)—that is, one might imagine, the realm of the dual one has already entered. "Even the gate over which he leant manifested no sympathizing movement to the words, and I think that circumstance determined me to accept the invitation" (13). What kind of determination—reading "that" as a conjunction—is "circumstance"? Having "entered the court," Heathcliff calls, "Joseph, take Mr. Lockwood's horse; and bring up some wine"; and the reflecting narrator splits himself grammatically (goes to the deuce) in reporting, "'Here we have the whole establishment of domestics, I suppose,' was the reflection suggested by *this compound order*. 'No wonder the grass grows up between the flags'" (13; italics added). Lockwood's reflection, then, compounds the sorry state or order of the compound ("compound, or courtyard," OED) with Heathcliff's "compound order."

The reader deciding among the compound visions and linguistic duplicities of *Wuthering Heights* finds the critical task painfully arbitrary. Where Charlotte Brontë's doubles are wont "to mount into the window-seat" or cockpit of consciousness and enjoy "the clear panes of glass, protecting, but not separating" (*JE* 5), Emily Brontë's others cannot stand the pane of separation and strive repeatedly to cross the lattice. These images can stand for radically different perspectives about language and writing—its transparency or opacity, the degree to which the lettered lattice of the text can in fact offer a door to the wind (and its derivatives, spirit/anima/psyche). Where Charlotte Brontë's narrator tries to look frankly at the past and assure us that "now . . . I see it clearly" (*JE* 12), Emily Brontë's reflects obscurely that "you'll judge as well as I can, all these things; at least you'll think you will, and that's the same" (152).

8
Hypograms, Hypocrits, and Hippos: Conrad's *Heart of Darkness*

> *His flowing English seemed to be derived from a dictionary compiled by a lunatic.*
> —CONRAD, *Lord Jim*

Is the difficulty with *Heart of Darkness* the portentous mysteriousness so regretted by E. M. Forster and F. R. Leavis, or with its being, in the author's words, "too symbolic or rather symbolic at all"? Or . . . or is the horror of *Heart of Darkness* the apparently endless circulation of its signs in lies and irony? Inasmuch as the story raises questions of lies, hypocrisy, and ambiguity, it concerns the duplicity of language, the preeminent medium of the existence and expression of those conditions. As the imagined written record of an imagined oral yarn, some distinction between "sound" and "unsound" method looms large. And as the product of a fluently trilingual author obsessed with ambiguity, hypocrisy, and lies—his own not least—Conrad's Congo book solicits watchful reading.

The more one reads of Conrad's life, the more one finds in the celebrated words from the preface to *The Nigger of the "Narcissus"* (1897 [NN]) another schizoid instance of someone's addressing the self in disguise: "My task which I am trying to achieve is, by the power of the written word, to make you hear, to make you feel—it is, before all, to make you see" (59). Brave words these, especially when one sees the author argue shortly thereafter that "half the words we use have no meaning whatever and of the other half each man understands each word after the fashion of his own folly and conceit" (14 January 1898, *Collected Letters* [CL] 2:17). "If I succeed, you shall find," continues the preface, offering, in addition, "perhaps, also that glimpse of truth for which you have forgotten to ask" (59). Evidently Conrad had already forgotten his dictum of the previous year that "the truth is . . . that one's own personality is only a ridiculous and aimless masquerade of something hopelessly unknown" (24 March 1896, CL 1.267). But he had strong reasons for seeing to it that he forgot and we not find (that is, "if I succeed, you shall fail").

The detailed biographies by Frederick Karl (1979) and Zdisław Najder (1983) demonstrate how the facts pertaining to Conrad's unimaginable childhood are (as always) involved in illusion retrospectively created by the interpretation that cites (and sites) them. But whether his father was a noble democrat or a hopeless romantic and however his mother felt about her husband's political activities, one cannot doubt the searing impress of early experience on their only child, Józef Teodor Konrad Nałęcz Korzeniowski. Two days after Conrad's birth (3 December 1857), his father, Apollo, commemorated the occasion and his own patriotic preoccupation with a poem "To My Son Born in the Eighty-fifth Year of Muscovite Oppression, A Song," which urged:

> Baby son, tell yourself
> You are without land, without love,
> Without country, without people,
> While *Poland—your Mother* is entombed.
>   (Najder 11–12)

When his son was almost four, the father, active in clandestine resistance to Poland's Russian occupiers, was arrested, and the small family was condemned to join a tiny, desolate community of exiles in northern Russia. Konrad evidently spent most of his early youth without playmates. A few months after he turned seven, his long-declining mother died of tuberculosis, and he was left with an increasingly melancholy and ailing father who eked out small funds translating and writing. Finally, returned to Poland with his ten-year-old son, Apollo published his *Studies on the Dramatic Element in the Works of Shakespeare* just in time to serve as a kind of testament for the son who shortly saw "entombed" Poland receive his father's body to the accompaniment of a demonstration by university students in

Cracow. So Konrad passed to the practical care of his mother's brother, Tadeusz Brobowski.

Little wonder, then, that when not yet seventeen, Konrad sheered off from the landlocked scene of all that woe and paternal writing for Marseilles and the sea, where, after three desultory years, he attempted a more definitive break with his past by shooting himself in the chest. Much later, in the different fiction of *A Personal Record* (PR) Conrad looks back at the boy Konrad and "the mysteriousness of his impulses to himself" and notes that there was "no precedent" for "a boy of my nationality and antecedents taking a, so to speak, *standing jump* out of his racial surroundings and associations" (121; italics added). Konrad's departure from Poland has led critics to compare Conrad's Lord Jim's desertion of his ship, the *Patna*: " 'I had jumped . . .' He checked himself, averted his gaze. . . . 'It seems,' he added" (*Lord Jim* [*LJ*] 125). Marlow reports that Jim's "references to 'my Dad' "—the *pater* with whom Jim will never have any further contact—gave the patriarchal image of "about the finest man that ever had been worried by the cares of a large family since the beginning of the world" (101). There was indeed among the overdeterminations of the real world a ship named *Patna* (to which nothing occurred like the *Jeddah* incident used in the novel), but as early as 1930 Gustav Morf suggested that the name of this ship was chosen for its resemblance to *Polska* (Poland)—and hence, also, that nation-ship's rescue by France in the form of a French vessel (Meyer, *Conrad* 63). But a more graphic instance of condensation might evoke all "enfants de la patrie" and that sentiment engraved on monuments all over Europe: *Pro Patria* (and cited in *PR* 35). In this case, *r i* literally, graphically, coalesces to *ri* or *n* and enacts the denial of the feminine native land as *Patria* becomes *Patna*.

One consideration in Konrad's jump to the sea must have been the memories reverberating from within a year of his mother's death, when he read aloud the proofs of his father's translation of Hugo's *Les travailleurs de la mer* ("my first introduction to the sea" [*PR* 72]). So did the sea perhaps become for a little boy who had never seen it a maternal figure: sailors on the *Narcissus* hear "a beshrouded ocean whisper its compassion afar—in a voice mournful, immense, and faint" (129). One character writes in his diary to his beloved: "And also I was afraid of your mother. I never knew mine. I've never known any kind of love. There is something in the mere word" (*Under Western Eyes* 360). Perhaps in this "mere" word one sees the mother (*mère*), whose French homophone makes her "the mirror of the sea" (*mer*). In *A Personal Record* Conrad remembers his mother as "a mere loving, wide-browed, silent, protecting presence, whose eyes had a sort of commanding sweetness" (24).

Konrad's imagination was thus shaped by "the greatest misfortune that can assail a child—the loss of its Parents" (as his uncle wrote him in 1869 after his father's death [Najder 31]); and the overwhelming sense of what he missed, of what was missed, and of the massive deprivations to his narcissism (*intensified* by proximal satisfaction) made life a mystery that, wish what he might, could never be solved by a word or story: "Art . . . like life itself, is . . . obscured by mists" (NN 60). So the missed story, the mystery of "my story" (as Conrad might see it) must—like the Ancient Mariner's—be endlessly reformulated, bearing witness to how, "young at sea" ("Youth" 42), "I missed my late helmsman awfully—I missed him" (*Heart of Darkness* [*HD*] 51). When Jim tells Marlow that "Some day one's bound to come upon some sort of chance to get it all back again. Must!" Marlow thinks, "I did not even know what it was he wished so much to regain, what it was he had so terribly missed. It might have been so much that it was impossible to say" (*LJ* 174). And when Jim blazes out, "Ah! what a chance missed! My God! what a chance missed!" Marlow comments that "the ring of the last 'missed' resembled a cry wrung out by pain" (104—in the earlier story Marlow imagines "the mist itself" to scream in "mournful uproar" [*HD* 41]). This intimation of what he has missed constitutes (in yet another author's appropriation of Acts 17:28) "the mist in which [Jim] moved and had his being" (136); he has come "from home" into the present, "with his miserable trouble and his shadowy claim, like a man panting under a burden in a mist" (206).[1]

Conrad believed that "the power of sound has always been greater than the power of sense" (*PR* xi), and this recurrent sound association of mystery/ mist [story]/missed [story] can help explain how earlier critics, interested like F. R. Leavis in "charged concreteness" (rather than charged semantics) could not make sense of Conrad's "adjectival insistence upon inexpressible and incomprehensible mystery" (177) or would wonder, like E. M. Forster, about "a central obscurity" that left Conrad "misty in the middle as well as at the edges" (173). But Conrad knows that the author "is only writing about himself" (PR xiii), especially, his "young days, the days when one's habits and character are formed" (PR xx): for him, such effort means encountering "billowing mists from . . . the dead" and seeking "discourse with the dead" (PR 87, xv). So this would-be honest author has to reiterate "the mysteriousness of his impulses to himself," and that what "perhaps must remain for ever obscure even to [oneself], will be [one's] unconscious response to the still voice of that inexorable past" (PR 24–25). Such an inexorable but unacceptable past constitutes the region of Conrad's wandering: the "grands éspaces remplis des formes vagues" where "les spectres se changent en chair vivante, les vapeurs flottants se solidifient" (29 March 1894, CL 1:150 ["great spaces filled with vague forms where ghosts transform into living flesh, floating vapours turn solid"]).[2]

"Mistah" Kurtz, in *Heart of Darkness*, is one of Korzeniowski's revenants: "He rose, unsteady, long, pale, indistinct like a vapour exhaled by the earth, and swayed slightly, misty and silent before me" (64). Kurtz originates in the "misseds" of time—after the brief attack by the natives, Marlow concludes that Kurtz is now missing—"vanished"—and confesses, in his most intimate moment, that his sorrow at this thought "had a startling extravagance of emotion." Seized with "lonely desolation," he feels as if he had "been robbed of a belief or had missed [his] destiny in life" (48). This sense of lack helps us understand why Conrad's Marlow "was anxious to deal with this shadow by myself alone"—even though, he adds, "to this day I don't know why I was so jealous of sharing with anyone the peculiar blackness of that experience" (64). He is, so to speak, niggard of his narcissism: he cannot truly share experience, coming as it does out of his past, because, being known, it would no longer be his unique, individual, peculiar past, and he would then no longer be his present self. As an author "unconsciously compelled now to write volume after volume" (PR 18), he no doubt feels unconsciously compelled to protect his (self-)investment. Besides, as Marlow says of his fellow man upon his return from the depths of Congo-Conrad's "Inner Station," "I felt so sure they could not possibly know the things I knew" (70)—and why? "I had no clear perception of what it was I really wanted" (71). Critics now commonly point to Marlow's nervous disorder at the end (hence, beginning) of the tale, but above that narrator (like the eye above the writing hand) is another who, paradoxically, writes so as not to be understood—so to have the job, the *occupation* of going-on-not-being-understood—and so as not to understand himself. "The inner truth is hidden—luckily, luckily" (36).

When this subtle psychological machine functions ("You are so subtle, Marlow" [*LJ* 112]), Conrad has the pregnant satisfaction of experiencing the "brooding gloom," "gloom brooding" whose inspiring presence he signals no less than five times at the beginning of *Heart of Darkness*. Later he confides to his old friend Edward Garnett, "Before everything switch off the critical current of your mind and work in darkness—the creative darkness which no ghost of responsibility will haunt" (11 August 1920, Garnett 273). But working with mystery, in darkness, in dream, unconsciously—"all my work is produced unconsciously" (24 September 1895, *CL* 1:246)—one rarely finds anything definite, words least of all. In *The End of the Tether*, for instance, a father decides on the name Ivy for his daughter "because of the sound of the word, and obscurely fascinated by a vague association of ideas" (174).

The more duplicitous Marlow gives this challenge regarding Kurtz: "I did not see the man in the name any more than you do" (29). He draws attention to the name again with "Kurtz—Kurtz—that means 'short' in German—don't it?" (59). Well, yes, "short," or "brief," or "concise," but the spelling is *kurz*. One critic details similarities between Kurtz and Apollo Korzeniowski, beginning with the likeness of their names (Crews 522n.), and another argues that "to call his villain Kurtz . . . was to memorialize this phase of his life when he was not yet Joseph Conrad but still Konrad Korzeniowski—a name prone to be shortened to Korz" (Ellmann 18). No evidence is offered for such shortening, but it's hardly necessary given the text's clear suggestion of a curtailed Korzeniowski. The connection is pressing enough to be made earlier, as Marlow discovers on the copy of *An Inquiry into Some Points of Seamanship* by "Towser, Towson—some such name," "a signature, but it was illegible—not Kurtz—a much longer word" (39)—implying that the name at least began *Kur*—or *Kor*. (One might remark the pivotal role of the word *cur* in drawing together Marlow and Jim [*LJ* 94–102]). Conrad writes, anyway, that "the name was as true as everything else in his life—and death" (59; never mind who it is: Konrad is as dead—or alive—as Apollo).

"I am missing innumerable shades," says Marlow; "—they were so fine, so difficult to render in colourless words" (*LJ* 112).[3] Absence of color is absence of light, and in *Heart of Darkness* we hear the trick of using black, dark, colorless words to render some of the missing shades—as with the women so dramatically absent from the narrative, for example. Forgetting his Nietzsche, Marlow remarks that "it's queer how out of touch with truth women are!" (16).[4] Then, emphasizing the truth of the phrase crediting their being in the present ("women are"), he continues: "They live in a world of their own and [shifting graphemes] there [shifting tenses] had never been anything like it and [arrogating perspective] never can be." Their world that he imagines "*is* too beautiful altogether," and "if they *were* to set it up it would go to pieces" [italics added]. To appreciate the pun that then follows, note that Conrad had already written a female acquaintance that "women have a more penetrating vision, and a greater endurance of life's perversities" (27 January 1897, CL 1:334): "Some confounded fact which *we men* have been living contentedly with ever since the day of creation, would start up and knock the whole thing over" (italics added). The confounded fact, it seems, is patriarchy itself. In an adjacent pun Marlow remarks that to his aunt's eyes "it appears however that I was also one of the Workers, with a capital—you know" (15). What we know is that with no Capital he is, following Marx, a Worker indeed. Though considered by his aunt "something like a lower sort of apostle," Marlow casts off the prophet motive by venturing "to hint that the Company was run for profit" (16).

The way to the realm of the missed lies beyond "the door of Darkness" (14). To get to his story Marlow comes to "a city that always reminds me of a whited sepulchre" (13), and passes through "narrow and deserted streets" to arrive at a house "as still as a house in a city of the dead" (14). Slipping through a crack, he ends up before two women dressed in black, whose knitting has for some critics associated them with the first two Fates, Lachesis and Clotho, though their activity might equally evoke one of Conrad's fantasies of "it": a universal "knitting machine" that "knits us in and it knits us out. It has knitted time, space, pain, death, corruption, despair and all the illusions—and nothing matters" (20 December 1897, CL 1:425). One knitter "wore a starched white affair on her head" and seems to know all about Marlow, because, he reports, "an eerie feeling came over me. She seemed uncanny and fateful. Often far away there [appropriately weird syntax] I thought of these two, guarding the door of Darkness" (14). The uncanny, Freud argues, comes from experiencing, dimly perceiving, our compulsion to repeat—and certainly Conrad's narrator has been nearby this door before (in 1869) and will be there again (in 1914). In "Poland Revisited" (1915) the author relates how a return visit to Cracow the previous year brought back the memory of "a small boy of eleven," beset by "a private gnawing worm of my own" at "the time of my father's last illness" (223). Recalling his return from school each evening, he continues:

> I walked all the way to a big old house in a quiet narrow street. . . . There, in a large drawing-room, panelled and bare, with heavy cornices and a lofty ceiling, in a little oasis of light made by two candles in a desert of dusk, I sat at a little table to worry and ink myself all over till the task of my preparation was done. The table of my toil faced a tall white door, which was kept closed; now and then it would come ajar and a nun in a white coif would squeeze herself through the crack, glide across the room, and disappear. There were two of these noiseless nursing nuns. (223–24)

The "prep" finished, "I would have had nothing to do but sit and watch the awful stillness of the sick room flow out through the closed door and coldly enfold my scared heart. I suppose that in a futile childish way I would have gone crazy. But I was a reading boy" (224–25). Become a writing man, he pens through Marlow a greeting suitable for Korzeniowski *père et fils*: "Ave! Old knitter of black wool. *Morituri te salutant*" (HD 14).

One imagines inevitable misrepresentations to and by Konrad concerning his father's—and earlier, his mother's—health, so that their deaths emphatically canceled all hope of security, stripping off, as he writes, "my simple trust in the government of the universe" ("Poland Revisited" 225). More particularly, after the death of his father, Konrad was cared for and instructed by his hardworking, commonsensical uncle Tadeusz who, though he prided himself on his justice, had little sympathy for his nephew's paternal memories, since he held Apollo responsible for his beloved sister's death. Growing up with competing visions of the past, Konrad would have to conclude that someone was not telling the truth—or that no one was—or perhaps, finally, that there was no one truth. Hence, also, a concern for hypocrisy and the conscious or unconscious motives for dissembling; these Conrad could study in himself, if he chose, since he "altered facts, confused dates, and changed effects into causes, even in his private correspondence" (Najder 39). Finally, as an acutely sensitive writer Conrad lived with a daily awareness of what was missed in words—his fore-note to *A Personal Record* contains what almost sounds a private joke: "Let me only find the right word! Surely it must be lying somewhere" (xii). Someone who wants truth—an answer—will forego direct questions in favor of silent attentiveness, like the frame narrator of *Heart of Darkness*: "I listened, I listened on the watch for the sentence, for the word that would give me the clue to the faint uneasiness inspired by this narrative" (30). This tells us how to proceed as readers of Conrad's narrative.

We begin with the passage that leads up to the frame narrator's anxiety. Marlow senses "the silence of the land" in his own "very heart—its mystery, its greatness, the amazing reality of its concealed life" (*HD* 28). While the brickmaker runs on in the background, we read:

> What were we who had strayed in here? Could we handle that dumb thing, or would it handle us? I felt how big, how confoundedly big, was that thing that couldn't talk and perhaps was deaf as well. What was in there? I could see a little ivory coming out from there and I had heard Mr. Kurtz was in there. I had heard enough about it too—God knows! Yet somehow it didn't bring any image with it. (29)

As the brickmaker "jabber[s] about himself," so our narrator gives vent to his profound confusion about "it." "What is life worth if one cannot jabber to one['s] heart's content?" asks Conrad in 1896 (22 February, *CL* 1:262), but in fact the problem is that the real content of the heart cannot be addressed; "in my case when the heart is full the words are scarce," he confesses (27 September 1885, *CL* 1:11), and much later he puts the dynamic to Henry James in a pun: "Quand je suis ému je deviens muet" (Karl 772). The "thing that couldn't talk" is then the heart, the unconscious, but also, recalling Plato's famous image in the *Phaedrus* (275d), anything written: a text: this story ("What was in there?"). One tangible good seems to be ivory, but even there the actual word that "rang in the air, was whispered, was sighed" (26) would have been *ivoire*, mocking the claim of what "I" am able "to see" (*voir*). In any event, "I believed it in the same way one of you might believe there are inhabitants in the planet Mars," and one notes that "lie" is the heart of "be*lie*ve."

Marlow then digresses to tell of a Scottish sailmaker so certain in his belief that there were "people" in Mars he would offer to fight at the slightest doubt. Then this:

> I would not have gone so far as to fight for Kurtz, but I went for him near enough to a lie. You know I hate, detest, and can't bear a lie, not because I am straighter than the rest of us, but simply because it appals me. There is a taint of death, a flavour of mortality in lies—which is exactly what I hate and detest in the world—what I want to forget. It makes me miserable and sick, like biting something rotten would do. (29)

Going "near enough to *a lie*," Marlow becomes in sound and fact "an *ally*, a helper, an accomplice" (*LJ* 111; italics added) of Kurtz's; that Marlow "did not go to join Kurtz there and then" (69) only raises the suggestion of later alliance. In fact, soon enough Marlow will say, "I laid the ghost of his gifts at last with a lie" (49).[5] This lie, to draw on Marlow's formulation in *Lord Jim*, would be "for the laying of what is the most obstinate ghost of man's creation, of the uneasy doubt uprising like a mist, secret and gnawing like a worm, and more chilling than the certitude of death—the doubt of the sovereign power enthroned in a fixed standard of conduct" (80). Lies are to allay doubt, but doubt leads us to expect lies. No wonder the frame narrator grows uneasy.

So he suggests, in effect, that one listen, listen "on the watch for the sentence, for the word" that might supply some clue. One word for what he wants might be *hypogram*, the term used by Michael Riffaterre (taking it from de Saussure's remarkable anagrammatical speculations) to denote an under[*hypo*]lying key word or kernel or nucleus around which a body of text or discourse revolves (Riffaterre, *Semiotics* 12–13). After the interruption of the narrator's cue, the text reminds us that all this while Marlow is letting the brickmaker "run on." Then Marlow goes off about rivets— "Rivets I wanted" (30)—which he needs to get on with the work, and the author, analogously, to hold the story work together. The brickmaker, who now turns out to be the Central Station secretary, assumes a confidential air and offers to take Marlow's request "from dictation" (31). But listen with the frame narrator to the rivetting account:

> I demanded rivets. There was a way—for an intelligent man. He changed his manner; became very cold and suddenly began to talk about a hippopotamus; wondered whether sleeping on board the steamer (I stuck to my salvage night and day) I wasn't disturbed. There was an old hippo that had the bad habit of getting out on the bank and roaming at night over the station grounds. The pilgrims used to turn out in a body and empty every rifle they could lay hands on at him. Some even had sat up o' nights for him. All this energy was wasted though. "That animal has a charmed life," he said. (31)

Such a sudden and apparently unmotivated appearance gives "hippo" some promise of revealing itself as a hypogram, particularly as it roams through the ensuing narrative.[6] Marlow recalls the "fine fellows" of the native crew who, after all, didn't eat each other before his face, and, he adds, "they had brought along a provision of hippo-meat which went rotten and made the mystery of the wilderness stink in my nostrils. Phoo! I can sniff it now" (36). Later he dwells again on that nourishment:

> Certainly they had brought with them some rotten hippo-meat which couldn't have lasted very long anyway, even if the pilgrims hadn't, in the midst of a shocking hullabaloo, thrown a considerable quantity of it overboard. It looked like a high-handed proceeding, but it was really a case of legitimate self-defense. You can't breathe dead hippo waking, sleeping, and eating and at the same time keep your precarious grip on existence. (42)

In its last direct appearance, the word denotes a chief object of moral endeavor, as Marlow reflects that for most of us the earth "a place to live in, where we must put up with sights, with sounds, with smells too, by Jove!—breathe dead hippo so to speak and not be contaminated. And there, don't you see, your strength comes in, the faith in your ability for the digging of unostentatious holes to bury the stuff in" (50).

These accounts are somewhat contradictory—did the meat go rotten? or was it rotten when brought on board? or did it just offend delicate Western sensitivity, seeing as how the remaining meat evidently continues to be eaten? But clearly Marlow links hippo meat (dead hippo), nourishing and desirable though it be to some, to a lie, with its "taint of death" that makes him "sick like biting something rotten would do." Why? One explanation for this particular hypogram and its associations lies buried back in the early description of the city where "the Company's offices" are located (Bruxelles/Brussels) and which, reports Marlow, "always makes me think of a whited sepulchre." The allusion recalls Matthew 23:27–29:

> Woe unto you, scribes and Pharisees, hypocrits! for ye are like unto whited sepulchres, which indeed appear beautiful outward, but are within full of dead men's bones, and of all uncleanness.
>
> Even so ye also outwardly appear righteous unto men, but within ye are full of hypocrisy and iniquity.
>
> Woe unto you, scribes and Pharisees, hypocrits!

His appropriation of this harsh denunciation in part identifies Marlow with its original speaker, an identification strengthened a few paragraphs on by his reference to "all my sorrows" (14). Our new man of sorrows, Marlow is acquainted with the modern grief of pervasive doubt; according to his good news about life, "the most you can hope from it is some knowledge of yourself—that comes too late—a crop of unextinguishable regrets" (69). Marlow describes the self-encounter in the Congo as the "culminating point" of his experience and leaves us to infer that it muted his earlier "heavenly mission to civilise you" (11). Precisely in taking to heart the gospel injunction to the hypocrite, "First cast out the beam out of thine own eye" (Matthew 7:5), Marlow changes from a Jesus to a Buddha figure (at the story's beginning and end), Christ having been irrecoverably contaminated by the cultural hypocrisies committed in his name.

In denouncing the hypocrisy of others, one has necessarily to disclose, or at least hint at, the standards and beliefs assumed for one's own judgment. Marlow, for instance, scorns the "rot let loose in print and talk" (15–16) and "the philanthropic pretence" (27) of the imperial enterprise. But doing so, one is open to the relativizing *tu quoque* of a pervasive individualism: "Hypocrite lecteur,—mon semblable,—mon frère!" (Baudelaire, "Au Lecteur"). Such an alliance, however, with its suggestion of mutual recognition and understanding, threatens the narcissism that depends on the subject's mystery to itself and others (mystery permits [the illusion of] mastery). As Hegel sees it in the *Phenomenology of Spirit*, the denouncer of hypocrisy posits its judging as correct consciousness, "setting itself up in this unreality and conceit of knowing well and better above the deeds it discredits, and wanting its words without deeds to be taken for a superior kind of *reality*" (405). This places the judging consciousness on a level with what it denounces, but rather than advance to mutual recognition, the judging consciousness repels the prospect of "community of nature, and is the hard heart that is *for itself*, and which rejects any continuity with the other" (405). As a result the situation is reversed, and the judging consciousness is now the hypocrite whose "respect for duty and virtue" becomes "a mask to hide itself from its own consciousness, no less than from others" (401). So the narcissistically disordered subject will guard its commitments, its comments, the better to mysteriously occlude the dilemma posed by its desire to be known and open and by its desire to control:

> "My dear chap," I cried, "you shall always remain for them an insoluble mystery." Thereupon we were silent.
> "Mystery," he repeated, before looking up. "Well, then let me always remain here." (*LJ* 269)

One possible outcome to the mysterious burden of narcissistic deprivation is suicide; another is the ego-diminishing assumption of powerlessness and nihilism, as in Marlow's "flash of insight" that nothing matters, since "the essentials of this affair lay deep under the surface, beyond my reach and beyond my power of meddling" (40); another is simply to go on talking or writing, even if only to tell: "I don't know. I can't tell. But I went" (72). Writing was for Conrad like going to sea—a jump, an attempt at escape—and of those two "impulses" that ordered his life, he did not know which was the "more mysterious" (*PR* 18). Both involve transiting the abyss, but writing, more than sailing, never arrives. It was always so, but perhaps only with the advent of electromagnetic writing (tele*graph*, phono*graph*) and wide-scale advertising has "missing presence" become a critical part of social experience and the human archive. At the same time, not coincidentally, hypocrisy became banalized, replaced by the more private, psychologized concerns of "sincerity" or "authenticity." According to Nietzsche, "Hypocrisy has its place in ages of strong belief" (77), which would not give it much to do with Marlow's sense of "ultimate wisdom," discovered "in a sickly atmosphere of tepid scepticism, without much belief in your own right, and still less in that of your adversary" (69). As a writer Conrad wants to believe in his own right and writing, but at the same time the "unsound method" of writing does not permit him to hear himself and so takes him further from self-presence and closer to death: "I heard him mutter, 'Live rightly, die, die. . . .' I listened. There was nothing more. Was he rehearsing some speech in his sleep, or was it a fragment of a phrase from some newspaper article? [Curious article that would be!] He had been writing for the papers and meant to do so again, 'for the furthering of my ideas. It's a duty'" (*HD* 68). Kurtz's "duty," à la Hegel, is "consciousness of duty" as itself "the hypocrisy which wants its judging to be taken for an *actual* deed, and instead of proving its rectitude by actions, does so by uttering fine sentiments" (403). So, "uttering fine sentiments" or, more particularly, writing them—because the "unsound method" facilitates unctuousness, lies, and manipulation—becomes equivalent to hypocrisy. The writer who sees this comes to a difficult position, the more so as any desire to write against hypocrisy must first confront the hypocrisy of writing "I" when that itself is mystery and contradiction.

In fact, Conrad's contradictions cannot decide themselves, and his doubts, duplicities, and dilemmas of ambivalence continually shuttle from one form of sublimation to another, ever reinscribing themselves: himself ("a novelist . . . is only writing about himself" [*PR* xiii]). Even in trying to name his condition to a compatriot he tropes himself: "Homo duplex has in my case more than one meaning" (5 December 1903, *CL* 3:89). Another key word, then, for considering the art of Conrad's darkness, is *or*. Even "the word 'ivory'" rings in the air (26, 36). *Or* is the sign of undecidability, hence indecision, inaction, and lack of care. Concerning some recently landed soldiers, Marlow reports, "Some I heard got drowned in the surf, but whether they did or not nobody seemed particularly to care" (16). Later he claims to "have a voice" that, ambiguously, "for good *or* evil . . . cannot be silenced" (38). Just as quickly, however, he asks, "What did it matter what any one knew *or* ignored?" (40). A later equivocation concludes, "I don't know which"; and another, "I won't pretend to say" (50).

Readers are quick to pick up the theme: "Is Marlow Kurtz's antagonist, critic and potential redeemer? *Or* is he Kurtz's pale shadow and admirer, his double, finally one *more* idolator in a *story* full of fetishists and devil worship?" (Brantlinger 264; italics added here and all following instances). Another finds that the novel "embodies an insight which has been brought home to humanity time and time again during the Twentieth Century: elevated words can serve the light *or* the dark depending upon the way their embodied ideas and aims are, *or* are not, put into practice" (McLauchlan 390). Another sees that "we are left with the question: does the mind seek order *or* truth?" (Said 112). All of this can perhaps encourage us to hear Kurtz's memorable last words in a way worthy of Kurtz's "unsound method" and of the story's self-avowed "dream sensation, that commingling of absurdity, surprise, and bewilderment," the sense of what it calls "the terrific suggestiveness of words heard in dream" (30, 65). Conrad, after all, knows that aitches can be dropped ("Yer bloomin' lot of yrpocrits" [*NN* 174]) and elsewhere imagines making "experimental essays in combining detached letters and loose syllables" (*Victory* 153);[7] more important, the doubled phrasing of Kurtz's summing up signals an impossible choice. Worse then, than any either-or is "The h*orror!* The h*orror!*" (68). "Scorching last words," one reader subvocalizes (Stewart 365). Another finds "horror" the "culminating instance of . . . almost punning Conradian concepts engendering an unmistakable moral assessment out of an intuitive psychic spasm" (Levenson 404)—which one might reconceive as *words* that engender a misty moral assessment out of an intuitive lexical spasm.

Marlow, of course, latches onto Kurtz's curt formula as if it offered some absolution: "He had summed up—he had judged. 'The horror!' He was a remarkable man" (69). By one view Kurtz heroically articulates a deathbed self-condemnation for past lack of restraint, one according with Conrad's "positive *horror* of losing for one moving moment that full possession of myself which is the first condition of good service" (*PR* xvii; italics added). His is the horror, then, of glimpsing himself "hollow at the core," a "hollow sham" (58, 67), and his "supreme moment of complete knowledge" (68) at one with the "moving moment" of self-dispossession dreaded by Conrad. But we might feel this "expression of some sort of belief" with what Marlow describes as its "candour," "conviction," and "note of revolt" (69) rather undercut by the repeated description immediately leading up to it, of Kurtz "lying on his back" like "a man who is lying at the bottom of a precipice," and, in his own words, "lying here in the dark"—though the light is "within a foot of his eyes" (68). Someone, at any rate, is obviously lying when Kurtz *cries* out "in a whisper" (68). And as Marlow reflects further, the very sounds begin to betray him: "It was an affirmation, a moral victory paid for by innumerable defeats, by abominable terrors, by abominable satisfactions. But it was a victory" (70).[8] The way in which "The horror! The horror!" resounds through the final interview foregrounds that phrase as the embodiment of the novel's contradictions or ambiguities or pluralities—or whatever one chooses (if one can decide) to call them. Conrad's sense that the final scene "locks in—as it were—the whole" (31 May 1902, CL 2:417; or, so to speak, the hole) has not stopped one anxious admirer from disparaging its "cheaply ironic double-talk" as "a jumble of melodramatic tricks" (Mudrick 188).

Marlow begins the intended ending, one of literature's great "double sessions," outside a door, finding that "while I waited he seemed to stare at me out of the glassy panel. . . . I seemed to hear the whispered cry, 'The horror! The horror!'" (72). Kurtz, evidently, is now Marlow's direct reflection at the same time that Marlow is the object of Kurtz's cry. Admitted to the Intended's drawing room, Marlow sees Kurtz and her "together—I heard them together. She had said with a deep catch of the breath, 'I have survived'" (73), and the scene becomes for us a kind of phantasmagoria or horror show in which the undead Kurtz now possesses Miss Intended's body and says "with a deep catch of the breath, 'I have survived'" (73). The "cruel and absurd mysteries" that follow in the form of painful conversation pose the undecidable as drawing-room norm for a culture that affords no vocabulary, much less sympathy, for the unconscious. "I knew him as well as it is possible for one man to know another," Marlow says, asking us to decide what it means for one man "to know" another.[9]

For her part, Miss Intended has a kind of double discourse that enables her to say what we hope she understands despite herself. She enacts the inevitable failure of repression which lies behind the whole story: the hidden comes to light in accordance with Freud's dictum that "the influence of thoughts that lie outside the intended speech . . . determines the occurrence of the slip" (*Psychopathology* 80). "It is not pride," the Intended begins, characterizing her desire to have Marlow know that she has been "worthy" of Kurtz. Then, after the pause, "Yes! I am proud" (74). Then, having referred to Kurtz's ability to speak, she cries, "But you have heard him. You know!" Her exclaimed assumption neatly completes the reader's long-developing wariness concerning the text's many chummy "you know"s, so that one hears Marlow's response, "Yes, I know," as affirming a negative.

And when the Intended says that she is "unhappy for—for life" (74), or that she "cannot . . . cannot believe—not yet" (75), one has hopeful evidence of a new kind of strength and intelligence able to respond to Marlow's "We shall always remember him" as she does, initially, "No! . . . It is impossible" (74). One critic notes that with her remark "He died as he lived," the Intended "has unwittingly summarized the nature of a corrupt life coextensive with death and equivalent to it" (Stewart 374), so complimenting what can be read as an intended witty summary. Then comes the great closing moment where she wants to hear Kurtz's last words; as Marlow is later to say of Jim's Jewel, "She wanted an assurance, a statement, a promise, an explanation—I don't know how to call it: the thing has no name" (*LJ* 269). Since such states are calling for an answer to loss and lack, some way out of the endless circulation of signs with its unavoidable lies, hypocrisies, and ambiguities, what better way to trip the circuit than to answer with "your name," you know?[10]

9

Sylvia on Aurelia Plath

> *Mother, you are the one mouth*
> *I would be a tongue to . . .*
> —SYLVIA PLATH, *"Poem for a Birthday"*

Some readers of Sylvia Plath's work have remarked to an unusual degree on the sense that it "seems an encoded message" (Schwartz and Bollas 150) or is structured around "an underlying code" or "pre-ordained scheme" (Lavers 101) or "predetermined meaning" (Kroll 19) that is to be revealed by "a laborious decoding" (Holbrook 239). While differing as to the specific contents of her cipher, most critics agree that these concern aspects of her biography, particularly in its unconscious dimension. The impinging pressure of her unconscious shows up not just in some themes of her writing—anger at mother, feelings of inadequacy, jealousy, dreams, ambivalence—but even more so in their repetitive nature. Take for example a discrete image set that appears in the selected "Juvenilia" (pre-1956) section of the collected poetry. In "To a Jilted Lover" the speaker, lying "cold on my narrow cot," looks "in sorrow" through "my window-square of black" and imagines that

> from the moon, my lover's eye
> chills me to death
> with radiance of his frozen faith.
> (CP 309)[1]

Now there is "nowhere . . . to hide," for "moon and sun reflect his flame," but when noon comes, her love will see how she is "blazing" still in her "golden hell."

In "Tongues of Stone," a story dating from January 1955, the twenty-two-year-old Plath turns to her experience in McLean Hospital after her breakdown and attempted suicide of less than eighteen months before. Here the protagonist ("the girl") feels "dead inside" and unreachable by any laughter or love: "As from a distant moon, extinct and cold, she saw their *supplicant*, sorrowful faces, their hands stretching out to her, frozen in attitudes of love" (JP 266; italics added). There was, she feels, "nowhere to hide." Over four years later, in a journal entry for 13 October 1959, Plath records feeling "very depressed today," and adds, "Menacing gods. I feel outcast on a cold star, unable to feel anything but an awful helpless numbness. I look down into the warm, earthly world. In to a nest of lovers' beds . . . and feel apart, enclosed in a wall of glass" (J 291). Finally, in the brief poetic memoir of her early childhood, "Ocean 1212-W," composed in 1962, Plath evokes her depressed response to the birth of her one sibling, Warren, when she was two and a half: "As from a star I saw, coldly and soberly, the *separateness* of everything. I felt the wall of my skin: I am I. That stone is a stone. My beautiful fusion with the things of this world was over" (JP 23). The repetitive insistence of these similar images of separateness spread over at least seven years of writing and twenty-four years of experience points to the absence of time in the unconscious and asks us to ponder the origin of this particular feeling and expression. The appearance of the image in poem, journal, and fiction bears out as well what one critic considers "the almost perfect continuity and agreement between her direct statements about herself and the descriptions of events and feelings" of her fictional protagonists and poetic personae (Orgel 271).

In fact, the antecedent of the image components picked out above can be found in a story that dates from the early 1950s, "Among the Bumblebees." Through her protagonist, Alice, Plath returns to her childhood—the younger brother in the story is even named Warren—and summons up a picture of her relation to her father when he was wasting away from diabetes mellitus during the summer of her seventh year. Entering the sickroom of the man she has been shown to adore and idealize, Alice comes to the sleeping figure, leans over his chest, and "from somewhere, very faint and far off" hears his faint heartbeat. Then: " 'Father,' she said in a small pleading voice. 'Father.' But he did not hear, withdrawn as he was into the core of himself, insulated against the sound of her *supplicant* voice."

Lost and betrayed, she slowly turned away and left the room" (*JP* 312; italics added). With the father's withdrawal into deep inner space, this scene seems a kind of inversion of the others; but taken together they suggest a possible psycho-logical sequence of variations consequent on an internalization and then reprojection of this splitting/distancing. In "To a Jilted Lover" the writer addresses herself; she first makes the beloved a kind of man in the moon, chilling her with rejection, but ends by identifying with his (lunar) perspective of her in her aureate, "golden hell." This duality reflects a kind of splitting of a primordial object, after which the two entities rush apart, one deep within and the other far without—except of course that both are still "inside." In "Tongues of Stone" the author, "dead inside," fully assumes the lunar perspective and sees, as it were, the mirror of her own earlier state in "supplicant, sorrowful faces." The journal entry four years after shows the deepening of this particular attitude and formula, but the still later occurrence in "Ocean 1212-W" introduces a fascinating modification as the original splitting is pushed back well before her father's death to Warren's birth. Even here, however, one senses that not so much the advent of the sibling as circumstances it crystallized are at issue—the little girl left, while her mother was at the hospital, with her maternal grandparents (as was again often to be the case during her father's long demise): "She had been gone three weeks. I sulked. I would do nothing. Her desertion punched a smoldering hole in my sky. How could she, so loving and faithful, so easily leave me?" (*JP* 23).[2]

Plath saw her life, it seems, in terms of betrayal and loss, though one discovers therein nothing to indicate gross "developmental failures." Instead, one can consider her work as bearing witness to invisible, unconscious structuring—overdetermining—aspects of her existence. There is first of all her real genetic endowment; this included not just great verbal facility and a 160 IQ (Scigaj 249) but a history of depression in her father's family that her mother, though learning of it after her daughter's breakdown, never thought to relate to her. There is the psychosociology of a recently established immigrant family: Plath's father, Otto, had arrived at sixteen from "some manic-depressive hamlet in the black heart of Prussia" (*BJ* 27); and though her mother's mother had as a girl presented flowers to the Austrian emperor Franz Josef (*CP* 149), the mother herself had been stoned by schoolmates in the anti-German outpouring after America entered World

War II. The desire to master the language her parents spoke as children and at times taught reappears throughout Plath's journal,³ as does the occasional passing fantasy of exchanging the agnosticism bequeathed by her father for her mother's Catholic roots. Such diffuse social insecurity, exacerbated by the surrounding Massachusetts Yankeeism, helps account for Plath's large investment in the imaginary "culture" retailed by the magazines she doted on and wrote for, like *Seventeen, Mademoiselle, Ladies Home Journal*, and the *New Yorker*.

Still more pervasive in the structuring of Plath's being are the many subtle complexities of her family dynamics and history. Plath's mother, Aurelia, was twenty-five when she unwittingly gave up her hard-won career as a teacher of English and German to marry the polymath entomologist and occasional German professor twenty-one years her elder, Otto Plath. If Aurelia, having been raised "in a matriarchy" (*LH* 3) that arose after her father lost money and nerve, was seeking a strong father figure, she seems to have gotten more than she bargained for in the figure she recalls as "*der Herr des Hauses*" (*LH* 13). The narrator of *The Bell Jar*, Esther, reports her mother's telling how, just after the marriage, "my father said to her, 'Whew, that's a relief, now we can stop pretending and be ourselves'" and "from that day on my mother never had a minute's peace" (*BJ* 69). One wonders as well about forty-six-year-old Otto's projection onto young Aurelia's mother, also named Aurelia, who chaperoned the couple on their cross-country auto trip to get married and who proved to be a constant presence in Sylvia Plath's childhood. His daughter, at any rate, could imagine seeking "a young man with a brilliant father. I could wed both" (*J* 117). When his daughter was born, promptly nine months after his marriage, Otto Plath announced to his colleagues, "I hope for one more thing in life—a son, two and a half years from now" (*LH* 12). Aurelia Plath comments that at Warren's birth, "only two hours off schedule," Otto was greeted as "the man who gets what he wants when he wants it" (*LH* 12). In Sylvia Plath's "Among the Bumblebees," the protagonist claims to be "her father's pet" and notes with approval the way he looked "when he scolded Mother sometimes, strong and proud" (*JP* 308), and Aurelia Plath refers to her husband's "explosive outbursts of anger" (*LH* 18) as he began to tire from the diabetes he refused (fearing cancer) to have diagnosed. The respected author of *Bumblebees and Their*

Ways died just after his daughter turned eight, leaving a legacy of anger and frustration, and no insurance.

The leg that was amputated in his terminal hospitalization became a powerful signifier for Otto Plath's survivors. Some thirty-five years afterward, Aurelia Plath pauses in her introduction to *Letters Home* to explain, "I had talked with the doctors concerning the type of help a wife must give to restore confidence to a husband who has been mutilated by surgery and I understood the compelling necessity to make him feel a 'whole man' and completely acceptable to me" (24). Her daughter seems to have thought she could have done the job better, and at twenty reports to her mother her "best baby yet," a story "about a vet with one leg missing and a girl meeting on a train" (*LH* 84). In *The Bell Jar* Plath anticipates and exposes her mother's pieties via Esther's memory of her mother's having said, "What a merciful thing it was for him [Esther's father] he had died, because if he had lived he would have been crippled and an invalid for life, and he couldn't have stood that, he would rather have died than had that happen" (137). A recurring double for the author's mother, Mrs. Tomolillo, voices outrage in a 1959 story after accidentally reading the "Lies, lies, lies" in the "record book" of her psychiatric treatment, but quiets at the sight of a "man on crutches, one pants leg empty and folded up in a neat tuck" (*JP* 128). The author, however, had to deal with dreams such as that of a man with a great sword hacking off legs, "whereupon the men fell down like ninepins with their leg stumps and lower legs scattered. I believe they were supposed to dig their own graves on their leg stumps" (*J* 269–70). Given her own psychotherapy and reading, Plath could make some obvious oedipal interpretations and ask in her journal, "If I really think I killed and castrated my father may all my dreams of deformed and tortured people be my guilty visions of him or fears of punishment for me?" (*J* 273). A scene deleted from the final version of *The Bell Jar* shows Esther struggling with the missing leg in a different way, as she complains to her psychiatrist, "I feel so cut off." "No! no!" she is told; "It is not *you* who are cut off! . . . It is your father's *leg* that was cut off!" (Kroll 112). And although she can be glad that "it was my father's leg, and not me, that had been cut off" (Kroll 112), the very fact that she *does* feel so cut off ("outcast," "as from a star," etc.) suggests that in some way she is or would be "her father's leg." Plath's pen is her means of undoing the cut-off state and making things right; at least for its moment, writing can restore Daddy and happiness: "I felt happier than I had been since I was about nine and running along the hot white beaches with my father the summer before he died" (BJ 60). But the copy of Daddy's *Roget's Thesaurus* which Plath kept by her as fetish and bible (cf. J 88) supported her concomitant attempt not to restore but to appropriate and rewrite her father's legacy. Unfortunately, the question of where to lay responsibility for (and file psychic claims against) her father's death is never adequately resolved, and in that uncertainty Plath vacillates between self-castigation and blaming her mother, who, in turn, she imagines, "feels I killed him" (J 253).

With her father's death Plath's immediate environment was reconstituted. The family moved inland, where they were joined by the grandmother, also named Aurelia, whose husband lived away during the week, working as a steward in a country club. The matriarchy Plath's mother had experienced arose again in what Plath later described as "a smarmy matriarchy of togetherness" in "the little white house on the corner with a family full of women" (J 242). Deprived of "mirroring" from her father, Plath had to make do with feedback from the cultural authority of the women's "slicks" and their image of woman in the Name-of-the-Father. Writing for these magazines offered Plath a way in which the mystery of acceptance/ rejection by such authority could be mastered concretely. But the oedipal romance with the father and its aborted conclusion, immensely formative and haunting though it was, permits in its failure a glimpse of the anterior, preoedipal structure it would have sublated. One might say that with her father's death Plath was condemned to repeat her infantile situation with her first "leg," her mother—even down to sharing a bedroom with her. "Narcissistic women seek to replace the absent father, whom the mother has castrated, and thus to reunite themselves with the mother of earliest infancy," summarizes Christopher Lash (299), and it was Plath's unhappy fate to find this phantasy completely realized.

Students of psycho-Plathology have commented on Plath's "unusually, even disconcertingly, close" relationship with her mother (Bennett 99) and have seen in her astonishingly voluminous *Letters Home* a desperate attempt "to delimit where Aurelia ends and Sylvia begins" (Kamel 223). It is Mrs. Plath herself who makes the disturbing observation that "between Sylvia and me there existed—as between my own mother and me—a sort of psychic osmosis," and then proceeds to relate how she and her daughter read together Edna St. Vincent Millay's "Renascence," which "particularly moved" Sylvia with the lines

> A man was starving in Capri;
> He moved his eyes and looked at me;
> I felt his gaze, I heard his moan,
> And knew his hunger as my own.
> (*LH* 32)

Aurelia Plath emerges as the "dominant parent" who hungrily lives out "her own fantasies of an ideal girlhood—of what she wanted for herself as a child—through her daughter" (Bundtzen 42, 63). After Sylvia had had a "special" date, reports Mrs. Plath, "ah, then she'd picture the evening for me, and I'd taste her enjoyment as if it had been my own" (*LH* 38). For psychoanalytically oriented critics Plath's investment in the letters home, her history of aggressive achievement, her breakdown and final suicide "raise questions about the earliest maternal attachment" (Brink 217) and seem rooted in "a failure in the early months of her life to find herself consistently reflected in the human environment" (Schwartz and Bollas 167): she "seems to have experienced the mother's handling in infancy, for whatever reason, as something meaningless and bewildering" (Holbrook 27–28) and to have felt throughout her life "the effects of her fissured pre-Oedipal union with her mother and of their subsequent hyper-symbiosis or 'osmosis'" (Axelrod 179). Such speculations are not to criticize Plath's mother, "a remarkable woman, a true survivor" (Rich 230) in her own right and one whose own needs (from a psychodynamic perspective) had themselves never been fully attended to (cf. Bennett 99, 163), but to see if they may open ways into Plath's writing that—"substitute for [her]self" (*J* 255). Aurelia Plath was, indeed, overly solicitous of her daughter (that is, her own self-projection): Linda Wagner-Martin reports that toward the end of Sylvia Plath's junior-high years, Mrs. Plath was offered the attractive and rewarding position of dean of women at Northeastern University. On hearing the possibility of her mother's no longer being able to return home from work before her every day (Warren was soon to be off at boarding school), Sylvia complained angrily that "for your self-aggrandizement you would make us complete orphans!" (41). Mrs. Plath declined the advancement.

As we have already recorded in previous chapters, Melanie Klein and an ongoing strand of "object-relations" psychoanalytic theory attribute "fundamental importance to the infant's first object relation—the relation to the mother's breast and to the mother" and conclude that the secure "introjection" of this primal (and not "merely physical") object is the basis of a satisfactory development for the ego (*Envy* 178, 180). Aurelia Plath is, significantly enough, eager to be heard on this issue, and her language merits attention. After describing how she was "totally imbued" with the desire to be a good mother and how even if, supposing, she had been "inclined to rigidity" she would have been "strongly opposed" by her husband's "constantly voiced . . . recollections" of his (surely idealized) nurture, Aurelia Plath reports that she "quietly followed the 'demand feeding' accepted as modern today" though she would "never confess to it in front of my contemporaries, who conscientiously followed the typed instructions of their children's pediatricians" (*LH* 10, 12). A tone of defensive insecurity lurks around these claims, and one might recall Klein's observation that a "too anxious attitude" over demand feeding can increase the infant's anxiety (*Envy* 186). Late in her life Plath offered a comment that suggests her sense of her mother's general attitude: "For goodness sake, stop being so frightened of everything, Mother!" (unpublished; quoted Wagner-Martin 223). But Plath's most telling comment on the "mother somehow not there" (*J* 259) is the picture of Esther in a doctor's waiting room, vainly watching a mother and baby "for some clue to their mutual satisfaction" (*BJ* 182). Aurelia's breast becomes again her daughter's focus with the birth of Warren:

> The one difficult period was when I nursed the baby; it was always then that Sylvia wanted to get into my lap. Fortunately, around this time she discovered the alphabet from capital letters on packaged goods on the pantry shelves. With great rapidity she learned the names of the letters and I taught her the separate sounds of each. From then on, each time I nursed Warren, she would get out a newspaper, sit on the floor in front of me and pick out the capital letters to "read." (*LH* 16)

Learning to milk the word opened the way for Sylvia "to lay in her mother's lap" self-substitutes of "poems and prizes" (Rich 230) and artfully to remind her, as she does at age seven, that

> When mother goes away from me
> I miss her as much, as much can be.
>   (Unpublished; quoted Stevenson 1)

In her frequently cited discussion of "Narcissistic Object Choice in Women," Annie Reich presents the case of a young woman whose mother's own narcissistic disturbance or insecure sense of self "made it impossible for the child to develop any feeling of depth in relation to the mother, but kept her on the level of imitation" (310). Such a mother does not offer the child a reassuring mirror and good feelings about self (positive narcissistic nurture) but rather an inconstant, vacillating, or even antagonistic (à la *Snow White*) reflection. Such inconstancy, the internalization of which begins at the breast, amplifies the developing psyche's inherent adaptive tendency to split good object from bad and so massively confirms what might otherwise be passing, tentative ambivalence into a permanent aspect of personality—ambivalence such as is often noted in Plath (Bundtzen 36, Williamson 54). In the case Reich relates, the woman as a child was sent away to school rather than, like Plath, to nearby grandparents, but on weekends at age four she regularly witnessed her brother's breastfeeding. This scene reactivated and augmented earlier ambivalence so that the mother's breast, "which was denied to her in such drastic fashion, became something to be hated; she wanted to destroy it, to tear it to bits. . . . any wish for the mother was superseded by the feeling: 'She makes me sick; I am not incorporating something wonderful but something poisonous'" (Reich 314). Here the incorporation occurs through the eye and revives a sickening, poisonous feeling or affect which *is* the timeless, split-off, internal bad object made up of the child's archaic and still unresolved (inadequately mirrored, uninterpreted) anger, disappointment, envy, jealousy, regret. Reich's conclusion, published the year of Sylvia Plath's first breakdown, seems prophetically to address the poet's dynamic:

> The mother, the mother's breast—later superseded by the paternal phallus—represented the core of the rather unsublimated ego ideal

which she wanted to be in order to undo the intense, narcissistic injuries, particularly feelings of being deserted and castrated, that she had experienced. The heterosexual love object represented this ideal; but her aggression against the original, homosexual, love object made her devalue the ideal and destroy the partner. However, she was so fused with the object, which after all she had elevated into her own ego ideal, that by destroying it she destroyed herself. (314)

"I notice women's breasts and thighs with the calculation of a man choosing a mistress," Plath writes in her journal at age nineteen (J 22). Her "delicately flat little bosom" (J 21) or "small inadequate breasts" (J 32) contrast with the "full breasts under the taut black jersey" she singles out on another (J 13), "full breasts" that she longs for even as she "abhor[s] the sensuousness which they bring. . . . I desire the things which will destroy me in the end" (J 22). The breasts she desires would be nurturing with "full milky love" (J 83), a love transferred to Esther's favorite dishes, "full of butter and cheese and sour cream" (BJ 20). A dream shortly before her twenty-seventh birthday has Plath "drinking milk from a gold chalice & repeating a name" (J 289), and one recalls that the name Aurelia embodies associations to gold (Lt. *aureolus*, "golden") and—via *areola*—breast and nipple. When she wants to deflate the phantasy, Plath mocks herself as having been "lulled in the arms of a blind optimism with breasts full of champagne and nipples made of caviar" (J 73). But a fantastically "good feed," the caviar-surfeited Esther later discovers, carries the risk of ptomaine poisoning (BJ 22, 35–36).

In another dream Plath "drank from a plastic cylindrical bottle with a red tip and realized in horror it was starch-poison I put in it" (J 221). Her husband's comment that it was a "dream of conception" does not go very far, though it may remind one of the apparent interchangeability of penis and breast in some unconscious imagery (see Klein, *Envy* 199). More interesting is the anomalous formulation of "starch-poison." Perhaps, primed by her mother's old joke about "jellyfish" as the second of the two meanings of *Aurelia*, the poet's ear had noted *starch* as a dialect term for "the jelly-fish" (OED, s.v. "starch, sb.," 3.b). In any event, a very late poem invokes the pseudoconcern of "talkers," like Aurelia, asking, "You all right?" to comment, blankly: "The starched, inaccessible breast" ("Paralytic," CP 266).

So, in "I Want, I Want," which seems to recall the mother's and grandmother's "cocoa butter on the nipples so they won't crack" (J 243), Plath imagines "the baby god" who

> Cried out for the mother's dug.
> The dry volcanoes cracked and spit,
>
> Sand abraded the milkless lip.
> (CP 106)

"Medusa"—itself the name of genus of jellyfish synonymous with *Aurelia* (noted by Kroll 252)—opens with a vision of "that landspit of stony mouthplugs," and that stony Winthrop (Massachusetts) strand of Plath's childhood leads to images of breasts like stones and "dry-papped stones" ("The Detective," CP 209; "Point Shirley," CP 111).

Before entering into stranger connections in Plath's imagery, we ought to pause and consider some examples of the associations she wrought. As Judith Kroll notes, in Plath's discourse metaphors are "strikingly frequent, and similes have the immediacy of metaphor" (16). In "The Courage of Shutting-Up" eye pupils suggest "black disks" that, via the link of brain/electronic brain/tape spools, lead to the image of "the disks of the brain" revolving "like the muzzles of cannon" (CP 210). In an explicit but illogical simile, flat circles have become mouths of cannon, and we experience a wrenching jump from (as it were) two to three dimensions. A little over a month later the simile marker drops out altogether as the poet presents a train in "Getting There":

> . . . the wheels move, they appall me—
> The terrible brains
> Of Krupp, black muzzles
> Revolving . . .
> (CP 248)

When we are told that "the moon, for its ivory powders, scours the sea" ("Stings," CP 215), one imagines that this "ravenous" reader of even "the instructions on soap-flake boxes" (JP 208) has associated back to Ivory soap and the Proctor and Gamble logo. For some critics, poetic transformations such as these from the later poems exhibit "the 'concrete attitude' of the schizophrenic for whom the distance between the use of metaphor and the recognition of it *as* metaphor collapses. Words then become an equivalent of experience rather than mediating or reparative symbols" (Schwartz and Bollas 153). Other critics argue, more "positively," that "when she comes to see that reality resides in her own mind, words and poems become as real as anything else"—though one may wonder how, given such a sense of "reality," one "never ceases to know the *difference* between art and life" (Juhasz 102).

Several associations to the name complex *Aurelia* have already been mentioned, but the author who for years composed with the thesaurus open beside her would no doubt have noted cognates of *Aurelia*—*aureole* and *aureate*—and a synonym for the latter, *yellow*.[4] So, in "Candles," the flames' "pale, tentative yellows" lead the speaker to remember her "maternal grandmother," Aurelia (CP 149), and the association figures still more prominently elsewhere. With the discovery of her father's grave, and the name of the "yellow gravel" trail leading to it, Plath coyly addresses Aurelia Plath in the guise of "Electra on Azalea Path" (CP 116–17)—the attempt never quite gels, though, torn between Plath's guilty sense that her desire killed her father (heightened by an accusing dream of her mother's [J 244 and 253]) and her desire to lay that responsibility on her mother. On the other hand, recurring fears of losing her mother (e.g., J 253) help determine the weird image of "absence" as "an Australia gum tree—/ Balding, gelded" ("For a Fatherless Son," CP 205). To see *Aurelia* in *Australia* would hardly tax Plath's "crazy eye for anagrams" (J 176).

The father's name, Otto, lurks in Plath's repeated images of getting to the b*otto*m, as well as in the first line of "Daddy," which struggles, almost babylike, to articulate his name: "Y oudo n otdo, y oudo n otdo" (line respaced). Other critics have noted the pertinence for Plath of the German *platt* and French *plate*, both of which mean "flat" (Kroll 35, Lavers 218). One can see her constructing onomastic puns as she writes to her friend Gordon Lameyer shortly before her initial suicide attempt: "God on le mer. Or filial reward for the mother: e.g. Guerdon la mère" (Stevenson 45). *The Bell Jar* offers some outrageous puns, as when Esther reports Constantin's asking if she "would like to come up to his apartment to hear some balalaika records," and her response that she was "very fond of balalaika music" (65). This joke turns out to be on Esther, since Constantin does not like to ball at all. Another oblique sexual pun might gloss the phrase "masturbating a glitter" ("Death & Co.," *CP* 254), which one reader finds "perhaps the most perplexing . . . in all Sylvia Plath's poetry" (Holbrook 168). A poet who wants "to shoot off in all directions myself, like the colored arrows from a Fourth of July rocket" (*BJ* 68) would delight, one might suppose, in manipulating the sound/image of a "glittering clitoris." Puns offer one way for the expressing and coordinating of ambivalence, which is the lifelong task of the split subject convinced that "Either way we choose, the angry witch / will punish us for saying which is which" ("Metamorphoses of the Moon" ["Juvenilia"], *CP* 308). Where "concrete" declarations are feared, language itself can be sought as an absolute—as though if one could master language one might finally formulate the unspeakable and deliver oneself in answerable style of the burden of deep inner conflict. But the conflict, not having been encoded in or by language (however much it may lie in the difference between language and felt perception) cannot for all the puns and leaps of metaphor be answered by or in that activity which is its own displacement. What is needed are not more "words dry and riderless"—and the creation of yet another "psychic landscape poem" (Bassnett 61)—but some way of telling *how* "from the bottom of the pool, fixed stars / Govern a life" ("Words," *CP* 270).

One further aspect of Plath's relation to language concerns her involvement with letters themselves. Approaching her breakdown, Esther looks at a printed page and finds that "the letters grew barbs and rams' horns. I watched them separate, each from the other, and jiggle up and down in a silly way. Then they associated themselves in fantastic, untranslatable shapes, like Arabic or Chinese" (*BJ* 102). The letter *o* in particular obsesses Plath (one of her links to Keats). It is "the dead syllable" ("Widow," *CP* 164), "O so much emptiness" ("Three Women," *CP* 181), the "O moon of illusion" ("Moonsong at Morning," *CP* 316), the "O embryo" ("Nick and the Candlestick," *CP* 241), the o-pen "O-mouth" ("The Rival," *CP* 166; "Three Women," *CP* 182), and the "opus" ("Lady Lazarus," *CP* 246). O marks the figure of one who could feel "I was nothing . . . a zero" (Steiner 44); indeed, the well-known conclusion to "Ariel" shows I as an arrow driving into its target, "the red / Eye [O], the cauldron [O] of morning" (*CP* 240). This image is not far from Plath's fictionalized little girl who, explaining how she punishes her doll, says, "I bang her eyes in" (*JP* 142). The wish to see I enter O can be related to the curious presence of carbon monoxide in some later poems ("The Rival," *CP* 166; "A Birthday Present," *CP* 207; "Poppies in October," *CP* 240). In her at last unbridled drive to recover a zero-degree state of difference/split/separation ("There is nothing between us" ["Medusa," *CP* 226]), even the puns fuse—"Coal gas is ghastly stuff" ("The Tour," *CP* 238)—and we see O enter I in CO as a way, the way Plath chose, to death ("Sweetly, sweetly I breathe in, / Filling my veins with invisibles . . ." ["A Birthday Present," *CP* 207]).

As with Keats, the moon (another O) hangs over Plath's poetry and, as for Keats, seems bound up with unconscious phantasies concerning the mother and the maternal breast. "The moon is my mother," announces "The Moon and the Yew Tree": "She is bald and wild" (*CP* 173). More evocatively, in "Barren Woman" "The moon lays a hand on my forehead, / Blank-faced and mum as a nurse"—a description which recalls the curious note in *Letters Home* where Plath's "Mum" (as she is often addressed) relates, in indecipherable tones, how her daughter and son-in-law drove up five days ahead of a scheduled visit: "After a few minutes' conversation, however, I realized this early arrival had a purpose behind it other than just our mutual pleasure. I placed my hand on Sylvia's forehead in the old maternal gesture; it was burning hot" (333). The relative rarity of the "day-moon" makes it apt for comparison to "a sorry mother" ("Sleep in the Mojave Desert," *CP* 144) and contrasts to the more typical "moon . . . a stone madonna" ("The Net-Menders," *CP* 121). The association of moon and breast appears already in Plath's "Juvenilia" with "nippled moons" and "milk of moon" ("*Danse macabre*," *CP* 321) or ". . . lunar globes / of bulbous jellyfish / [which] glow milkgreen" ("Aquatic Nocturne," *CP* 306). The "mother's dug. / The dry volcanoes" already cited doubles the environment of "the moon's man" "chattering among the leprous / Peaks and craters of those extinct volcanoes" ("The Everlasting Monday," *CP* 62). This latter poem testifies to Plath's dislike of Mondays (11 February 1962 was a Monday) and has as epigraph, "Thou shalt have an everlasting / Monday and stand in the moon." In a letter to her Mum, Plath expresses the wish that "all the destructive people could be sent to the moon" (*LH* 438).

As in Keats, the breast/moon is the eye of the "blank moon-mother's face that stares from Sylvia Plath's poems" (Holbrook 141). The "moon's ball"

("The Everlasting Monday," CP 62) becomes "the bald moon" ("Candles," CP 149), a type of the "small bald eye" ("Love Letter," CP 147) or "bald, white tumuli" of eyes ("The Colossus," CP 129) writ still larger in the breastlike "bald hill" and its "crest of grass" ("Parliament Hill Fields," CP 152).[5] Eyes which are "lidded / And balled" ("Death & Co.," CP 254) offer less danger than

> pupils
> whose moons of black
> transform to cripples
> all who look.
> ("On Looking into the Eyes of a Demon Lover," CP 325)[6]

Images of being "impaled upon a stern angelic stare" ("The Trial of Man," CP 312), or of being able to "kill with my mind, my ice-eye" (J 193) or of eye-beam war—"She glared at me and I gave her a mad wild still stony glare that snuffed hers out" (J 215)—suggest Plath's familiarity with the "evil eye" that builds on the infant's lack of felt loving reflection or "mirroring" from the mother's eyes (those other nipples at which it feeds). So Esther, with a similar past, longs for someone who could "see through" to what she really is (BJ 60) but paints a sad picture of yet another failed mirroring as she watches her sleeping new acquaintance wake: "His eyelids lifted and he looked through me and his eyes were full of love. I watched dumbly as a shutter of recognition clicked across the blur of tenderness and the wide pupils went glossy and depthless as patent leather" (BJ 69). The eyes Plath sees more frequently, however, are "like transparent agate marbles" (BJ 4), "solid quartz" (JP 159), or "pebbles" (BJ 177—these last providing a link back to nipples in the form of "stony mouth-plugs" ["Medusa," CP 224]). Hence, aggressive phantasies about the mother can center on the unnourishing eye-nipples and produce the "image of mother dead with the Eye Bank having cut her eyes out. Not a dream, but a vision" (J 285). But she, not her mother, dies, and in what may be her ultimate poetic effort she imagines that even faced with her dead body, the moon (the "bony mother" ["Moonrise," CP 98])

> . . . has nothing to be sad about,
> Staring from her hood of bone

> She is used to this sort of thing.
> Her blacks crackle and drag.
> ("Edge," CP 273)

The need for nurture suggested by Plath's concern with breasts and eyes also figures in her recurrent mouth images. In positive manifestations a happy oral fusion can be recalled: "I fanned the hot milk out on my tongue as it went down, tasting it luxuriously, the way a baby tastes its mother" (*BJ* 164). But the suggestions of a "bad feed" are more likely, as after Esther has hurtled herself down a ski slope toward "the pebble at the bottom of the well, the white sweet baby cradled in its mother's belly" only to crash: "My teeth crunched a gravelly mouthful. Ice water seeped down my throat" (*BJ* 79). In "Among the Bumblebees" little Alice's jealousy at seeing Warren, whom she has kicked, comforted in her mother's arms, makes "the lump of pudding stop in the back of her throat as she was about to swallow, and she almost gagged" (*JP* 307). Much later, feeling betrayed by her husband, Plath writes, "Love has been an inexhaustible spring for my nourishment and now I gag" (*J* 212). The "fury [that] jams the gullet and spreads poison" (*J* 232) continues the rage of jealousy that begins with the awareness of deprivation, as in "Berck-Plage" where "a green pool opens its eye, / Sick with what it has swallowed" directly after images of "breasts and hips . . . titillating the light" (*CP* 197). Ambivalence about ingestion leads to conflicting claims about being "all mouth" ("Poem for a Birthday," *CP* 131) or being without one:

> The mouth first, its absence reported
> In the second year. It had been insatiable
> And in punishment was hung out like brown fruit
> To wrinkle and dry.

This poem, "The Detective" (*CP* 209), proceeds directly from brown fruit-like mouth to breasts; in *The Bell Jar*, on the other hand, Doreen's breasts are "like full brown melons" (*BJ* 14), though the closest Esther gets to mouthing them is to suck at her own salty knuckles while saying "I want Doreen" (*BJ* 89).

Self-destruction offers the radical resolution of oral ambivalence with its dangerous hatred of the mother's body, since by this means the real object, still desired, is preserved. Plath's striking lines in "Poem for a Birthday" in part speak to this idea:

> Mother, you are the one mouth
> I would be a tongue to. Mother of otherness
> Eat me.
> (CP 132)

But the formulation "a tongue," with its associated implications of "a language," offers other possibilities given a young author who finds it sad "only to mouth other poets" and wants "someone to mouth me" (J 30). If *she* could mirror the mother, supplying her with a tongue already known, then perhaps communion would be possible and death a small price. But since "the mother of mouths didn't love me," her only recourse is to "swallow it all" (CP 133). In one of Klein's most remarkable postulates, the infant's phantasied devouring onslaughts against the frustrating breast (the O-mouth versus the areola) give rise in turn to anxious phantasies of persecution by a devouring breast (anxieties that Klein sees as giving rise to the kind of chronic nightmares that Plath evidently suffered). This deep fear of talion punishment for the impulse "to suck dry, bite up, scoop out and rob the mother's body of its good contents" (Klein, "Notes" 183)—"vampiring dry of milk" the udder ("Goatsucker," CP 111)—surfaces in the following strangely mixed image from Plath's journal: "And again the dark eats at me: the fear of being crushed in a huge dark machine, sucked dry by the grinding indifferent millstones of circumstance" (J 119). Images elsewhere of "milling . . . breasts" ("Gigolo," CP 267) and "dry-papped stones" instilled with "milk" ("Point Shirley," CP 111) point to some phantasy of the indifferent, milkstone breasts of "the Dark Mother. The Mummy" (J 288), ma-maw, which might grind the poet to fragments. "The mother of pestles diminished me. / I became a still pebble" ("Poem for a Birthday" ["7. The Stones"], CP 136; see Kroll 241 for a possible prompt from African folklore).

The phantasies noted all lead to and then manifest a concern with inner contents or objects. The inner dynamic would develop as follows: If I feel bad then it must be that I have been fed poison and must vomit it out to save myself. If I feel conflicting emotions then perhaps there are several of me, or I am disintegrating into fragments—in any event I do not know what (or who) is inside, and perhaps must not if my "I" is to endure. In the space of six weeks in early 1953, Plath's fascination with inner contents ranges from food:

> the good corn-thickened soup and tuna salad, lush with mayonnaise and pink succulent laced shreds of meat, and sliced quarters of hard-boiled egg, slick rubbery white crescents cradling the brilliant yellow powdery yolk, cool long gulps of milk, the savory brown resilience of gingerbread—and tonight the warm glutinous cheese-curded macaroni, green lima beans mealy and good on the tongue, and a sweet syrupy mash of peach slices . . . (J 68)

to the "illicit sensuous delight" she gets from picking her nose:

> I always have, ever since I was a child. There are so many subtle variations of sensation. A delicate, pointed-nailed fifth finger can catch under dry scabs and flakes of mucous in the nostril and draw them out to be looked at, crumbled between fingers, and flicked to the floor in minute crusts. Or a heavier, determined forefinger can reach up and smear down-and-out the soft, resilient, elastic greenish-yellow smallish blobs of mucous, roll them round and jellylike between thumb and forefinger, and spread them on the undersurface of a desk or chair where they will harden into organic crusts. How many desks and chairs have I thus secretively befouled since childhood? Or sometimes there will be blood mingled with the mucous: in dry brown scabs, or bright sudden wet red on the finger that scraped too rudely the nasal membranes. God, what a sexual satisfaction! (J 64–65)

to the puzzle of excrement:

> Remember how you used to lock the bathroom door (they told you not to because it might stick, and then the firemen would have to come in the window and get you) and squat in fascinated discovery over the hand mirror on the floor and defecate? (J 66)

In connection with this last, one recalls that Esther, according to her mother, had been "perfectly trained at a very early age and [had] given her [mother] no trouble whatsoever" (BJ 166); the self-control reflected in the early formulation of her "old wish to get reward for elimination" (J 293) and "old need of giving Mother accomplishments, getting reward of love"

(*J* 252) breaks down behind locked doors under the greater need for a more physical mirroring. "Nowhere does one find an indication that Sylvia Plath was loved for herself," comments Steven Axelrod (92).

Plath's anxieties over inner contents surface in her many images of food "turning to poison" (*J* 186) and, more pathetically, images of what she terms in the journal "that old corruption I always feared would break out from behind the bubbles of my eyes" (*J* 91—this closely echoes "Tongues of Stone," written a year earlier [see *LH* 155], which describes "poisons . . . gathering in her body, ready to break out behind the bright, false bubbles of her eyes at any moment crying: Idiot! Imposter!" [*JP* 264]). In her psycho-anatomy the mouth opens on "a large darkness," "the blind cave behind the face" where "the dybbuk" hides (*BJ* 82): "I feel behind my eyes a numb, paralyzed cavern, a pit of hell, a mimicking nothingness" (*J* 55). This "gaping void in her own head" (*JP* 208) can be viewed as "merely" hollow while the ego is strong enough to maintain a force-field of repression around negative contents, but whenever that strength or cohesiveness falters (as it does repeatedly), they spew forth as a "great poisonous store of corrosive ashes" (*J* 58), a "dark pestilence" (*J* 55), the "poison" of fury (*J* 232), a mass of "bewildered, chaotic fragments" (*J* 58). The self's pressing concern, then, is how to "keep from flying to fragments—disintegrating, in one wild dispersal" (*J* 233), but "where is the integrating force going to come from?" (*J* 55). One tack, evidently, is to project or displace the fragmenting attack onto others. So, confronting a girl who was stealing rhododendron branches for a school dance, Plath reports how she "stared that sassy girl down, and [had] a blood-longing to [rush] at her and tear her to bloody beating bits" (*J* 216).

Less than a year earlier, however, Plath had denominated herself as the "fresh, brazen stubborn girl Sassy" in her story about "dynamite under high tension" struggling with a dominating mother ("Trouble-making Mother"; *J* 151–52). In a dream on Halloween night 1959, Plath returns to her childhood home and encounters two juvenile delinquents throwing out "our saucepan of milk" (left for witches? [cf. *J* 254]): "In a fury, I flew at one and actually started tearing him apart with my teeth and hands. The other had said he was going into the house, and I thought he would ruin it and hurt Mother" (*J* 295). This image, and several others of biting (*JP* 143, 186; *J* 102, 301), point to repercussions from some childhood incident(s) of her biting someone (Warren?), and back still further to phantasied oral attacks on the breast. The nexus of anger and fragmentation achieves remarkable expression in *The Bell Jar,* as Esther overthrows a "tray of thermometers" to secure her cure in "a ball of mercury": "I opened my fingers a crack, like a child with a secret, and smiled at the silver globe cupped in my palm. If I dropped it, it would break into a million little replicas of itself, and if I pushed them near each other, they would fuse, without a crack, into one whole again" (*BJ* 150). Both striving for perfection and writing represent ways of defending against and disproving disintegration.

Plath's attempt to be perfect fills her biographies and reaches from an entry in her diary made when she had just turned seventeen, which laments, "Never, never, never will I reach the perfection I long for with all my soul—my paintings, my poems, my stories—all poor, poor reflections" (*LH* 40), to the last of the collected poems, which mocks the effort and the etymology with its opening, "The woman is perfected. / . . . dead" ("Edge," *CP* 272).[7] Writing offered a means for attempting to perfect herself; by it she would be "a small god" able to "re-create the flux and smash of the world through the small ordered word patterns" she made (*J* 119). More dramatically, she writes: "I cannot live for life itself: but for the words which stay the flux. My life, I feel, will not be lived until there are books and stories which relive it perpetually in time" (*J* 150). In addition to giving her object permanence in the form of her own self-image, "*Writing breaks open the vaults of the dead*" (*J* 150), and so gives access (like the "secret passages" in *Rasselas*) to "some secret part of her, that long, blind, doorless and windowless corridor" (*BJ* 53) of the unconscious. When Plath decides that "writing is a religious act . . . an ordering, a reforming, a relearning and reloving of people and the world as they are and as they might be" (*J* 246), one hopes to have come upon some expression of truly reparative potential in her endeavor; but nine months on, the issue is still defense: "My sickness is when words draw in their horns and the physical world refuses to be ordered, recreated, arranged and selected. I am a victim of it then, not a master" (*J* 291). Writing, then, is in part a way to mastery and self-presence, as in the signature formula offered by the seventeen-year-old self-described "girl who wanted to be God": "I am I—I am powerful—but to what extent? I am I" (*LH* 40). But this repeated formula, with its theological grandiosity (cf. *JP* 155, "messages from the great I Am") itself stumbles on its shifting reference, as when the author writes, "*Who am I angry at? Myself.*

No, not yourself. Who is it?" (*J* 247). Her writing cannot bridge the gap it records between her "good," "essential" self and the "demon of negation," the "black cloud which would annihilate my whole being with its demand for perfection and measure, not of what I am, but of what I am not" (*J* 160, 161, 162). "I am what I am," she concludes, unable to imagine how she is what she (thinks she) is not and so see what she (thinks she) grasps concerning her mother, how "her conscious mind always split off, at war with her unconscious" (*J* 202).

Plath can be astute at realizing her duality in other people; regarding her boyfriend model for Buddy Willard in *The Bell Jar*, she writes in a 1952 journal entry, "Is there not a sort of duality, then, in him—a desire, born of childhood, to be 'mothered,' to be a child, suckling at the breast (a transfer of eroticism from mother to girlfriend)—and yet to *escape* the subtle feminine snare and be free of the insidious female domination he has sensed in his home all these years?" (*J* 40). Four years on, she is still telling her mother, "I feel like being 'babied,'" and longing for someone to "tell me they love me" (*LH* 217). Only several years and some psychotherapy later does she characterize her own childhood household as a "smarmy matriarchy" and ask, "What do I expect or want from Mother? Hugging, mother's milk? But that is impossible to all of us now. Why should I want it still?" (*J* 242, 260). The psychodynamic thesis, of course, is that she wants "it" because she lacks "it," having been deprived at very early developmental stages of the nurture and mirroring suitable to her particular psychic endowment (one of the reasons Esther loves Dr. Nolan is that she "hugged me like a mother" [*BJ* 173]); in the timelessness of the unconscious, that "lack of mother love" ("Stillborn," *CP* 142) is always, "still," and ongoing, and in Plath's case was perhaps retroactively intensified with her father's death. Evidence of what Plath feels she lacks comes with the mother's first appearance in the published *Journals:* "She was in my room [their shared sleeping room] when I came home, fussing with clothes, and she didn't even sense that something had happened [a kissing incident]. She just kept scolding and chattering on and on" (*J* 5). Lack of attention emerges in a different guise a few months later in a letter appropriately addressed "Dear Mum": "I had a strange experience in history today. As I always sit in the middle seat in the front row, it seems as if Mrs. Kafka [Koffka] is talking directly to me. I felt the oddest thrill" (*LH* 60). Eleven days later she describes to her mother "a friend" who thinks of suicide but whose mother "kept telling her she was foolish and could do it all." "Oh well," she signs off, with an irony that seems to have escaped Aurelia Plath, "maybe it's none of my business, but I love the girl and feel very inadequate and responsible. If you were her mother, she would be all right" (LH 64).

During the months leading up to Plath's August 1953 suicide attempt, which became the central incident in *The Bell Jar*, the author's rage toward her mother had begun to surface in "visions of yourself . . . murdering your mother in actuality" (J 79). A story written two years afterward describes how "the girl had lain awake listening to the thin thread of her mother's breathing, wanting to get up and twist the life out of the fragile throat, to end at once the process of slow disintegration" (JP 265; cf. BJ 101). But instead of murder, the girl crawls "into bed with her mother" only to experience "with growing terror the weakness of the sleeping form" and creep back to her own bed (JP 265). In light of these accounts, Plath's passionate cry that summer, "Oh, Mother, the world is so rotten! I want to die! *Let's die together!*" (LH 124) is a barely restrained attack. "Slow disintegration" of ego-syntonicity and "weakness" of the good object lead to the welling up of "uncontrollable dangerous hatred" from which the subject "by his suicide is in part struggling to preserve his real objects" (Klein, "Contribution" 132).

It seems clear that Plath expected her first suicide attempt to succeed, and it seems just as evident that nothing changed when her relationship with her mother was unexpectedly resurrected: "We'll take up where we left off," Esther's mother tells her; "We'll act as if all this were a bad dream" (BJ 193). To fulfill her mother's good dream, Plath was driven to present a false self, and the language of some of her early letters home from England, where she had time and distance for her idealizing phantasy to flourish, makes for painful reading. In January of 1956 she gushes, "Oh, Mummy, I am so happy that you are coming, there are tears in my eyes!" (LH 206); two months later, her Fulbright grant having been renewed, she begins, "Dearest darling beautiful saintly Mother!!! Hold on to your hat and brace yourself for a whistling hurricane of happiness" (LH 227); and a week later, effusing over Aurelia's upcoming visit, "I want a rosy, fat mummy to meet me in June!" (LH 231). Reading Plath's journal for these months, however, we see a completely different young woman in the overlapping process of disposing of one "eternal" love and installing another. As her relationship with Ted Hughes deepens, she writes her mother at the end of April, "radiance and love just surge out of me like a sun. I can't wait to set you down in its rays. Think, I shall devote two whole weeks of my life to taking utter care and very special tendering of you" (*LH* 243). The upshot, in perfectly overdetermined fashion, was that Plath took the occasion of her mother's arrival to marry Hughes (with Mrs. Plath as the only family present), at once deftly shifting the focus to herself, obviating her previously offered solicitude ("Think . . ."), and upstaging her brother's recent graduation (the son's rays).

A second psychotherapy, in 1958–59, with Dr. Ruth Beutscher (Dr. Nolan in *The Bell Jar*), who had greatly helped her after the suicide attempt, seems to have put Plath in much closer touch with feelings of rage against her mother. But in giving Plath the "permission to hate [her] mother" which was so enthusiastically received (*J* 242, 250), Dr. Beutscher released a djin which circumstance did not permit to be transferred and worked through in the "holding environment" of the therapeutic situation.[8] Dr. Beutscher became the good object and Aurelia Plath the bad, a simplification that must have considerably complicated Plath's ongoing internal object world. She was, however, now free to articulate her negative feelings and the preverbal contradictions of her psyche. In one entry she writes that she feels "only the Idea of Love" from her mother and that "I felt cheated: I wasn't loved, but all the signs said I was loved: the world said I was loved: the powers-that-were said I was loved" (*J* 244). She realizes that in her "satisfactory" letter-relationship carried on from England, "we could both verbalize our desired image of ourselves in relation to each other: interest and sincere love, and never feel the emotional currents at war with these verbally expressed feelings. I feel her disapproval. But I feel it countries away too" (*J* 255). So, "The Rival" complains, "No day is safe from news of you, / Walking about in Africa maybe, but thinking of me" (*CP* 167). As she moved toward and into her first pregnancy, the repressed returned in the new form of "magical fear Mother will become a child, my child: an old hag child" (*J* 260). She dreams of "my mother furious at my pregnancy" (*J* 289), and shortly after, of "my mother having a little son: my confusion: this son of mine is a twin to her son" (*J* 294). Frieda—not the expected son—was born four months after Plath and Hughes returned to England in late 1959. With the subsequent birth of her son in early 1962, Plath now mirrored her own sibling environment and increased the possibilities for role confusion. "I have the queerest feeling of having been reborn with Frieda," she writes her mother after the birth of Nicholas. "I suppose it's a case of knowing what one wants. I never really knew before"; and then, for the seeming fruit of that knowledge: "I hope I shall always be a 'young' mother like you" (*LH* 450). In Plath's dream life, however, her mother appears "snoopy" and "old" (*J* 301), like the "bastardly nanny," "snoopy old bitch" whom Plath "can't wait to get rid of" (*LH* 471, 472). Even as she struggles with this last incident, she complains to Warren that their mother "identifies much too much with me" (*LH* 472) and even writes her directly, ten weeks before the suicide, "Why do you identify so with me?" (unpublished; quoted Bundtzen 88).[9]

Plath's journal as published by Hughes (and only in America) essentially ends in late 1959, so consideration of her ongoing struggle with her Aurelia's imago must turn to her poetry and "fiction" (Plath's quotation marks), that "naked reflection of what I felt, as a child and later, must be true" (*J* 290). Readers have long recognized that *The Bell Jar*, written largely during 1961 but incorporating material from her journal and "fiction" of at least the preceding six years, is preoccupied with the protagonist's "hatred of her mother" (Holbrook 31) and "the indefinable hostility surrounding the mother's character" (Berman, *Cure* 145)—that there is hardly any "portrait of a parent in modern fiction so damaging as this one" (Brink 220). The novel figure of Joan Gilling, however, who appears suddenly to occupy the final fifth of the text, has struck many as a thematic and structural oddity, not least for her sudden suicide, which forms the story's climax and appears, amidst the rampant autobiographical reference, "the only purely imagined event in the book" (Butscher 342).

The name Joan, first of all, is significant in Plath's private iconography, dating at least from March 1954 when she saw a silent French version of the "Temptation of Saint Joan." The film made a profound impression, which she describes in detail to her mother (*LH* 135), and over four years later Plath notes in her journal how "nightmares haunt me: Joan of Arc's face as she feels the fire and the world blurs out in a smoke, a pall of horror" (*J* 206). "Gilling" perhaps was appropriated from the "very intuitive" director of an amateur production of *Bartholomew Fair* who cast Plath as "a screaming whore in a yellow dress. A mad poet. How clever of Dick Gilling" (*J* 93).

Joan is evidently a complex, composite double for Esther, who describes her as "the beaming double of my old best self, specially designed to follow and torment me" (*BJ* 167) and later builds on a paraphrase of Isaiah (55:8) to say, "Her thoughts were not my thoughts, nor her feelings my feelings, but we were close enough so that her thoughts and feelings seemed a wry, black image of my own" (179). So, Esther continues, "sometimes I wondered if I had made Joan up. Other times I wondered if she would continue to pop in at every crisis of my life to remind me of what I had been" (179). But then again, she thinks, "in spite of my profound reservations, I thought I would always treasure Joan. It was as if we had been forced together by some overwhelming circumstance, like war or plague, and shared a world of our own" (184). These ambivalent descriptions, together with the obsessive emphasis on Joan's "starey," nipplelike "pebble eyes" (48, 164, 177, 179, 189), suggest that with the "character" we verge upon almost unmediated permutations of the ma-imago. Anxious over her regained equilibrium, Esther imagines her rival's intention to "suck up by mere nearness" the "sweetness of recovery" (177).

The progression of scenes that unfold around Joan point to homosexual attraction as the idea against which the narrator needs most to defend herself. She recalls coming upon Joan and the older DeeDee in bed, and one suspects that the author sent her into that room seeking "two-part sheet music" (cf. the earlier "balalaika music") for the sake of the further double entendre in Joan's saying, "Wait for me, Esther, I'll come play the bottom part with you" (179). The incident leads Esther to ask good-mother Dr. Nolan about lesbianism and to the disturbing response that "tenderness" might be what a woman can see in another woman that she can not see in a man (179; cf. *J* 263). That single word "shuts up" Esther because it is, in fact, the master term for what she herself most wants (Holbrook notes Plath's "continual images of yearning for tender care" [296]). Esther then jumps to the memory of a "minor scandal" at her college dormitory involving a grandmotherly, "matronly-breasted senior" and a gawky freshman who had once been discovered "embracing." Under questioning, the reported "embrace" is found to have consisted in "Theodora . . . lying on the bed, and Milly . . . stroking Theodora's hair" (180). Long before, when Constantin happened to stroke her hair, Esther detailed the considerable infantile charge bound up in such contact: "A little electric shock flared through me and I sat quite still. Ever since I was small I loved feeling somebody comb my hair. It made me go all sleepy and peaceful" (70). In "The Moon and the Yew Tree," written shortly after Plath had finished her novel (cf. J 248), the speaker invokes the Holy Mother and sighs,

> How I would like to believe in tenderness—
> The face of the effigy, gentled by candles,
> Bending, on me in particular, its mild eyes.
> (CP 173)

But no sooner does Esther posit the attractive possibility of motherly-daughterly tenderness than she recoils again to her memory of a lesbian couple at college, a famous poet and an old classical scholar, and the poet's staring condemnation at hearing of Esther's wish to have children. On that slender basis Esther reflects: "Why did I attract these weird old women? There was the famous poet, and Philomena Guinea, and Jay Cee, and the Christian Scientist lady and lord knows who, and they all wanted to adopt me in some way, and, for the price of their care and influence, have me resemble them" (180). All these figures can be identified, with the exception of "lord knows who"—though Plath probably knew her as the mother of whom she writes, "I think I have always felt she uses me as an extension of herself" (J 255). The entire sequence with Joan is punctuated and concluded by Joan's telling Esther, "I like you" (179, 180), and bracketed by Esther's violent desire physically to expel the sickening tension which that utterance creates: "That's tough, Joan," she says. "Because I don't like you. You make me puke, if you want to know" (180; cf. 179). In a one-sentence coda, Esther exits the scene, "leaving Joan lying, lumpy as an old horse" across Esther's own bed. Horsiness, one might note, is, along with her pebbly eyes, emphatically associated with Joan. A clue to its import can be found in a letter of 5 May 1953, apparently first reported by Lynda Bundtzen, in which Plath "imagines a life with her 'twin' Aurelia, both of them as creative writers: 'I am elated by the way you are to be a ghost-writer. *Dobbin nothing!* You have a gift in your own line, and between the two of us we should make a lovely life. I owe all I am to you anyway, for you have made all possible'" (Bundtzen 76; italics added—Plath is evidently responding to some horsy self-characterization by her mother).

Esther's involvement with Joan culminates with the author's killing Gilling in the melodrama of Joan's surprise suicide. In terms of the psycho-logic of the narrative, Joan is responding to the return on her repeated "I like you" advances, which is that Esther goes out and loses her virginity to a Warren-like projection, hemorrhages from the encounter (as did Plath, cf. *J* 248), then uses Joan for help without at all confiding the truth of her experience. Instead, she fobs off on Joan the notion of some problem concerning her period. The account here does not match the biographical record, reported by her roommate at that time, Nancy Steiner, but does suit Plath's experience of a mother who "could never accept Sylvia's sexual involvements" (Wagner-Martin 123). The narrative then capitalizes on Esther's surname, taken from the senior Aurelia's maiden name, as Joan's psychiatrist—a woman with "an abstract quality that appealed to Joan" (183)—drops by in the hope that "Miss Greenwood" "might have an idea" concerning Joan's whereabouts (191). Esther now wants "to dissociate [herself] from Joan completely" and seems unmoved by the report that Joan "was alone." But later, as she tries to sleep, "Joan's face floated before me, bodiless and smiling, like the face of the Cheshire cat. I even thought I heard her voice" (192). The import of this vision becomes clear on the next page—after news of Joan's having hanged herself and a chapter break—as Esther reports another vision: "My mother's face floated to mind, a pale, reproachful moon," and recalls "her sweet, martyr's smile" (193). The double image of the martyred "mother/Joan" echoes "Johnny Panic and the Bible of Dreams"—Plath's earlier breakthrough story—and its narrator's discovery that

> whatever the dream I unearth, by work, taxing work, and even by a kind of prayer, I am sure to find a thumbprint in the corner, a malicious detail to the right of center, a bodiless midair Cheshire cat grin, which shows the whole work to be gotten up by the genius of Johnny Panic, and him alone. He's sly, he's subtle, he's sudden as thunder, but he gives himself away only too often. He simply can't resist melodrama. Melodrama of the oldest, most obvious variety. (*JP* 156–57)

In the novel's penultimate scene, Esther attends Joan's funeral; where, before, she "wondered" if she had made Joan up, now she says, oddly, "I wondered what I thought I was burying" (198). Joan's coffin, like Plath's text, is "the black shadow of something that wasn't there" (198). But Plath's anger and phantasized killing of her mother are all too present, and Aurelia Plath's description of the book as representing "the basest ingratitude" of a "raging adolescent voice" (see Ames 215 and Rose 75) was surely anticipated by the author. Among the overdeterminations for Plath's suicide, it seems that once again she came too close to actually attacking her mother and had, again, to introject her anger. The novel was published pseudonymously on 14 January 1963, and two days later Plath wrote her mother—to whom she had divulged little about the book—that if only she could "have some windfall, like doing a really successful novel," then she "could almost be self-supporting" (*LH* 495). But by the first week of February it was clear that the novel, though respectfully noted, was not to elicit the impossible complete and total public affirmation that would force the mother to acquiesce to a now psychically emancipated daughter's vision. And without that self-won support, there would be again, as at the end of the "Johnny Panic" story, the mother figure saying, "I'll have that little black book" while her "own baby," the transcriber, protested futilely "against her whopping milkless breasts" and her castigating "Naughty naughty" (*JP* 165, 166).

Notes

1   Lexis Complexes and Intentions in Tension

1. The perennial fantasy of legislating language to make perception a proprietary right achieved memorable expression in the (unsuccessful) suit brought by Mead Data Central, holder of the registered trademark Lexis,® against the Toyota Motor Corporation over the latter's use of the name Lexus for a new automobile (*Mead Data Cent., Inc., v. Toyota Motor Sales*, 875 F2d 1026 [2d Cir 1989]).
2. A possibility abetted, perhaps, by the familiar 7-Up advertising slogan "You like it [Ike], it [Ike] likes you."
3. In *Philosophical Investigations* Ludwig Wittgenstein writes: "Suppose someone said: every familiar word, in a book for example, actually carries an atmosphere with it in our minds, a 'corona' of lightly indicated uses. Just as if each figure in a painting were surrounded by delicate shadowy drawings of scenes, as it were in another dimension, and in them we saw the figures in different contexts.—Only let us take this assumption seriously!—Then we see that it is not adequate to explain *intention*" (181e). And he adds later, "Now, I say nothing about the causes of this phenomenon. They *might* be associations from my childhood" (216e).
4. Discussing psychoanalytic interventions, Roy Schafer writes: "One cannot distinguish sharply what the analyst finds and what the analyst introduces as a narrative organization; no absolute distinction between analytic subject and object is tenable; all perception is interpretation in context" (184). And Wordsworth, in the memorable formulation of "Tintern Abbey," describes "all the mighty world / Of eye and ear, both what they half-create, / And what perceive."
5. Cf. OED, s.v., which cites Charles Kingsley, 1853, on Keats's "mighty yearn after . . . beauty."
6. Compare the (self-)recognition scene of Browning's quester in "Childe Roland to the Dark Tower Came" (172–76):

> When, in the very nick
> Of giving up, one time more, came a click
> As when a trap shuts—you're inside the den!
>
> Burningly it came on me all at once,
> This was the place!

7   Cf. Stanley Fish's disarming admission that "in the analysis of [the] lines from *Lycidas* I did what critics always do. I 'saw' what my interpretive principles permitted or directed me to see, and then I turned around and attributed what I had 'seen' to a text and an intention" (in Ray 162).

2   Before the Milk of the Word: Nipple-Eyes

1   *The Rime of the Ancient Mariner* is of course *Christabel*'s companion, as would have been made clear if the second edition of *Lyrical Ballads* had been produced as initially planned. Though not immediately germane to the present discussion, the poem does seem to envision breast ice, if not eyes. Consider first the following notebook entry of December 1803 (no. 1718), in which Coleridge records his interest in the experience of what to his editor, Kathleen Coburn, suggests Isakower phenomena:

> When in a state of pleasurable & balmy Quietness I feel my Cheek and Temple on the nicely made up Pillow in Caelibe Toro meo [my celibate couch] . . . O then as I first sink on the pillow, as if Sleep had indeed a material *realm*, as if when I sank on my pillow, I was entering that region & realized Faery Land of Sleep—O then what visions have I had, what dreams—the Bark, the Sea, t̶h̶e̶ all the shapes & sounds & adventures made up of the Stuff of Sleep & Dreams, & yet my Reason at the Rudder / O what visions, μαστοι [Gk. *mastoi*, "breasts"] as if my Cheek & Temple were lying on me gale o' mast on [i.e., μεγαλόμαστον, "large-breasted"]—Seele meines Lebens! [Soul of my Life!]—& I sink down the waters, thro' Seas & Seas—yet warm, yet a Spirit— /
> ⟨οι⟩
> Pillow==mast high

As Coburn notes with regard to the pun on "mast high" and "*mastoi*," in Coleridge's "Devonshire dialect the difference between the dipthong of 'high' and '[h]oi' is very slight" (*Notebooks*).

To return to the Ancient Mariner, whose "glittering" and "bright" eyes have a fascinating power similar to that of the Lady's in *Christabel*, one of the first things "STC" has him see (you see) is "i[-]ce, mast-high," which in the "wondrous cold" floats by "as green as emerald" (53–54). Perhaps, like Christabel, the Mariner is caught in a projection of envy on the *mastoi* of the archaic mother (the *mère old* with the "bosom cold," "bosom old" that Christabel saw). The curious plural in a notebook entry of January 1804 (no. 1816)—"Mrs C. is to me all *strange,* & the Terra incognita always lies near to or under the frozen Poles"—seems to denote icy *mastoi.* The ice surrounding the Mariner makes strange sounds, "Like noises in a swound!" (62), a state perhaps analogous to the "dizzy trance" which comes on a Christabel "o'er-mastered" (mastoied?) because she had "drunken in / That look" of Geraldine's (589, 607; 620; 601–2).

2   Barbara Gelpi reports Shelley's "appalled reaction" to his first wife's refusal to nurse their infant, and comments that "he considered it enormously significant either that his mother nursed him herself, thus establishing him in his subjectivity—the nurse's soul entering the child—or that she, like Harriet, did not, and by this refusal made him all the more obsessed with an *ideal* of the maternal that would literally fulfill him: fill him full" (91). In the course of her study of *Prometheus Unbound* Gelpi quotes two passages in which "the metaphor of breast-feeding, with eyes displacing breasts, is obvious" (260).

3   Restless Wrestling: Johnson's *Rasselas*

1   Compare Johnson's description of an individual's "ruling passion," which "operates upon the whole system of life either openly or more secretly" ("Life of Pope" 520).

2   In "The Vision of Theodore" Johnson says of the chain of Habit that "each link grew tighter as it had been longer worn" (168).

3   Hester (Thrale) Piozzi reports that "when Mr Johnson felt his fancy, or fancied he felt it, disordered, his constant recurrence was to the study of arithmetic; and one day that he was totally confined to his chamber, and I enquired what he had been doing to divert himself, he shewed me a calculation which I could scarce be made to understand, so vast was the plan of it, and so very intricate were the figures: no other indeed than that the national debt, computing it at one hundred and eighty millions sterling, would, if converted into silver, serve to make a meridian of that material, I forget how broad, for the globe of the whole earth, the real *globe*" (87).

4   A coney is a rabbit, but see entries in Henke for "cony," "coney-berry," and "cony-catching," which show how "the bawdy sense of 'cony/cunny' was a commonplace" (60). In the 1741 erotic allegory A *Voyage to Lethe,* "Captain Samuel Cock" lists his father as "*Sampson Cock* of *Coney-Hatch*" (Boucé 81).

5 On "nothing" in Shakespeare, see Pyles; Rubinstein 172–73; and Booth 164; and for other Renaissance drama, Henke 179.
6 Cf. *Rambler* 89 (22 January 1751): "This invisible riot of the mind, this secret prodigality of being, is secure from detection, and fearless of reproach."
7 "To ask this question, for a mind as ardent as Johnson's, is to stand at the brink of an abyss" (McIntosh 190).
8 Cf. Charles Wesley's hymn "Looking to Jesus": "Thee my restless Soul requires; / Restless till / Thou fulfill / All its large Desires" (156).
9 "A quibble is to Shakespeare what luminous vapors are to the traveler; he follows it at all adventures; it is sure to lead him out of his way and sure to engulf him in the mire. It has some malignant power over his mind, and its fascinations are irresistible. Whatever be the dignity or profundity of his disquisition, whether he be enlarging knowledge or exalting affection, whether he be amusing attention with incidents or enchaining it in suspense, let but a quibble spring up before him and he leaves his work unfinished. A quibble is the golden apple for which he will always turn aside from his career to stoop from his elevation. A quibble, poor and barren as it is, gave him such delight that he was content to purchase it by the sacrifice of reason, propriety, and truth. A quibble was to him the fatal Cleopatra for which he lost the world and was content to lose it" ("Preface" 309).

See Einbond, however, on "the large number of Johnson's allegorical metaphors which are also good puns" and "the effect of such puns on the nature of his allegory" (45ff.).
10 Ehrenpreis points to "an anagram of 'Michael,' the name of Johnson's father" in "Imlac," though he is "confident that the author did not realize the fact" (102) and goes on to mock this "presumed insight" (107). The Arabs as "sons of *Ishmael*" (120; italics added) offer more interesting anagrammatic possibilities to conjure with for "Michael," particularly considering their leader, the rambling "Rover" who seizes Pekuah. Gwin J. Kolb finds that the appearance of an "Icon-Imlac" in a 1682 history of Ethopia owned by Johnson "almost certainly provided the name of the poet" (xxviii). Johnson, however, did not shy from even overt personifications, as we see, for instance, in the "Tom Double," "Will Puzzle," and "Ned Smuggle" of *Idler* 92 (19 January 1760).
11 On Easter Sunday 1759, a few months after writing *Rasselas*, Johnson prays, "So sanctify my affliction, O Lord, that I may be converted and healed; and that, by the help of thy holy spirit, I may obtain everlasting life through Jesus Christ our Lord"; and in his last prayer (December 1784), in a formulation suppressed by the first editor, he writes, "Forgive and accept my late conversion" (Wain 202, xi). John Wain comments, "By conversion he meant not a

change from non-belief to belief, but a change of heart, a progression from an unblessed to a blessed state of life" (xi). But Johnson defines conversion as "1. Change from one state into another, transmutation; 2. Change from reprobation to grace, from a bad to a holy life; 3. Change from one religion to another" (*Dictionary*, s.v.). If, with Wain, one plumps for the second sense, what is there to be accepted and forgiven?

12 Johnson's "God," for instance, might offer an example of what Joseph H. Smith, following Lacanian feminist analysis, calls the "imaginary phallus." Smith's discussion of this term seems directly applicable to Johnson: the "imaginary phallus," he writes, is an effort to repress

> the mother of symbiosis, the mother as a figure of death, the yearning for the early, life/death, mother lost. It represses, that is, grief, which then returns as depression or abjection.
>
> It is an effort to repress the original emptiness with which one entered the world. It is an effort to repress desire, or, at least, honest desire—desire that does not deny its origins in the original splitting, emptiness, indigence, and guilt.
>
> But the turning toward the hope of wholeness and life remains driven, empty, and imaginary until or unless one can, in that turning, simultaneously face the fear of lack and death that the rejected mother of symbiosis comes to represent. (1059–60).

13 The extraordinarily lengthy illustration accompanying this definition of *mummy*—a 376-word passage from Hill's *Materia Medica*—suggests some unusual investment by the lexicographer.

4 Mary Godwin's Remonstrance

1 The show enjoyed extended success, and Mary Godwin's journal entry for 28 December 1814 notes, "Go to Garnerin's Lecture of electricity, the gasses, and the phantasmagoria" (*Mary Shelley's Journal* 31). In *The Last Man* she draws upon her knowledge of the spectacle, writing that "futurity, like a dark image in a phantasmagoria, came nearer and more near, till it clasped the whole earth in its shadow" (186).

2 The drowned, gravid body of Shelley's wife, Harriet, was discovered on 10 December 1816; Percy Shelley and Mary Godwin learned of the suicide on the fifteenth and were married two weeks later, on the thirtieth. With the marriage she dropped her patronymic and assumed the name of Mary Wollstonecraft Shelley; *Frankenstein* was at this point well in hand. This discussion uses the name that accords best with the immediate reference.

3 The spelling *phantasy* is used to mark the distinction between the unconscious dynamic that figures largely in object-relations psychoanalytic theory and the more specific mental process of Freudian (and everyday) "fantasy" (see Greenberg and Mitchell 124).

4 Mary Shelley, then in Italy, sent the manuscript of *Mathilda* to her father for help in getting it published; he made no move to do so and refused her requests for its return (xi). Undeterred, she sent him her next novel, *Valperga*, and let him keep its earnings; this effort he did revise, informing her, "I have taken great liberties with it, and am afraid your *amour propre* will be proportionally shocked" (Locke 310).

5 The subvocalization of "Franklin" in "Frankenstein" encourages one to consider the fate of the name in our century, when cinematic treatments associated it with a rather different story. Already in 1921 William Carlos Williams imagined a benign "St. Francis Einstein of the Daffodils" who "has emerged triumphant" (Friedman and Donley 195–98). But with an actual Franz or Frank Einstein in place as the most widely recognized scientist of his time, one wonders whether James Whales's 1931 Universal Studios film *Frankenstein* could have become the classic popular representation of the scientist unleashing uncontrollable energy: the contradiction would have been too blatant, too conscious, and for that reason the competing signifier of the book title would perhaps not have worked for the film. Consciousness pretends to the law of identity and strives to avoid images divided against themselves—when it confronts figure-ground reversals (the duck/rabbit, the goblet/profiles), it usually settles on one and suppresses the other. Unlike consciousness, which cannot long hold two contradictory images, imagination facilitates its identifications by polysemy and paronomasia—hence Albert Einstein, good scientist, and his brother "Frank" as projected alter ego. Hence also the persistent confusion between Frankenstein and his creation, "the monster," who is never named in the story but now, as dictionaries attest, often labeled "Frankenstein." Martin Amis's 1987 title, *Einstein's Monsters*, testifies to the persistence of this particular subvocal theme.

6 Even the monster seems to enact this kind of projection: though full of "revenge and hatred," "rage of anger," and "fury" (*Frankenstein* 134) over the failure of his plan to befriend the De Lacys and thus resolved to burn their cottage, he waits with "forced impatience" and "eyes . . . fixed" in the direction of the descending moon until a "part of its orb was at length hid"; only when "the eye of the quiet moon" (164) has sunk does he, "with a loud scream," fire the home with "flames, which clung to it, and licked it with their forked and destroying tongues" (134–35).

5 Keats, Teats, and the Fane of Poesy

1 Keats's letters are cited from *Letters*, ed. Rollins, by date, followed by volume and page numbers—here 24 September 1819, 2:214.
2 See also Hamilton for the argument "that poetry represented for Keats an attempt to work through the mourning process" (497).
3 As G. M. Hopkins puts it, "The keener the consciousness, the greater the pain" ("Meditation on Hell," in *Sermons* 138). For Brink, Keats's "poetry began in conflict, in doubt about readiness for life. It held in aesthetic abeyance forces of disintegration too unsettling to face directly until poetry itself made it impossible to ignore them" (144).
4 Keats's publisher, John Taylor, interviewed the poet's former guardian and reported that Keats's mother "at an early Age . . . told my Informant, Mr. Abbey, that she must & would have a Husband; and her passions were so ardent, he said, that it was dangerous to be alone with her" (Rollins 1:303–5). In part from this description of Frances Jennings's "unusual importunity," Brink infers an "obsessional will to dominate in relations with men" that in turn masked underlying insecurity (163). The "Fanny-filled" image of woman Keats projected is evident in an early poem that begins: "Woman! when I behold thee flippant, vain, / Inconstant, childish, proud, and full of / fancies."
5 The analyst André Green notes that for Kleinians now *breast* is just another way of denominating *mother* (or primary caretaker). But, he adds, "One must retain the metaphor of the breast, for the breast, like the penis, can only be symbolic. However intense the pleasure of sucking linked to the nipple, or the teat, might be, erogenous pleasure has the power to concentrate within itself everything of the mother that is not the breast: her smell, her skin, her look and the thousand other components that 'make up' the mother. The metonymical object has become metaphor to the object" (148).
6 Though it appears long after Keats, one might note the use of the term *to moon* to describe the prank of displaying the naked posterior or "fanny." As a euphemism for the buttocks, *fanny* seems a twentieth-century Americanism—English, however, has *fan* (from Fr. *fin*) in Shakespeare (see F. Rubinstein, s.v.). Bertram Lewin speculates that buttocks may replace breasts in phantasy since "the real size of the buttocks, say for a child of two, might coincide very well with the virtual size of the retained memory of the breasts" (179).
7 A reading more in harmony with the shape and form of the urn, and its "Cold Pastoral!" associations of past oral satisfactions, than Kenneth Burke's analysis that "body is turd, turd body" (see Burke, *Rhetoric* 728, which leaves no doubt as to this hearing of the urn's dictum, "Beauty is truth, truth beauty").

8   Compare the beginning of the second stanza of "Take those lips away," in Percy's *Reliques of Ancient English Poetry*, where the forsaken lover regrets "those hills of snowe, / Which thy frozen bosom beares" (122).

9   Lewin records a dream that consisted entirely of "a slab of white marble coming toward the dreamer, on which he could see blue veins. Here again the [dream-]screen is hard and inedible, but the blue veins are in all probability additions derived from observations later than the earliest nursing period" (187).

10 As Sylvia Plath also knows in "All the Dead Dears":

> All the long gone darlings: they
> Get back, though, soon,
> Soon: be it by wakes, weddings,
> Childbirths or a family barbecue:
> Any touch, taste, tang's
> Fit for those outlaws to ride home on,
>
> And to sanctuary . . .

11 See also another of Almansi's patients in the article cited in chapter 2, a woman who dreams of a "Mother- or Wife-of-the-Year" figure pinned with "a corsage of two clusters of dark purple grapes. They hang down from the stem in such a way that one cluster hangs from one breast and the second cluster from the other breast. They look as if they were springing from each nipple, ripe and very full." She continues: "My gaze travels upward and I see her eyes. I am amazed to see that they are very large and of the same rich purple color as the grapes" (51–52).

12 As in Isidore of Seville's homophonic "etymology": "Ubera dicta, vel quia lacte uberta, vel quia uvida" ("*Ubera* comes either from '*lacte UBERtA*,' i.e. 'abounding in milk,' or from '*UvidA*' . . . that is full of milk as a grape is full of juice") (Lecercle 193).

6 Tears, Ay, Dull Tears: Tennyson's Idle Idol-Idyl

1   Lines 331–33. Tennyson is cited throughout from Ricks's 2d edition of *The Poems of Tennyson*, 3 vols.; here, 3:276.

2   T.—"But the man I count greater than them all—Wordsworth, Coleridge, Byron, Shelley, every one of 'em—is Keats . . ."
[Aubrey] De V[ere].—"He doesn't pall upon you?"
T.—"No."

>   *De V.*—"Shelley used to be a great idol of yours."
>   *T.*—"O yes."
>   (Allingham 295)

3   In Emily Brontë's *Wuthering Heights* (published the same year as *The Princess*), Nelly Dean says that Hindley "has room in his heart only for two idols—his wife and himself" (60); Anne Brontë condemns "idle egotism" in *The Tenant of Wildfell Hall* (334). Another I-doll, Victor Frankenstein claims to have been his parents' "plaything and . . . idol" (234).

4   Ricks's edition does not mention the exclamation mark as a variant; it appears in William E. Buckler's text in *The Major Victorian Poets: Tennyson, Browning, Arnold* (Boston: Houghton Mifflin, 1973); in Douglas Bush's *Selected Poetry of Tennyson* (New York: Modern Library, 1951); in W. H. Auden's *A Selection from the Poems of Alfred, Lord Tennyson* (Garden City, N.Y.: Doubleday, Doran, 1944), and the many different anthologies and critical editions published by Norton. Leo Spitzer is so taken with the poem's "exclamational pattern" that in his outline of the refrain words he supplies "the exclamation point evidently intended by the poet, but reserved for the last stanza—in which [announces Spitzer] I shall use a double exclamation mark" ("Tears" 196).

5   Cf. Ferdinand de Saussure's comment regarding the anagrams he found dispersed through Latin poetry: "I make no secret of the fact that I myself am perplexed—about the most important point: that is, how one should judge the reality or phantasmagoria of the whole question" (Starobinski 105–6).

7 Under Brontëan Thunder

1   Freud's contemporary Théodor Flournoy coined the term *cryptomnesia* in his book-length study of the medium Helen Smith to discuss how her "romances of subliminal imagination" originated in cryptomnesias from books she had read as a child and later forgotten (see Ellenberger 171 and 317; the book *From India to the Planet Mars: A Study of a Case of Somnambulism* was published in 1899 and translated into English the following year).

2   The young, angry Jane Eyre, too, is described as "a mad cat" (9).

3   Cf. Byron's characterization of England as "a Country in all senses the most dear / To foreigner or native" (*Don Juan* 10.77.5–6).

4   Little wonder Charlotte Brontë was haunted by Mrs. Rigby's review of *Jane Eyre* and the contention that "altogether the auto-biography of Jane Eyre is preeminently an anti-Christian composition. There is throughout it a murmuring against the comforts of the rich and against the privations of the poor, which,

as far as each individual is concerned, is a murmuring against God's appointment—there is a proud and perpetual assertion of the rights of man, for which we find no authority either in God's word or in God's providence—there is that pervading tone of ungodly discontent which is at once the most prominent and the most subtle evil which the law and the pulpit, which all civilized society in fact has at the present day to contend with" (JE, "Backgrounds" 442).

5   Or rather, antiheroine, or perhaps even, to imagine a diminutive of *villain* (and *villein*), *villette* (cf. Joyce's "Stephen Hero")—such a title marking Charlotte Brontë's willing assumption of the sins of "hunger, rebellion and rage" (which Matthew Arnold, for example, saw in *Villette*) projected onto her (the earlier Jane Eyre, rejecting that sacrificial assumption, refers to "my villainy" [53]).

6   That Madame Heger's maiden name was Parent might have furthered such kinship (and *kindisch*) associations.

7   Like Bertha Mason, sealed in the third story, and Charlotte Brontë herself, "buried" alive in Haworth (25 March 1845, WS 2:25). In view of her brother's poem "Azrael; or, Destruction's Eve," which offers a tirade against religion delivered at Methuselah's grave, one wonders whether the patriarch's name might have been one of the children's joking ways of referring to their aging father (who lived to bury them all).

8   One might note here Freud's account (reporting work by V. Henri and C. Henri) of "a professor of philology whose earliest memory, dating back to between the ages of three and four, showed him a table laid for a meal and on it a basin of ice. At the same period there occurred the death of his grandmother which, according to his parents, was a severe blow to the child. But the professor of philology, as he now is, has no recollection of this bereavement; all that he remembers of those days is the basin of ice" ("Screen Memories" 50). In an 1836 vision of characters who appear nowhere else in her sprawling juvenilia, Brontë sees a "Dr. Charles Brandon" (C.B.) who has evidently just performed an operation and is "washing his bloody hands in a bason," "a bason of water on a slab" (JE, "Backgrounds" 415). The picture leaves the twenty-year-old author "confounded and annoyed," and feeling "a heavy weight." In *Villette* Lucy sees M. Paul wash his hands "in a little stone bowl" (506). Note also Melanie Klein, who writes of a child who "had also discovered the wash basin as symbolizing the mother's body" ("Symbol Formation" 104), and Irene Tayler, who sees in Charlotte's hollows and dells "the fetal retreat to which she . . . so many times alluded over the years" (262).

Given the mediating term of "Bassompierre" and its reference to "Home," one might pursue another possible determination and posit that "stone-basin" = "home," recalling Freud's invocation of the womb as "the former *Heim*

9   The emotional etymology of truth: truth is troth, troth is trust.
10 "It was very odd but [Henry's] sister [Elizabeth] did not think a pin the worse of him for all his Dishonour—it is private meanness—not public infamy that degrade a man in the opinion of his relatives—Miss Hastings heard him cursed by every mouth—saw him denounced in every newspaper. Still he was the same brother to her he had always been—still she beheld his actions through a medium peculiar to herself— . . . —natural affection is a thing never rooted out where it has once really existed" (*Novelettes*, 242).
11 The verses to which she seems to refer include these lines: "Yet, brother, it were ill to weep, when life hath been so drear, / That we are left alone to keep its painful vigil here. / 'Twere ill if thou hast trod the way to count the labouring hours, / Or mourn that sorrow fill'd thy cup with hastier hand than ours" (Dobell 33).
12 Cf. Brontë's Elizabeth Hastings, "always burning for warmer, closer attachment—she couldn't live without it—but the feeling never woke & never was reciprocated—O for Henry" (*Novelettes* 243–44).
13 Pointers owned by Charlotte Brontë's Branwellian Henry Hastings and Zamorna (*Novelettes* 244, 291) are also named Juno.

8   Hypograms, Hypocrits, and Hippos: Conrad's *Heart of Darkness*

1   Cf. Keats and his concluding quotation of Wordsworth's "Tintern Abbey": "This Chamber of Maiden Thought becomes gradually darken'd and at the same time on all sides of it many doors are set open—but all dark—all leading to dark passages—We see not the ballance of good and evil. We are in a Mist—We are now in that state—We feel the 'burden of the Mystery'" (3 May 1818).
2   Blake also knows this misty space where texts take shape, which he describes in a letter as a "Land of Abstraction where Spectres of the Dead wander" (11 September 1801).
3   "And now . . . these Shades may be allowed to return to their place of rest"; "literary life must . . . seek discourse with the shades" (*PR* x, xv).
4   Later Marlow will say that women "are out of it—should be out of it" and must be helped to stay "in that beautiful world of their own" (49); but less than a year before writing that, Conrad confided to a friend that "reason is hateful" because "it demonstrates . . . that we, living, are out of life—utterly out of it" (14 January 1898, *CL* 2:16).
5   Kimbrough's text here prints "least" for "last."

6 Gary Adelman notes the oddity of the digression, only to ask, "Is this meant as an allegory of [Marlow's] own inexplicable behavior, and of his thick-skinned temperament?" (84).

7 Cf. Freud on the "analysis and synthesis of syllables—a syllabic chemistry" which he finds in a great number of jokes (*Interpretation* 332).

8 Benita Perry, one might add here, sees "the joining of disparities in unorthodox and unexpected conjunctions" as "a deliberate and ostentatious feature of the novel's discourse," and points to the phrase "abominable satisfactions" in particular as one of the work's "overt signs of its heterogenous and incompatible meanings" (39). But "covert" signs can be as much at work in cuing response as overt ones.

9 Regarding the inevitable homoerotic suggestion, consider how Marlow saw the Russian and Kurtz: "They had come together unavoidably, like two ships becalmed near each other, and lay rubbing sides at last." The Russian lad recalls that Kurtz talked of "'everything! . . . Of love too.' 'Ah, he talked to you of love!' I said much amused. 'It isn't what you think,' he cried almost passionately" (55). Indeed—the son's homoerotic desire for a father[-figure] remains a neglected dimension of infantile sexuality.

10 "Even as he signed his novels and stories Joseph Conrad, he was writing to Polish friends and relatives as Korzeniowski, but with unusual variations. He signed, alternately, Konrad Korzeniowski, Jph Conrad Korzeniowski, J. C. Korzeniowski, K. N. Korzeniowski, Konrad N. Korzeniowski, simply Konrad, Conrad Korzeniowski, Conrad N. Korzeniowski, Joseph Conrad (Korzeniowski), J. Conrad K., Konrad Korzeniowski (Joseph Conrad); or, on occasion, J. Conrad, Conrad, Joseph Conrad. To non-Polish friends, he signed Jph. Conrad, Joseph Conrad, J. Conrad, Conrad, even Jph Cd" (Karl 20).

9   Sylvia on Aurelia Plath

1 The following abbreviations are used in citing titles of Plath's work: *CP, The Collected Poems; J, The Journals of Sylvia Plath; LH, Letters Home by Sylvia Plath; BJ, The Bell Jar; JP, Johnny Panic and the Bible of Dreams: Short Stories, Prose, and Diary Excerpts.*

2 The nineteenth-century Italian Giacomo Leopardi's dream-poem, "The Terror by Night," written when the author was twenty-one, describes a dream "in which the moon falls out of the sky and burns itself out in a field. The dreamer then looks up at the sky and is frozen with terror at the sight of the hole from which the moon has been torn" (Rycroft 29). In the case of a female patient's somewhat similar dream, Rycroft concludes that "the moon repre-

sents the [mother/]breast" (36). Given the the curious parallel, one notes, apropos of *The Bell Jar* (discussed below), that according to his translator Leopardi "'committed to his notebook one of the most terrible indictments ever penned by a son against his mother' even though 'he always treated her outwards with the most scrupulous respect'" (Rycroft 35).

3 So perhaps to attempt to unlock the meaning of the opening to a German song she had as a child from her mother, a refrain "running through the various texts of Plath's writing . . . *'Ich weiss nicht was sol es bedeuten'* ['I do not know what it means']" (Rose 112; see *CP* 287).

4 In her copy of Sir James Frazer's *The Golden Bough* (a gift from her mother), Plath underlined the remark that "primitive man regards his name as a vital portion of himself" (Axelrod 234).

5 Cf. "Berck-Plage": "A crest of breasts, eyelids and lips / Storming the hilltop" (*CP* 200); and "Three Women": "I am a river of milk. / I am a warm hill" (*CP* 183).

6 The Latin *pupilla* is the diminutive of *pupa* or *puppa*, used in vulgar Latin to indicate the nipple, and in modern Italian as a vulgar word for the female breasts (Almansi 61; cf. the English areola).

7 Cf. Brink: "She had also become master of a new ironically mocking language in which the psychotic vindication of archaic hurt pours forth" (232).

8 The overdetermination here is aptly suggested by Axelrod, who comments that "we might hypothesize how her reason for acquiescing [in late 1959] in Hughes's return to England was not that he would be 'his best' there but that she could escape her analysis there, could escape those resonant questions, 'Would you have the guts to admit you'd made a wrong choice?' and 'Does Ted want you to get better?'" (190).

9 With her interest in the magic of names, Plath would perhaps by this time have been particularly struck by Peter Quennell's remark regarding two late works by the French writer and suicide Gérard de Nerval, that *Aurélia* "is the matrix of confusion, from which *Sylvie* has been drawn. The writer's cloudy preoccupations had grown so vast, so overweening that the narrow chambers of art proved scarcely ample enough to house them" (92).

Works Cited

Abraham, Nicolas, and Maria Torok. "Introjection—Incorporation: Mourning or Melancholia." In *Psychoanalysis in France,* translated and edited by Serge Lebovici and Daniel Widlöcker. New York: International University Press, 1980.

———. *The Wolf Man's Magic Word: A Cryptonymy.* Translated by Nicholas Rand. Theory and History of Literature. Minneapolis: University of Minnesota Press, 1986.

Adelman, Gary. *"Heart of Darkness": Search for the Unconscious.* Boston: Twayne, 1987.

Ahl, Frederick. "Ars Est Caelare Artem (Art in Puns and Anagrams Engraved)." In *On Puns: The Foundation of Letters,* edited by Jonathan Culler. Oxford: Blackwell, 1988.

Aitchison, Jean. *Words in the Mind: An Introduction to the Mental Lexicon.* Oxford: Blackwell, 1987.

Allingham, William. *William Allingham's Diary.* 1907. Reprint. Carbondale: Southern Illinois University Press, 1967.

Allott, Miriam, ed. *Keats: The Complete Poems.* Corrected edition. Annotated English Poets. London: Longman, 1972.

Almansi, Renato J. "The Face-Breast Equation." *Journal of the American Psychoanalytic Association* 8, no. 1 (1960): 43–70.

Altick, Richard D. *The Shows of London.* Cambridge, Mass.: Harvard University Press, 1978.

Ames, Lois. "Sylvia Plath: A Biographical Note." In *The Bell Jar,* by Plath.

Axelrod, Steven Gould. *Sylvia Plath: The Wound and the Cure of Words.* Baltimore: Johns Hopkins University Press, 1990.

Bakhtin, M[ikhail] M[ikhailovich]. *The Dialogic Imagination: Four Essays.* Edited by Michael Holquist; translated by Caryl Emerson and Michael Holquist. Austin: University of Texas Press, 1981.

Baldick, Chris. *In Frankenstein's Shadow: Myth, Monstrosity, and Nineteenth-Century Writing.* Oxford: Clarendon Press, 1987.

Bassnett, Susan. *Sylvia Plath.* Totowa, N.J.: Barnes and Noble, 1987.

Bate, W. Jackson. *John Keats*. Cambridge, Mass.: Harvard University Press, 1963.
———. *Samuel Johnson*. 1975. Reprint. New York: Harcourt Brace Jovanovich, 1979.
Beaugrande, Robert de. "Text, Attention, and Memory in Reading Research." In *Understanding Readers' Understanding: Theory and Practice*, edited by Robert J. Tierney, Patricia L. Anders, and Judy Nichols Mitchell. Hillsdale, N.J.: Erlbaum, 1987.
Bennett, Paula. *My Life a Loaded Gun: Female Creativity and Feminist Poetics*. Boston: Beacon Press, 1986.
Berman, Jeffrey. *Narcissism and the Novel*. New York: New York University Press, 1990.
———. *The Talking Cure: Literary Representations of Psychoanalysis*. New York: New York University Press, 1985.
Bettelheim, Bruno. *The Uses of Enchantment*. New York: Vintage Books, 1977.
Booth, Stephen, ed. *Shakespeare's Sonnets*. New Haven: Yale University Press, 1977.
Boswell, James. *Life of Johnson*. Oxford Standard Authors. London: Oxford University Press, 1969.
———. *London Journal 1762–1763*. Edited by Frederick A. Pottle. New York: McGraw-Hill, 1950.
Boucé, Paul-Gabriel. "The Secret Nexus: Sex and Literature in Eighteenth-Century Britain." In *The Sexual Dimension in Literature*, edited by Alan Bold. London: Vision; Totowa, N.J.: Barnes and Noble, 1982.
Brantlinger, Patrick. *Rule of Darkness: British Literature and Imperialism, 1830–1914*. Ithaca: Cornell University Press, 1988.
Brink, Andrew. *Loss and Symbolic Repair: A Psychological Study of Some English Poets*. Hamilton, Ont.: Cromlech Press, 1977.
Bromberg, David. "On the Occurrence of the Isakower Phenomenon in a Schizoid Disorder." *Contemporary Psychoanalysis* 20 (1984): 600–624.
Brontë, Anne. *The Tenant of Wildfell Hall*. 1848. Reprint. Penguin English Library. Harmondsworth, England: Penguin Books, 1979.
Brontë, Charlotte. *An Edition of the Early Writings of Charlotte Brontë*. Edited by Christine Alexander. Vol. 1, *The Glass Town Saga, 1826–1832*. Oxford: Blackwell, 1987.
———. *Five Novelettes*. Edited by Winifred Gérin. London: Folio Press, 1971.
———. *Jane Eyre*. Edited by Richard J. Dunn. 2d ed. Norton Critical Edition. New York: Norton, 1987.
———. *The Poems of Charlotte Brontë*. Edited by Tom Winnifrith. Oxford: Blackwell, 1984.

———. *Shirley*. 1849. Edited by Andrew Hook and Judith Hook. Reprint. Penguin English Library. Harmondsworth, England: Penguin, 1982.
———. *Villette*. 1853. Edited by Mark Lilly; introduction by Tony Tanner. Reprint. Penguin English Library. Harmondsworth, England: Penguin, 1983.
Brontë, Emily. *Wuthering Heights*. Edited by William M. Sale, Jr. Rev. ed. Norton Critical Edition. New York: Norton, 1972.
Brontë, Patrick. *Brontëana: The Rev. Patrick Brontë, A.B., His Collected Works and Life*. Edited by J. Horsfall Turner. 1898. Facsimile reprint. New York: AMS Press, 1978.
Brontë, Patrick Branwell. *The Poems of Patrick Branwell Brontë*. Edited by Tom Winnifrith. New York: New York University Press, 1983.
Brooks, Cleanth. *The Well Wrought Urn: Studies in the Structure of Poetry*. 1947. Reprint. New York: Harcourt, Brace and World, Harvest Books, n.d.
Bundtzen, Lynda K. *Plath's Incarnations: Woman and the Creative Process*. Ann Arbor: University of Michigan Press, 1983.
Burke, Kenneth. *A Grammar of Motives* and *A Rhetoric of Motives*. 1945, 1950. Reprint. 2 vols. in 1. New York: World Publishing, Meridian Books, 1962.
Burton, Robert. *The Anatomy of Melancholy*. 3 vols. Everyman's Library. London: Dent; New York: Dutton, 1964.
Butscher, Edward. *Sylvia Plath: Method and Madness*. 1976. Reprint. New York: Washington Square Press, Pocket Books, 1977.
Byrd, Max. "Johnson's Spiritual Anxiety." *Modern Philology* 78 (1981): 368–78.
Campbell, Thomas. *Dr. Campbell's Diary of a Visit to England*. Edited by James L. Clifford. Cambridge: Cambridge University Press, 1947.
Carroll, Michael P. "On the Psychological Origins of the Evil Eye: A Kleinian View." *Journal of Psychoanalytic Anthropology* 7, no. 2 (Spring 1984): 171–87.
Cavell, Stanley. *Must We Mean What We Say? A Book of Essays*. New York: Scribner's, 1969.
Chase, Karen. *Eros and Psyche: The Representation of Personality in Charlotte Brontë, Charles Dickens, and George Eliot*. London: Methuen, 1984.
Chitham, Edward. *A Life of Emily Brontë*. Oxford: Blackwell, 1987.
Cleland, John. *Fanny Hill; or, Memoirs of a Woman of Pleasure*. Edited by Peter Wagner. Harmondsworth, England: Penguin, 1985.
Clifford, James L. *Young Sam Johnson*. New York: McGraw-Hill, 1955.
Coleridge, Samuel Taylor. *Collected Letters of Samuel Taylor Coleridge*. Edited by Earl Leslie Griggs. Vol. 1, 1785–1800. Oxford: Clarendon, 1956.
———. *The Notebooks of Samuel Taylor Coleridge*. Edited by Kathleen Coburn. Bollingen Series, no. 50. Vol. 1, 1794–1804. 2 parts. New York: Pantheon, 1957.
Conrad, Joseph. *The Collected Letters of Joseph Conrad*. Edited by Frederick R.

Karl and Laurence Davies. Vol. 1, 1861–1897. Vol. 2, 1898–1902. Vol. 3, 1903–1907. Cambridge: Cambridge University Press, 1983–88.

———. *Congo Diary and Other Uncollected Pieces.* Edited by Zdzisław Najder. Garden City: N.Y.: Doubleday, 1978.

———. "The End of the Tether." In *"Youth," "Heart of Darkness," and "The End of the Tether."* Collected Edition, vol. 5. London: Dent, 1967.

———. *Heart of Darkness.* Edited by Robert Kimbrough. Norton Critical Editions. 3d ed. New York: Norton, 1988.

———. *Lord Jim.* Edited by Cedric Watts and Robert Hampson; introduction by Cedric Watts. Penguin Classics. Harmondsworth, England: Penguin, 1986.

———. *The Nigger of the "Narcissus."* In *Great Short Works of Joseph Conrad,* edited by Jerry Allen. Perennial Classics. New York: Harper and Row, 1967.

———. *A Personal Record: Some Reminiscences.* Collected Edition, vol. 8. London: Dent, 1960.

———. "Poland Revisited." In *Notes on Life and Letters.* London and Toronto: Dent, 1921.

———. *Under Western Eyes.* Collected Edition, vol. 11. London: Dent, 1963.

———. *Victory.* Garden City, N.Y.: Doubleday, Anchor Books, 1957.

———. "Youth." In *"Youth," "Heart of Darkness," and "The End of the Tether."* Collected Edition, vol. 5. London: Dent, 1967.

Crews, Frederick. "The Power of Darkness." *Partisan Review* 34 (1967): 507–25.

Darwin, Erasmus. *The Botanic Garden: A Poem, in Two Parts. Part I, Containing The Economy of Vegetation. Part II, The Loves of the Plants. With Philosophical Notes.* 1791. Facsimile reprint. Menston, England: Scholar Press, 1973.

———. *The Temple of Nature; or, The Origin of Society: A Poem, with Philosophical Notes.* London: Johnson, 1803.

Davies, Stevie. *Emily Brontë.* Bloomington: Indiana University Press, 1988.

Davis, Philip. *In Mind of Johnson: A Study of Johnson the Rambler.* Athens: University of Georgia Press, 1989.

de Man, Paul. *The Resistance to Theory.* Minneapolis: University of Minnesota Press, 1986.

Derrida, Jacques. "Foreword: *Fors:* The Anglish Words of Nicolas Abraham and Maria Torok." Translated by Barbara Johnson. In *The Wolf Man's Magic Word,* Abraham and Torok.

Deutelbaum, Wendy. "Two Psychoanalytic Approaches to Reading Literature." In *Bucknell Review* 26, no. 1: *Theories of Reading, Looking, and Listening,* edited by Harry R. Garvin. Lewisburg, Pa.: Bucknell University Press, 1981.

Dixon, Norman F. *Preconscious Processing.* Chichester, England: Wiley, 1981.

Dobell, Sydney. *The Poems of Sydney Dobell.* London: Scott, 1887.

Dunn, Jane. *Moon in Eclipse: A Life of Mary Shelley*. New York: St. Martin's, 1978.
Eco, Umberto. *The Limits of Interpretation*. Bloomington: University of Indiana Press, 1990.
Edelman, Gerald M. *Bright Air, Brilliant Fire: In the Matter of Mind*. New York: Basic Books, 1992.
Ehrenpreis, Irvin. "*Rasselas* and Some Meanings of 'Structure' in Literary Criticism." *Novel* 14 (1981): 101–17.
Einbond, Bernard L. *Samuel Johnson's Allegory*. The Hague: Mouton, 1971.
Ellenberger, Henri F. *The Discovery of the Unconscious: The History and Evolution of Dynamic Psychiatry*. New York: Basic Books, 1970.
Ellmann, Richard. *Golden Codgers: Biographical Speculations*. London: Oxford University Press, 1973.
Empson, William. *The Structure of Complex Words*. 1951. Reprint. N.p.: University of Michigan Press, 1967.
Forster, E. M. "Joseph Conrad: A Note." In *Abinger Harvest*. Harmondsworth, England: Penguin, 1967.
Freidman, Alan J., and Carol C. Donley. *Einstein as Myth and Muse*. Cambridge: Cambridge University Press, 1985.
Friedman, Susan Stanford. *Penelope's Web: Gender, Modernity, H.D.'s Fiction*. Cambridge: Cambridge University Press, 1990.
Freud, Sigmund. "Address Delivered in the Goethe House at Frankfort." In *Standard Edition*, 21:208–12.
———. *Beyond the Pleasure Principle*. Translated by James Strachey. New York: Norton, 1975.
———. *Collected Papers*. Translated by Alix Strachey and James Strachey. 5 vols. New York: Basic Books, 1959.
———. *The Complete Letters of Sigmund Freud to Wilhelm Fliess, 1887–1904*. Translated and edited by Jeffrey Moussaieff Masson. Cambridge, Mass.: Harvard University Press, 1985.
———. *The Interpretation of Dreams*. Translated and edited by James Strachey. Reprint of *Standard Edition*, vols. 4–5. New York: Avon, 1965.
———. *Jokes and Their Relation to the Unconscious*. Translated and edited by James Strachey. New York: Norton, 1963.
———. "Mourning and Melancholia." In *Standard Edition*, vol. 14. London: Hogarth Press, 1958.
———. "Notes upon a Case of Obsessional Neurosis." In *Collected Papers*, vol. 3.
———. "On the History of the Psycho-Analytic Movement." In *Collected Papers*, vol. 1.

———. "Psycho-analysis and the Ascertaining of Truth in Courts of Law." In *Collected Papers*, vol. 2.

———. *The Psychopathology of Everyday Life*. Translated by Alan Tyson; edited with introduction and additional notes by James Strachey. New York: Norton, n.d.

———. "Screen Memories." In *Collected Papers*, vol. 5.

———. *The Standard Edition of the Complete Psychological Works of Sigmund Freud*. Translated and edited by James Strachey et al. 24 vols. London: Hogarth Press, 1961.

———. "The 'Uncanny.'" In *Standard Edition*, vol. 17.

Freud, Sigmund, and Josef Breuer. *Studies on Hysteria*. Translated and edited by James Strachey et al. Reprint of *Standard Edition*, vol. 2. New York: Basic Books, n.d.

Frye, Northrop. *Anatomy of Criticism: Four Essays*. 1957. Reprint. Princeton: Princeton University Press, 1971.

Garnett, Edward, ed. *Letters from Joseph Conrad, 1895–1924*. 1928. Reprint. Indianapolis and New York: Bobbs-Merrill, Charter Books, 1962.

Gass, William. *On Being Blue: A Philosophical Inquiry*. Boston: Godine, [1976].

Gazzaniga, Michael S. *The Social Brain: Discovering the Networks of the Mind*. New York: Basic Books, 1985.

Gelpi, Barbara Charlesworth. *Shelley's Goddess: Maternity, Language, Subjectivity*. Oxford: Oxford University Press, 1992.

Gérin, Winifred. *Branwell Brontë*. London: Nelson, 1961.

———. *Charlotte Brontë: The Evolution of Genius*. 1967. Reprint. Oxford: Oxford University Press, 1982.

Gilbert, Sandra M., and Susan Gubar. *The Madwoman in the Attic: The Woman Writer and the Nineteenth-Century Literary Imagination*. 1979. Reprint. New Haven: Yale University Press, 1984.

Gillett, Peter J. "Tennyson's Mind at the Work of Creation." *Victorian Poetry* 15, no. 4 (Winter 1977): 321–33.

Gittings, Robert. *John Keats*. Boston: Little, Brown, 1968.

———, ed. *Letters of John Keats*. London: Oxford University Press, 1970.

Godwin, William. *An Enquiry Concerning Political Justice and Its Influence on General Virtue and Happiness*. 1793. Edited and abridged by Raymond A. Preston. 2 vols. New York: Knopf, 1926.

———. *Enquiry Concerning Political Justice*. 3d ed. 1798. Edited by Isaac Kramnick. Harmondsworth, England: Penguin, 1976.

Gregory, Richard R., ed. *The Oxford Companion to the Mind*. Oxford: Oxford University Press, 1987.

Green, André. *On Private Madness*. London: Hogarth Press and the Institute of Psycho-analysis, 1986.
Greenberg, Jay R., and Stephen A. Mitchell. *Object Relations in Psychoanalytic Theory*. Cambridge, Mass.: Harvard University Press, 1983.
Greene, Donald, ed. *Samuel Johnson*. Oxford Authors. Oxford: Oxford University Press, 1984.
Grice, Paul. *Studies in the Way of Words*. Cambridge: Harvard University Press, 1989.
H.D. [Hilda Doolittle]. *Tribute to the Angels*. In *Trilogy*. New York: New Directions, 1973.
———. *Tribute to Freud*. Foreword by Norman Holmes Pearson. New York: New Directions, 1984.
Hagstrum, Jean. "Johnson and the *Concordia Discors* of Human Relationships." In *The Unknown Samuel Johnson*, edited by John J. Burke, Jr., and Donald Kay. Madison: University of Wisconsin Press, 1983.
Hair, Donald S. *Domestic and Heroic in Tennyson's Poetry*. Toronto: University of Toronto Press, 1981.
Hamilton, James W. "Object Loss, Dreaming, and Creativity: The Poetry of John Keats." *Psychoanalytic Study of the Child* 24 (1969): 488–531.
Hardy, J. P., ed. *The History of Rasselas, Prince of Abissinia*, by Samuel Johnson. London: Oxford University Press, 1968.
Harrison, G. Elsie. *The Clue to the Brontës*. London: Methuen, 1948.
Hartman, Geoffrey H. *Saving the Text: Literature/Derrida/Philosophy*. Baltimore: Johns Hopkins University Press, 1981.
Haydon, Benjamin Robert. *The Diary of Benjamin Robert Haydon*. Edited by Willard Bissell Pope. Vol. 2. Cambridge, Mass.: Harvard University Press, 1960.
Hazlitt, William. *Lectures on the English Poets* and *The Spirit of the Age: or, Contemporary Portraits*. Introduced by C. M. Maclean. Everyman's Library. London: Dent; New York: Dutton, 1967.
Hegel, G. W. F. *Phenomenology of Spirit*. Translated by A. V. Miller. Oxford: Oxford University Press, 1977.
Henke, James T. *Courtesans and Cuckolds: A Glossary of Renaissance Dramatic Bawdy (Exclusive of Shakespeare)*. New York: Garland, 1979.
Holbrook, David. *Sylvia Plath: Poetry and Existence*. London: Athlone Press, 1976.
Holmes, Richard. *Shelley: The Pursuit*. 1974. Reprint. New York: Viking Penguin, 1987.
Homans, Margaret. *Bearing the Word: Language and Female Experience in Nineteenth-Century Woman's Writing*. Chicago: University of Chicago Press, 1986.

Hopkins, Gerard Manley. *The Sermons and Devotional Writings of Gerard Manley Hopkins*. Edited by Christopher Devlin, S.J. London: Oxford University Press, 1959.

Irwin, George. *Samuel Johnson: A Personality in Conflict*. Auckland: Auckland University Press, 1971.

Isakower, Otto. "A Contribution to the Patho-psychology of Phenomena Associated with Falling Asleep." *International Journal of Psycho-analysis* 19 (1938): 331–45.

Jack, Ian. *Keats and the Mirror of Art*. Oxford: Clarendon Press, 1967.

Jakobson, Roman. "Closing Statement: Linguistics and Poetics." In *Style in Language*, edited by Thomas A. Sebeok. Cambridge, Mass.: M.I.T. Press, 1960.

Johnson, Barbara. "My Monster/My Self." *Diacritics* 12 (Summer 1982): 2–10.

Johnson, Samuel. *Diaries, Prayers, and Annals*. Edited by E. L. McAdam with Donald Hyde and Mary Hyde. Yale Edition of the Works of Samuel Johnson, vol. 1. New Haven: Yale University Press, 1958.

———. *The History of Rasselas, Prince of Abissinia*. Edited by D. J. Enright. Harmondsworth, England: Penguin, 1976.

———. *The Idler* and *The Adventurer*. Edited by W. J. Bate, John M. Bullitt, and W. F. Powell. Yale Edition of the Works of Samuel Johnson, vol. 2. New Haven: Yale University Press, 1963.

———. *A Journey to the Western Islands of Scotland*. Edited by Allan Wendt. Boston: Houghton Mifflin, 1965. Published with James Boswell, *The Journal of a Tour to the Hebrides with Samuel Johnson, LL.D.*

———. *The Letters of Samuel Johnson*, collected and edited by R. W. Chapman. Vol. 1, 1719–1774. Oxford: Clarendon Press, 1952.

———. "Life of Pope." In *Samuel Johnson: Selected Poetry and Prose*, edited by Frank Brady and W. K. Wimsatt. Berkeley and Los Angeles: University of California Press, 1977.

———. "Preface to the Plays of William Shakespeare." In *Samuel Johnson: Selected Poetry and Prose*, edited by Frank Brady and W. K. Wimsatt. Berkeley and Los Angeles: University of California Press, 1977.

———. *The Rambler*. Edited by W. J. Bate and Albrecht B. Strauss. Yale Edition of the Works of Samuel Johnson, vols. 2–4. New Haven: Yale University Press, 1969.

———. "Review of [Soame Jenyns], *A Free Inquiry into the Nature and Origin of Evil*. In *Samuel Johnson*, edited by Donald Greene. Oxford: Oxford University Press, 1984.

———. "The Vision of Theodore, the Heremit of Teneriff, Found in His Cell." In *Samuel Johnson*, edited by Donald Greene. Oxford Authors. Oxford: Oxford University Press, 1984.

Joost, Nicholas. "Whispers of Fancy; or, The Meaning of *Rasselas*." *Modern Age* 1 (Fall 1957): 166–73.
Joseph, Gerhard. "Frankenstein's Dream: The Child as Father of the Monster." *Hartford Studies in Literature* 7, no. 2 (1975): 97–115.
Joyce, James. *Finnegans Wake*. 1939. Reprint. New York: Viking, 1955.
———. *A Portrait of the Artist as a Young Man*. New York: Viking, 1964.
Juhasz, Suzanne. *Naked and Fiery Forms: Modern American Poetry by Women: A New Tradition*. New York: Harper and Row, Colophon Books, 1976.
Jung, C. G. "On the Doctrine of Complexes." 1913. In *Experimental Researches*, translated by R. F. C. Hull. In *The Collected Works of C. G. Jung*, Bollingen Series, no. 20. Vol. 2. Princeton: Princeton University Press, 1973.
———. "A Review of the Complex Theory." In *The Structure and Dynamics of the Psyche*, translated by R. F. C. Hull. In *The Collected Works of C. G. Jung*. Bollingen Series, no. 20. Vol. 8. 2d ed. Princeton: Princeton University Press, 1969.
Kamel, Rose. "'Reach Hag Hands and Haul Me In': Matriphobia in the Letters of Sylvia Plath." *Northwest Review* 20, no. 2 (1981): 198–208. Reprinted in *Sylvia Plath: The Critical Heritage*, ed. Wagner.
Karl, Frederick R. *Joseph Conrad: The Three Lives: A Biography*. New York: Farrar, Straus and Giroux, 1979.
Keats, John. *Complete Poems*. Edited by Jack Stillinger. Cambridge, Mass.: Harvard University Press, 1982.
———. *The Letters of John Keats, 1814–1821*. Edited by Hyder Edward Rollins. 2 vols. Cambridge, Mass.: Harvard University Press, 1958.
Keefe, Robert. *Charlotte Brontë's World of Death*. Austin: University of Texas Press, 1979.
Kernan, Alvin. *Printing Technology, Letters, and Samuel Johnson*. Princeton: Princeton University Press, 1987.
Keynes, Geoffrey, ed. *Blake: Complete Writings*. 1957. Reprint. Oxford: Oxford University Press, 1971.
Killam, John, ed. *Critical Essays on the Poetry of Tennyson*. New York: Barnes and Noble, 1960.
Kimbrough, Robert, ed. *Heart of Darkness*. Rev. ed. Norton Critical Editions. New York: Norton, 1971.
———. *Heart of Darkness*. 3d ed. Norton Critical Editions. New York: Norton, 1988.
Klein, Melanie. "A Contribution to the Psychogenesis of Manic-Depressive States." 1935. Reprinted in *The Selected Melanie Klein*, edited by Juliet Mitchell. New York: Free Press, 1987.

———. *Envy and Gratitude*. 1957. Reprinted in *Envy and Gratitude and Other Works, 1946–1963*, introduction by Hanna Segal. London: Virago, 1988.

———. "The Importance of Symbol Formation in the Development of the Ego." 1930. Reprinted in *The Selected Melanie Klein*, edited by Juliet Mitchell. New York: Free Press, 1987.

———. "Notes on Some Schizoid Mechanisms." 1946. Reprinted in *The Selected Melanie Klein*, edited by Juliet Mitchell. New York: Free Press, 1987.

Knoepflmacher, U. C. "Thoughts on the Aggression of Daughters." In *The Endurance of Frankenstein*, ed. Levine and Knoepflmacher.

Kolb, Gwin J., ed. *"Rasselas" and Other Tales*. Yale Edition of the Works of Samuel Johnson, vol. 16. New Haven: Yale University Press, 1990.

Koslow, Francine A. "Sex in Surrealist Art." In *Eros in the Mind's Eye: Sexuality and the Fantastic in Art and Film*, edited by Donald Palumbo. Westport, Conn.: Greenwood Press, 1986.

Kozicki, Henry. *Tennyson and Clio: History in the Major Poems*. Baltimore: Johns Hopkins University Press, 1979.

Kristeva, Julia. *Revolution in Poetic Language*. Translated by Margaret Waller. New York: Columbia University Press, 1984.

Kroll, Judith. *Chapters in a Mythography: The Poetry of Sylvia Plath*. New York: Harper and Row, 1976.

Krutch, Joseph Wood. *Samuel Johnson*. New York: Henry Holt, 1944.

Lacan, Jacques. *Ecrits: A Selection*. Translated by Alan Sheridan. New York: Norton, 1977.

———. *The Four Fundamental Concepts of Psycho-analysis*. Edited by Jacques-Alain Miller; translated by Alan Sheridan. Reprint. 1973. New York: Norton, 1981.

Lash, Christopher. *The Culture of Narcissism: American Life in an Age of Diminishing Expectations*. New York: Warner, 1979.

Lavers, Annette. "The World as Icon: On Sylvia Plath's Themes." In *The Art of Sylvia Plath: A Symposium*, edited by Charles Newman. Bloomington: Indiana University Press, 1970.

Law, William. *A Serious Call to a Devout and Holy Life*. Everyman's Library. London: Dent; New York: Dutton, 1961.

Leavis, F. R. *The Great Tradition: George Eliot, Henry James, Joseph Conrad*. 1948. Reprint. London: Chatto and Windus, 1973.

Lecercle, Jean-Jacques. *The Violence of Language*. London and New York: Routledge, 1990.

Levenson, Michael. "The Value of Facts in the *Heart of Darkness*." In *Heart of Darkness*, ed. Kimbrough, 3d ed.

Levine, George. "The Ambiguous Heritage of *Frankenstein*." In *The Endurance of Frankenstein*, ed. Levine and Knoepflmacher.
Levine, George, and U. C. Knoepflmacher, eds. *The Endurance of Frankenstein: Essays on Mary Shelley's Novel*. Berkeley and Los Angeles: University of California Press, 1979.
Levinson, Marjorie. *Keats's Life of Allegory: The Origins of a Style*. Oxford: Blackwell, 1988.
Lewin, Bertram D. "Reconsideration of the Dream Screen." *Psychoanalytic Quarterly* 22 (1953): 174–99.
Lobo, Jerónimo. A *Voyage to Abyssinia*. Translated [by Samuel Johnson] from Joachim Le Grand's French version, *Relation historique d'Abissinie* (1728), of a sixteenth-century Portuguese manuscript of Jerónimo Lobo; edited by Joel J. Gold. Yale Edition of the Works of Samuel Johnson, vol. 15. New Haven: Yale University Press, 1985.
Locke, Don. A *Fantasy of Reason: The Life and Thought of William Godwin*. London: Routledge and Kegan Paul, 1980.
Lynn, Steven. "Sexual Difference and Johnson's Brain." In *Fresh Reflections on Samuel Johnson: Essays in Criticism*, edited by Prem Nath. Troy, N.Y.: Whitston, 1987.
Mallowan, M. E. L. "Excavations at Brak and Chagar Bazar." *Iraq* 9 (1947): 1–266.
Marcel, Anthony J. "Conscious and Unconscious Perception." *Cognitive Psychology* 15 (1983): 197–237, 238–300.
Martin, Robert Bernard. *Tennyson: The Unquiet Heart*. Oxford: Clarendon Press, 1980.
Mauron, Charles. *Introduction to the Psychoanalysis of Mallarmé*. Translated by Archibald Henderson, Jr., and Will L. McLendon. Berkeley and Los Angeles: University of California Press, 1963.
McIntosh, Carey. *The Choice of Life: Samuel Johnson and the World of Fiction*. New Haven: Yale University Press, 1973.
McLauchlan, Juliet. "The 'Value' and 'Significance' of *Heart of Darkness*". In *Heart of Darkness*, ed. Kimbrough, 3d ed.
McSweeney, Kerry. *Tennyson and Swinburne as Romantic Naturalists*. Toronto: University of Toronto Press, 1981.
Mellor, Anne K. *Mary Shelley: Her Life, Her Fiction, Her Monsters*. New York and London: Methuen, 1988.
Meredith, George. *The Egoist*. 1879. Edited by George Woodcock. Reprint. Baltimore: Penguin, 1968.
Meyer, Bernard C. *Joseph Conrad: A Psychoanalytic Biography*. Princeton: Princeton University Press, 1967.

---. "Notes on Flying and Dying." *Psychoanalytic Quarterly* 52 (1983): 327–42.
---. "On the Application of Psychoanalysis in W. Jackson Bate's Life of Samuel Johnson." *Journal of the Philadelphia Association for Psychoanalysis* 6 (1979): 153–61.
---. "Some Observations on the Rescue of Fallen Women." *Psychoanalytic Quarterly* 53 (1984): 208–39.
Moers, Ellen. "Female Gothic." In *The Endurance of Frankenstein*, ed. Levine and Knoepflmacher.
Moglen, Helene. *Charlotte Brontë: The Self Conceived.* New York: Norton, 1976.
Mudrick, Marvin. "The Originality of Conrad." In *Heart of Darkness*, ed. Kimbrough, rev. ed.
Najder, Zdisław. *Joseph Conrad: A Chronicle.* Translated by Halina Carroll Najder. New Brunswick: Rutgers University Press, 1983.
Newton, Peter M. "Samuel Johnson's Breakdown and Recovery in Middle-Age: A Life Span Developmental Approach to Mental Illness and Its Cure." *International Review of Psycho-analysis* 11 (1984): 93–118.
Nietzsche, F. *Twilight of the Idols and the Anti-Christ.* Translated by R. J. Hollingdale. Harmondsworth, England: Penguin, 1972.
Norris, Christopher. *William Empson and the Philosophy of Literary Criticism.* London: Athlone Press, 1978.
O'Flaherty, Patrick. "Dr. Johnson as Equivocator: The Meaning of *Rasselas*." *Modern Language Quarterly* 31 (1970): 195–208.
Orgel, Shelley. "Sylvia Plath: Fusion with the Victim and Suicide." *Psychoanalytic Quarterly* 43 (1974): 262–87.
Oxford English Dictionary [OED]. Compact Edition. Oxford: Oxford University Press, 1971.
Paglia, Camille. "Christabel." In *Samuel Taylor Coleridge*, edited by Harold Bloom. New York: Chelsea House, 1986.
Parry, Benita. *Conrad and Imperialism: Ideological Boundaries and Visionary Frontiers.* London: Macmillan, 1983.
Partridge, Eric. *A Dictionary of Slang and Unconventional English.* 5th ed. 2 vols. in 1. New York: Macmillan, 1961.
Patterson, Annabel. "Intention." In *Critical Terms for Literary Study*, edited by Frank Lentricchia and Thomas McLaughlin. Chicago: University of Chicago Press, 1990.
Pattison, Robert. *Tennyson and Tradition.* Cambridge, Mass.: Harvard University Press, 1979.
Pearson, Hesketh. *Johnson and Boswell: The Story of Their Lives.* 1958. Reprint. London: Cassell, 1987.

Percy, Thomas. *Reliques of Ancient English Poetry.* 1765. Edited by Edward Walford. Reprint. London: Warne, 1880.
Peters, Margot. *Charlotte Brontë: Style in the Novel.* Madison: University of Wisconsin Press, 1973.
Phillips, Adam. *Winnicott.* Cambridge, Mass.: Harvard University Press, 1988.
Pilkington, Adrian. "Poetic Effects: A Relevance Theory Perspective." In *Literary Pragmatics*, edited by Roger D. Sell. London: Routledge, 1991.
Piozzi, Hester Lynch [Thrale]. *Anecdotes of the Late Samuel Johnson, LL.D., During the Last Twenty Years of His Life.* In *Memoirs and Anecdotes of Dr. Johnson*, edited by Arthur Sherbo. London: Oxford University Press, 1974.
Plath, Sylvia. *The Bell Jar.* 1963. Reprint, with a biographical note by Lois Ames. New York: Bantam Books, 1981.
―――. *The Collected Poems.* Edited by Ted Hughes. New York: Harper and Row, 1981.
―――. *Johnny Panic and the Bible of Dreams: Short Stories, Prose, and Diary Excerpts.* Introduction by Ted Hughes. New York: Harper and Row, 1978.
―――. *The Journals of Sylvia Plath.* Edited by Frances McCullough in consultation with Ted Hughes; foreword by Ted Hughes. Book Club Edition. New York: Dial Press, 1982.
―――. *Letters Home by Sylvia Plath: Correspondence, 1950–1963.* Selected and edited with commentary by Aurelia Schober Plath. New York: Harper and Row, 1975.
Porter, Roy. "'The Hunger of Imagination': Approaching Samuel Johnson's Melancholy." In *The Anatomy of Madness: Essays in the History of Psychiatry*, edited by W. F. Bynum, Roy Porter, and Michael Shepherd. Vol. 1, *People and Ideas*. London and New York: Tavistock, 1985.
Pyles, Thomas. "Ophelia's 'Nothing.'" *Modern Language Notes* 64 (May 1949): 322–23.
Pynchon, Thomas. *The Crying of Lot 49.* 1963. Reprint. New York: Bantam, 1967.
Quennell, Peter. *Baudelaire and the Symbolists.* London: Chatto & Windus, 1929.
Rackin, Phyllis. "Recent Misreadings of 'Break, Break, Break' and Their Implications for Poetic Theory." *Journal of English and Germanic Philology* 65, no. 2 (April 1966): 224–30.
Rapaport, Herman. "*Jane Eyre* and the *Mot Tabou.*" *Modern Language Notes* 94, no. 5 (December 1979): 1093–1104.
Ray, William. *Literary Meaning: From Phenomenology to Deconstruction.* Oxford: Blackwell, 1984.
Reed, Kenneth T. "'This Tasteless Tranquility': A Freudian Note on Johnson's 'Rasselas.'" *Literature and Psychology* 19 (1969): 61–62.

Rees, Jean. *Profligate Son: Branwell Brontë and His Sisters*. London: Hall, 1986.
Reich, Annie. "Narcissistic Object Choice in Women." 1953. Reprinted in *Essential Papers on Object Relations*, edited by Peter Buckley. New York: New York University Press, 1986.
Reid, Stephen A. "Keats's Depressive Poetry." *Psychoanalytic Review* 58 (1971): 395–418.
Reynolds, Joshua. *Discourses on Art*. 1797. Reprint. N.p.: Collier Books, 1966.
Rich, Adrienne. *Of Woman Born: Motherhood as Experience and Institution*. New York: Norton, 1976.
Rickman, John. "On the Nature of Ugliness and the Creative Impulse." *International Journal of Psycho-analysis* 21, no. 3 (July 1940): 294–313.
Ricks, Christopher. *Keats and Embarrassment*. 1974. Reprint. Oxford: Clarendon Press, 1984.
———. *Tennyson*. 2d ed. Berkeley and Los Angeles: University of California Press, 1989.
Riffaterre, Michael. *Semiotics of Poetry*. Bloomington: Indiana University Press, 1978.
———. *Text Production*. Translated by Terese Lyons. New York: Columbia University Press, 1983.
Rollins, Hyder Edward, ed. *The Keats Circle: Letters and Papers and More Letters and Poems of the Keats Circle*. 2d ed. 2 vols. Cambridge, Mass.: Harvard University Press, 1965.
Rose, Jacqueline. *The Haunting of Sylvia Plath*. London: Virago Press, 1991.
Rosen, Victor H. *Style, Character, and Language*. Edited by Samuel Atkin and Milton E. Jucovy. New York: Aronson, 1977.
Rubenstein, Marc A. "'My Accursed Origin': The Search for the Mother in *Frankenstein*." *Studies in Romanticism* 15 (Spring 1976): 165–94.
Rubinstein, Frankie. *A Dictionary of Shakespeare's Sexual Puns and Their Significance*. 2d ed. London: Macmillan, 1989.
Ryals, Clyde de L. *From the Great Deep: Essays on "Idylls of the King."* Athens: Ohio University Press, 1967.
Rycroft, Charles. *Imagination and Reality*. New York: International Universities Press, 1968.
Sadoff, Dianne F. *Monsters of Affection: Dickens, Eliot, and Brontë on Fatherhood*. Baltimore: Johns Hopkins University Press, 1982.
Said, Edward W. *Joseph Conrad and the Fiction of Autobiography*. Cambridge, Mass.: Harvard University Press, 1966.
St. Clair, William. *The Godwins and the Shelleys: The Biography of a Family*. New York: Norton, 1989.

Saussure, Ferdinand de. *Cours de linguistique générale.* Edited by Tullio de Mauro. Paris: Payot, 1983.

———. *Course in General Linguistics.* Translated by Wade Baskin. New York: McGraw-Hill, 1966.

Schafer, Roy. *The Analytic Attitude.* New York: Basic Books, 1983.

Schwartz, Murray M., and Christopher Bollas. "The Absence at the Center: Sylvia Plath and Suicide." *Criticism* 18 (1976): 147–72.

Scigaj, Leonard M. "The Painterly Plath That Nobody Knows." *Centennial Review* 32, no. 3 (1988): 220–49.

Seed, David. " 'Frankenstein': Parable or Spectacle?" *Criticism* 24 (1982): 327–40.

Shapiro, Theodore. *Clinical Psycholinguistics.* New York: Plenum Press, 1979.

Shelley, Mary Wollstonecraft [Godwin]. *Collected Tales and Stories.* Edited by Charles E. Robinson. Baltimore: Johns Hopkins University Press, 1976.

———. *Frankenstein; or, The Modern Prometheus (The 1818 Text).* Edited by James Reiger. 1974. Reprint. Chicago: University of Chicago Press, Phoenix Books, 1982.

———. *The Last Man.* Introduction by Brian Aldiss. London: Hogarth Press, 1985.

———. *The Letters of Mary Wollstonecraft Shelley.* Edited by Betty T. Bennett. Vol. 1. Baltimore: Johns Hopkins University Press, 1980.

———. *Mary Shelley's Journal.* Edited by Frederick L. Jones. Norman: University of Oklahoma Press, 1947.

———. *Mathilda.* Edited by Elizabeth Nitchie. Chapel Hill: University of North Carolina Press, 1959.

Shelley, Percy Bysshe. *The Letters of Percy Bysshe Shelley.* Edited by Frederick L. Jones. Vol. 1. Oxford: Clarendon Press, 1964.

———. *Poetical Works.* Edited by Thomas Hutchinson. New edition, corrected by G. M. Matthews. Oxford Standard Authors. London: Oxford University Press, 1970.

Sherwin, Paul. "*Frankenstein*: Creation as Catastrophe." *PMLA* 96, no. 5 (October 1981): 883–903.

Silverman, Kaja. *The Subject of Semiotics.* New York: Oxford University Press, 1983.

Smith, Joseph H. "Evening the Score." *Modern Language Notes* 104, no. 5 (December 1989): 1050–65.

Spitz, René. "The Primal Cavity: A Contribution to the Genesis of Perception and Its Role for Psychoanalytic Theory." *Psychoanalytic Study of the Child* 10 (1955): 215–40.

Spitzer, Leo. *Linguistics and Literary History: Essays in Stylistics*. Princeton: Princeton University Press, 1948.

———. "'Tears, Idle Tears' Again." 1952. In *Critical Essays*, ed. Killiam.

Starobinski, Jean. *Words upon Words: The Anagrams of Ferdinand de Saussure*. Translated by Olivia Emmet. New Haven: Yale University Press, 1979.

Steiner, Nancy Hunter. *A Closer Look at Ariel: A Memory of Sylvia Plath*. Introduction by George Stade. New York: Harper's Magazine Press, 1973.

Stevenson, Anne. *Bitter Fame: A Life of Sylvia Plath*. Boston: Houghton Mifflin, 1989.

Stewart, Garrett. "Lying as Dying in *Heart of Darkness*." In *Heart of Darkness*, ed. Kimbrough, 3d ed.

Sunstein, Emily W. *Mary Shelley: Romance and Reality*. Boston: Little, Brown, 1989.

Tayler, Irene. *Holy Ghosts: The Male Muses of Emily and Charlotte Brontë*. New York: Columbia University Press, 1990.

Tennyson, Alfred. *The Letters of Alfred, Lord Tennyson*. Edited by Cecil Y. Lang and Edgar F. Shannon, Jr. 2 vols. Cambridge, Mass.: Harvard University Press, 1987.

———. *The Poems of Tennyson*. Edited by Christopher Ricks. 2d ed. 3 vols. Berkeley and Los Angeles: University of California Press, 1987.

Tennyson, Hallam. *Tennyson: A Memoir*. London: Macmillam, 1899.

Tomarken, Edward. *Johnson, "Rasselas," and the Choice of Criticism*. Lexington: University Press of Kentucky, 1989.

Tucker, Herbert F. *Tennyson and the Doom of Romanticism*. Cambridge, Mass.: Harvard University Press, 1988.

Twitchell, James B. *The Living Dead: A Study of the Vampire in Romantic Literature*. Durham, N.C.: Duke University Press, 1981.

Ulmer, Gregory. "The Puncept in Grammatology." In *On Puns: The Foundation of Letters*, edited by Jonathan Culler. Oxford: Blackwell, 1988.

Veeder, William. *Mary Shelley and "Frankenstein": The Fate of Androgyny*. Chicago: University of Chicago Press, 1986.

Vendler, Helen. *The Odes of John Keats*. Cambridge, Mass.: Harvard University Press, 1983.

Wagner, Linda, ed. *Sylvia Plath: The Critical Heritage*. London and New York: Routledge, 1988.

Wagner-Martin, Linda. *Sylvia Plath: A Biography*. New York: Simon and Schuster, 1987.

Wain, John, ed. *Johnson on Johnson*. London: Dent, 1976.

Wasserman, Earl R. "Johnson's *Rasselas:* Implicit Contexts." *Journal of English and Germanic Philology* 74 (1975): 1–25.
Watt, Ian. *Conrad in the Nineteenth Century.* Berkeley and Los Angeles: University of California Press, 1981.
Wesley, Charles. *Representative Verse of Charles Wesley.* Selected and edited by Frank Baker. New York: Abingdon Press, 1962.
Williams, A. Hyatt. "Keats' 'La Belle Dame Sans Merci': The Bad-Breast Mother." *American Imago* 23 (1966): 63–81.
Williamson, Alan. *Introspection and Contemporary Poetry.* Cambridge, Mass.: Harvard University Press, 1984.
Wimsatt, W. K. "In Praise of *Rasselas:* Four Notes (Converging)". In *Imagined Worlds: Essays on Some English Novels and Novelists in Honour of John Butt,* edited by Maynard Mack and Ian Gregor. London: Methuen, 1968.
———. *Philosophic Words: A Study of Style and Meaning in the "Rambler" and "Dictionary" of Samuel Johnson.* 1948. Reprint. Hamden, Conn.: Archon, 1968.
Wimsatt, W. K., and Monroe C. Beardsley. "The Intentional Fallacy." In W. K. Wimsatt, Jr., *The Verbal Icon: Studies in the Meaning of Poetry.* N.p.: University Press of Kentucky, 1954.
Winnicott, D. W. *Home Is Where We Start From: Essays by a Psychoanalyst,* compiled and edited by Clare Winnicott. New York: Norton, 1986.
Wise, Thomas James, and J. A. Symington, eds. *The Brontës: Their Lives, Friendships, and Correspondence.* 1933. Reprint. 4 vols. in 2. Philadelphia: Porcupine Press, 1980.
Wittgenstein, Ludwig. *Notebooks, 1914–16.* Edited by G. H. von Wright and G. E. M. Anscombe; translated by G. E. M. Anscombe. 2d ed. Chicago: University of Chicago Press, 1979.
———. *Philosophical Investigations.* Translated by G. E. M. Anscombe. 2d ed. 1958. Oxford: Blackwell, 1974.
Wollstonecraft, Mary. *A Short Residence in Sweden.* Edited, with introduction and notes, by Richard Holmes. Harmondsworth, England: Penguin, 1987. Published with William Godwin, *Memoirs of The Author of "The Rights of Woman".*
———. *Thoughts on the Education of Daughters.* In *The Works of Mary Wollstonecraft,* edited by Janet Todd and Marilyn Butler. Vol. 4. New York: New York University Press, 1989.
Wordsworth, William. *The Prelude: 1799, 1805, 1850.* Edited by Jonathan Wordsworth, M. H. Abrams, and Stephen Gill. New York: Norton, 1979.
Wordsworth, William, and Dorothy Wordsworth. *The Letters of William and Dorothy Wordsworth: The Early Years, 1708–1805.* Arranged and edited by Ernest de Selincourt; revised by Chester L. Shaver. Oxford: Clarendon Press, 1967.

Wright, Elizabeth. *Psychoanalytic Criticism: Theory in Practice*. London: Methuen, 1984.
Young, Edward. *Night Thoughts*. Edited by Stephen Cornford. Cambridge: Cambridge University Press, 1989.

Index

Abraham, Nicolas, 121
Abyss, 43
Abyssinia, 42
Adelman, Gary, 198 (n. 6)
Allingham, William, 108, 112, 194 (n. 2)
Almansi, Renato, 23, 26, 27, 29, 194 (n. 11)
Ambiguity, 14
Ambivalence, 13, 32, 59, 60, 83, 84, 86, 87, 88, 109, 119; in Keats, 75, 76, 77; in Plath, 167
Anagrams, 7, 118; of "Villette," 135; in Plath, 170; in Johnson, 190 (n. 10); and de Saussure, 195 (n. 5)
Angria, 122, 132
Areola, 26, 168, 199 (n. 6)
Axelrod, Steven, 165, 177, 199 (n. 8)
Azrael, 133, 196 (n. 7)

Bakhtin, Mikhail, 15
Baldick, Chris, 57
Basin, 129, 196 (n. 8)
Bassnett, Susan, 171
"Bassompierre," 196 (n. 8)
Beaugrande, Robert de, 8
Beauty, for Keats, 85
Beckett, Samuel, 51
"Beef?, Where's the," 6
Bennett, Paula, 164, 165

Berman, Jeffrey, 182
Bettelheim, Bruno, 70
Beutscher, Ruth, 181
Birds, as idols, 112
Blake, William, 6–7, 12–13, 71, 107, 118, 197 (n. 2)
Bollas, Christopher, 159, 165, 170
Booth, Stephen, 14
Boss, bosom and, 33
Boswell, James, 46
Brantlinger, Patrick, 155
Breast, 4, 79, 84, 167–68; "good" and "bad," 32, 83, 93; and moon, 82; as penis, 168; "mastoi," 188 (n. 1); as mother, 193 (n. 5)
Brink, Andrew, 165, 182, 193 (n. 4), 199 (n. 7)
Bromberg, David, 24
Brontë, Anne, 138
Brontë, Charlotte, 119–35, 138–39, 141; *Jane Eyre*, 15, 29, 119, 120–24; *Shirley*, 124–25; *Villette*, 125–26, 127, 128–35
Brontë, Emily, 135–141; *Wuthering Heights*, 135–41
Brontë, Patrick, 124, 137
Brontë, Patrick Branwell, 132, 136–37
Brooks, Cleanth, 14, 15, 105
Browning, Robert: "Childe Roland to the Dark Tower Came," 187 (n. 6)

Bundtzen, Lynda, 203
Burke, Kenneth, 193 (n. 7)
Burton, Robert, 86, 92
Butscher, Edward, 182
Byrd, Max, 51
Byron, George Gordon, Lord, 32

Cairo, 49
Carroll, Michael, 26, 32
Cavell, Stanley, 8, 10
Charm, 81
Chitham, Edward, 135
Christianity, 10, 51, 101, 153
Circe, 82–83, 86
Cleland, John, 45
Click, 18
Clifford, James, 20, 44
Coburn, Kathleen, 188 (n. 1)
Coleridge, 59, 188 (n. 1); "Christabel," 32–33, 188 (n. 1); "The Rime of the Ancient Mariner," 188 (n. 1)
Complex, 1, 19, 20; as stimulus word, 3
Condensation, 3
Coney, 189 (n. 4)
Conrad, Joseph, 142–58
Cretinism, 126
Crews, Frederick, 147
Crypt, 55, 129, 130
Cryptomnesia, 195 (n. 1)
Cryptonymy, 121

Dainties, 83–84
Darwin, Erasmus, 68, 81, 85
Davies, Stevie, 125, 139
Deliria, 3
Depressive position, 31–32, 83, 93
Derrida, Jacques, 21

Despair, 111
Deutelbaum, Wendy, 20
Disintegration, 177
Displacement, in *Villette*, 135
Dixon, Norman, 8
Dobell, Sydney, 134, 197 (n. 11)
Dream screen. *See* Isakower phenomenon
Duplicity, 140, 142

Eco, Umberto, 11
Edelman, Gerald, 21
Ehrenpreis, Irvin, 43, 55, 190 (n. 10)
Eidolon, 87, 107, 109
Einbond, Bernard, 50, 190 (n. 9)
Einstein, Albert, 192 (n. 5)
Ellmann, Richard, 147
Emanation, 120
Empson, William: *The Structure of Complex Words*, 8–11
Envy, 32
Epicurus, 107
Eye: as nipple, 23, 29, 79, 94, 173; suspended in space, 27; as moon, 67
Eye-idol, 29

Fancy, 45, 107, 113; in Keats, 75; idol, 107
Fane, 74
Fate, 148
Figure-ground reversal, 14, 192 (n. 5)
Fish, Stanley, 188 (n. 7)
Flournoy, Théodore, 195 (n. 1)
Forster, E. M., 142, 145
Franklin, Benjamin, 63
Freud, Sigmund: on complex, 2; on condensation, 4; on jokes, 4, 19; on stimuli, 8; on melancholia, 73, 116;

on Goethe, 74; on the uncanny, 148–49; 196 (n. 8); on screen memories, 196 (n. 8); on syllabic chemistry, 198 (n. 7)
Frye, Northrop, 9

Gass, William, 125
Gaze, the, 34, 37, 69
Gelpi, Barbara, 188 (n. 2)
Geneva, 62
Glaucus, 82
Gloam, 87
Goat: connotation of, 44–45, 46
God: as guard, 53; as imaginary phallus, 191 (n. 12)
Godwin, Mary, 32, 56–71
Godwin, William, 57; *Political Justice*, 58–59; described by Hazlitt, 63; on Mary Wollstonecraft, 66
Green, André, 15, 193 (n. 5)
Greene, Donald, 49
Gregory, Richard L., 8
Grice, H. P., 11–13
Gules, 82

Hagstrum, Jean, 44
Hair, Donald S., 117
Hamilton, James W., 193 (n. 2)
Happy Valley, in *Rasselas*, 41
Hardy, J. P., 53
Harrison, G. Elsie, 125
Hartman, Geoffrey H., 104
Hazlitt, William: on Godwin, 63; on Godwin's *St. Leon*, 75
H.D. (Hilda Doolittle), 16, 24
Hegel, G. W. F., 153–55
Heisenberg uncertainty principle, 15
Hill, as breast, 86, 121, 194 (n. 8)

Hippo, 152
Holbrook, David, 159, 165, 170, 182, 183
Hollow, 128
Homans, Margaret, 120, 139
Homoeroticism, 183, 198 (n. 9)
Homophone, 21
Hopkins, Gerard Manley, 193 (n. 3)
Horror, 156
Hudson, R., 13
Hughes, Ted, 181, 199 (n. 8)
Hypocrisy, 149, 153; Hegel on, 153–55
Hypogram, 19, 151–53

Identity, 85
Idols, 58, 102, 195 (n. 3); as *eidola*, 106
Idyl, 108
Implication, 11
Inferencing, 12
Ingestion, 84; in Plath, 174
Intentions, 2, 6, 7, 8, 11, 19, 104; tensions in, 15
Introjection, 83, 166
Irwin, George, 50
Isakower phenomenon, 23–25, 188 (n. 1)
Isidore of Seville, 194 (n. 12)
Ivory, 150

Jakobson, Roman, 5, 6
Janus, 119
Jenyns, Soame, 52
Johnson, Barbara, 70
Johnson, Samuel, 38–55; and padlock, 40; on early habiats, 54–55; recurrence to arithmetic, 189 (n. 1); on puns, 190 (n. 9)
Joseph, Gerhard, 62

Joyce, James, 17–18, 107
Joy's Grape, 94
Jung, C. G., 2

Kamel, Rose, 164
Karl, Frederick, 143
Keats, Frances Jennings, 72, 78, 193 (n. 4)
Keats, John, 72–98; "Ode on Melancholy," 73, 74, 90–95; and Plath, 171
Keefe, Robert, 119
Ker, Alan, 100
Kernan, Alvin, 42
Key-words, 2
Kingsley, 187 (n. 5)
Klein, Melanie, 31, 32, 83, 167, 175, 180
Knoepflmacher, U. C., 57
Knotenpunkt, 4, 104; as homophone, 21; as nucleus or nodal word, 103
Kolb, Gwin J., 190 (n. 10)
Korzeniowski, Apollo, 143
Kristeva, Julia, 16, 25
Kroll, Judith, 159, 169
Krutch, Joseph, 42, 48

Lacan, Jacques, 34, 50, 115, 119; on mirror stage, 19, 123; on breast, 37; on gaze, 69
Lack, 47, 48, 146, 179
Lake: and lack, 68
Lash, Christopher, 164
Lattice, 141
Lavers, Annette, 159
Law, William, 46
Lawrence, D. H.: on Benjamin Franklin, 63

Leavis, F. R., 117, 142, 145
Lecercle, Jean-Jacques, 16
Leiris, Michel, 9
Leopardi, Giacomo, 198 (n. 2)
Levine, George, 71
Lewin, Bertram, 24–25, 193 (n. 6), 194 (n. 9)
Lexis, 1
Lexis complex: and poetic function, 5
Lie, 152; in *Heart of Darkness*, 142
Locke, Don, 58
Loss, 86; and Keats, 73
Lucretius, 107
Lynn, Steven, 42

Magritte, René, 34
Mahler, Margaret, 16
Mallowan, M. E. L, 29
Marcel, Anthony J., 8
Martin, Robert Bernard, 100
Martineau, Harriet, 126
Marvell, Andrew, 44, 112
Maternal body, 95
Mathew, G. F., 89
Matrix. *See* Hypogram
Mauron, Charles, 20
McIntosh, Carey, 190 (n. 7)
McLauchlan, Juliet, 156
McSweeney, Kerry, 117
Melancholy, 73, 91, 116
Mellor, Anne, 64
Memory, as idol, 115
Meredith, George, 111
Methusaleh, 128
Meyer, Bernard, 41, 144
Mill, 125, 128
Milton, John, 43, 69, 125
Mist, 77, 94, 145, 197 (n. 1)

"Mistah" Kurtz, 146
Moan, 89, 98
Moglen, Helene, 119
Moneta, 78, 97
Monster, 67
Moon, 67, 79, 80; woman as, 81; as word, 84; as breast, 129, 172–73; as eye, 159, 172–73, 192 (n. 6); as verb, 193 (n. 6)
Mourning, in Keats, 73, 78, 82, 88
Mudrick, Marvin, 157
Mum, 78–79, 83
Mummy, 55, 65, 191 (n. 13)
Mystery, 145

Najder, Zadisław, 143, 150
Narcissism, 153
Navel, of dream, 130
Nekuia, 41
Newton, Peter M., 40
Nietzsche, Friedrich, 154
Nile, 42, 48, 49
Nipple-eye, 29, 32, 68; in "Christabel," 34. *See also* Eye: as nipple
Nodal point, 3, 4. *See also* Knotenpunkt
Non-introjection, 129
Norris, Christopher, 9, 10, 11
Nothing, 45, 47, 190 (n. 5)

O, 171
Object, internalized, 40, 57, 83, 175; -relations, 10, 13, 31, 166; transitional, 16
Odysseus, 106
O'Flaherty, Patrick, 51
Ooman, 81

Or, 75, 92, 155–56
Oral deprivation, 29, 34, 68
Orb, 68, 81
Orgel, Shelley, 160
Overdetermination, 3, 4, 15, 17
Ovid, 1

Paglia, Camille, 32
Palgrave, F. T., 103
Paranoid-schizoid position, 31, 84
Paronomasia, 21
Passage, secret, 38, 50, 55, 178
Patterson, Annabel, 8
Pattison, Robert, 108
Pecunia, 50
Perception, multistage, 8
Percy, Thomas: *Reliques of Ancient English Poetry*, 194 (n. 8)
Peri-Banou, 135
Perry, Benita, 198 (n. 8)
Peters, Margot, 119, 123
Phallus, 34, 61
Phantasmagoria, 56–57, 64, 157, 191 (n. 1)
Phantasy, 67, 82, 175, 192 (n. 3)
Phantom, 46
Piozzi, Hester Thrale, 41, 47
Plath, Aurelia, 162–63, 165, 181
Plath, Otto, 162–63
Plath, Sylvia, 159–86; *The Bell Jar*, 162–86
Plato: *Phaedrus*, 150
Pleasure: Johnson on, 44
Poetic function of language, 5
Polidori, John William, 32, 33, 68
Polysemy, 14, 93
Pope, Alexander, 107
Porphyry, 89

Porter, Roy, 73
Pragmatic linguistics, 11
Preoedipal dynamics, 16, 67
Primal scene, of *Frankenstein*, 65, 66, 68, 70
Processing, parallel, 8, 104
Projection, 19, 83, 192 (n. 6)
Proserpine, 90, 94, 97
Psychocriticism, 20
Puns, 5, 20, 124; puncept, 21; in *Frankenstein*, 65; and poetry, 73, 88; and mastery of ambivalence, 85; in Plath, 170–72; coordination of ambivalence, 171
Pynchon, Thomas, 21–22

Quennell, Peter, 199 (n. 9)

Rackin, Phyllis, 114
Rapaport, Herman, 121
Redon, Odilon, 29
Reich, Annie, 167
Reid, Stephen, 93
Relevance, 12
Rest, 47
Revenge, 61
Rich, Adrienne, 165, 167
Rickman, John, 15
Ricks, Christopher, 85, 99, 103, 104, 110, 117
Riffaterre, Michael, 19, 151
Rigby, Elizabeth, 195 (n. 4)
Rosen, Victor, 16, 17
Rycroft, Charles, 198 (n. 2)

Saccade, 8
Sadoff, Dianne F., 119
Said, Edward, 156
Saint Paul, 125
Saussure, Ferdinand de, 7; on anagrams, 195 (n. 5)
Schafer, Roy, 187 (n. 4)
Schwartz, Murray, 159, 165, 170
Semele, 77–78
Sepulchre, whited, 148, 152
7-Up, 187 (n. 2)
Severn, Joseph, 72, 75, 79
Sexuality, infantile, 37
Shades, 91, 147, 197 (n. 3)
Shannon, Edgar, 103
Shapiro, Theodore, 16
Shelley, Mary Wollstonecraft. *See* Godwin, Mary
Shelley, Percy Bysshe: and nipple-eye, 33–34; as Victor Frankenstein, 64; writing in *Frankenstein*, 70
Sherburn, George, 42
Sign, arbitrary nature of, 7
Silverman, Kaja, 37
Smith, George, 135
Smith, Joseph H., 191 (n. 12)
Spitz, René, 25, 26, 37
Spitzer, Leo, 18, 19, 115, 195 (n. 4)
Splitting, 16, 123, 161
Stewart, Garrett, 158
Suicide, 50–51, 154, 174, 186
Switch word, 4

Tayler, Irene, 125
Taylor, James, 133, 134
Tennyson, Alfred, Lord, 99–118; on mother, 100; on punning, 101; "Tears, Idle Tears," 104–118; "Ulysses," 104–05; and Keats, 194 (n. 2)
Tennyson, Elizabeth, 99, 109–10

Tennyson, Hallam, 103
Thrale, Hester. *See* Piozzi, Hester Thrale
Torok, Maria, 121
Tree, 7; blasted, 60–61
Trilling, Lionel, 75
Truth, as trust, 197 (n. 9)
Tucker, Herbert F., 108
Twitchell, James B., 32

Ulmer, Gregory, 20
Underworld, 105
Urns, 86

Vendler, Helen, 94
Vere, Aubrey de, 85
Vortex, 21

Wagner-Martin, Linda, 165
Wain, John, 190 (n. 11)
Wasserman, Earl R., 42, 49
Whales, James, 192 (n. 5)
Williams, A. Hyatt, 86
Williams, William Carlos, 192 (n. 5)
Wimsatt, W. K., 21, 39, 49
Winnicott, D. W., 15, 57, 74
Wittgenstein, Ludwig, 51, 187 (n. 3); on intention, 9
Wolfman (Serge Pankejeff), 121
Wollstonecraft, Mary, 56–57
Words, 13; full, 37; as food, 84; as shadows, 109
Wordsworth, 16, 34, 39
Wright, Elizabeth, 34, 37

Young, Edward, 43